Rivers

CURRICULUM GUIDE

CHEMISTRY

*One of a series of six rivers-based units written
by teachers participating in the Rivers Curriculum Project
funded by the National Science Foundation*

Dr. Robert Williams, Project Director
Southern Illinois University at Edwardsville (SIUE)

Cynthia Bidlack, Project Coordinator, SIUE

Authors:

Dr. Virginia Bryan, SIUE

Allen Burbank, Chester High School

Dr. Jack Ballinger, Florissant Valley College

Dale Seymour Publications®

Aquatic E
Iowa Dep
2473 160th
Guthrie Center, Iowa   50115-8518

Managing Editor: Catherine Anderson

Project Editor: Christine Freeman

Production and Manufacturing Coordinator: Leanne Collins

Design Manager: Jeff Kelly

Text and Cover Design: Christy Butterfield

Cover Photograph: Nicholas Pavloff

Technical Art: Carl Yoshihara

This book is published by Dale Seymour Publications®,
an imprint of Addison Wesley Longman, Inc.

The blackline masters in this publication are designed to be used
with appropriate duplicating equipment to reproduce copies for
classroom use. Addison Wesley Longman grants permission to
classroom teachers to reproduce these masters.

Copyright ©1997 by Southern Illinois University (SIU)
Printed in the United States of America

Order Number DS 29722
ISBN 0-201-49367-5

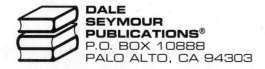

DALE
SEYMOUR
PUBLICATIONS®
P.O. BOX 10888
PALO ALTO, CA 94303

This product is printed
on recycled paper

1 2 3 4 5 6 7 8 9 10-ML-01 00 99 98 97 96

Acknowledgments

Rivers Project Curriculum

We cannot list all the teachers, scholars, and friends to whom we are indebted for the development of the Rivers Project curriculum units, but we want to mention some of these very important people.

To start, without the help and guidance of Mark Mitchell and Bill Stapp, GREEN Project at the University of Michigan, Ann Arbor, in the very early stages of the Rivers Project, we might not be where we are today. The same thank-you goes to Tanner Girard, Illinois Pollution Control Board Judge and former professor at Principia College in Elsah, Illinois, who has been helpful in so many ways. We owe so much to Don Humphreys and Ivo Lindauer, our National Science Foundation Program directors, who have believed in and supported the curriculum development since its inception and throughout the long and tedious job of writing, piloting, rewriting, and field-testing. We offer special thanks to the Illinois State Board of Education and the Illinois Higher Board of Education for beginning the project and for offering continuing support for Dwight D. Eisenhower teacher training.

No way exists for us to thank sufficiently each of the curriculum unit writers for the hours and hours of personal time devoted to their specific unit. Not only have they been writers but also trainers for new teachers entering the program, during both the school year and the summer training sessions.

We want to thank all the curriculum unit users for revision suggestions given to the writers. We are especially grateful to them for taking time away from their traditional classroom setting to give time to their students out on the river for hands-on activities.

To the university professors from across the country who read the units in their area and provided professional opinions and suggestions for improvement, we are sincerely thankful.

Finally, to Pat, Jack, Bill, Michele, and all the many university student workers and graduate assistants who have come and gone over the course of the last four years, what would we have done without you?

Dr. Robert Williams, Project Director
Cindy Bidlack, Project Coordinator

Cynthia Lee (Cindy) Bidlack died of cancer shortly after her 46th birthday. She gave so much to this project. For all her efforts, we can only say thanks. We remember her often and miss her much.

Rivers Chemistry Unit

The writing of *Rivers Chemistry* owes much to Bob Considine, Thornwood High School, and to Marvin Mondy, Alton High School. Bob, "Skip," Considine shared more ideas and suggestions that any single manual could hold. If *Rivers Chemistry* could be a series of books, Bob has enough material to do them all. Marvin Mondy has been our expert on testing for fecal coliform throughout the development, writing, and training sessions for this project. His help has allowed many chemistry teachers to complete this adventure into the life sciences with confidence.

Contents

RIVERS CURRICULUM PROJECT

When many of us think of rivers, we picture the fun times we have around them—boating, swimming, frolicking, watching wildlife, just enjoying being where land meets water. We may also appreciate the benefits that rivers give to us, such as drinking water, plentiful food sources, recreation, electric power, and an efficient means of transportation. While tallying up all these good things about rivers, however, we may grow concerned about threats to the health of our rivers.

Rivers and streams confront many forms of pollution—industrial waste, acid rain, sewage spills, and thermal pollution. Fortunately, scientists, environmentalists, and the public have instigated regulatory and technical changes that seem to be reducing some of these risks. What kinds of river pollution, and effects of pollution, need further attention? What other threats do rivers and streams face?

Scientists increasingly tell us that the main threat to America's rivers today comes not from pollution, but the physical and biological transformation of rivers and their watersheds. As rivers are altered to provide water transportation, generate power, reduce flood hazards, and provide water for farms, cities and industries, their physical, chemical, and biological processes are damaged or destroyed. The loss of riverside and aquatic habitat has led to the decline or extinction of more than one-third of North America's fish species and an even higher proportion of its native mussel species.

Healthy river systems are incredibly dynamic. As nutrients, sediments and organisms are transported downstream, water and organic materials are constantly added to the mix. Most of these materials come from the surrounding terrestrial system, with the land-water boundary, known as the "riparian zone," acting as a critical valve or filter that regulates the exchange. Riparian zones and their associated wetlands also act as natural sponges, absorbing and filtering polluted floodwaters over time. Where the banks of streams are cleared, straightened, and replaced with rocks or concrete to reduce flooding, the ability of associated wetlands and floodplains to control and filter runoff, provide habitat, and add nutrients is lost.

When rivers flood, they alter the shape of the stream, scouring new channels, inundating riverside land, depositing sediments, and building new banks and beaches. These functions are as important to healthy river ecosystems as natural fires are to healthy prairies and forests. For many fish species, this flood "pulse," called the "natural hydrograph" by scientists, not only triggers spawning and migration but also allows fish to reach seasonally inundated floodplain nurseries and spawning habitats.

Scientists have made significant progress in understanding how changing natural hydrologic cycles has contributed to the destruction of aquatic ecosystems. Numerous local communities have taken the lead in adopting cost-effective storm water, floodplain, and water-supply management programs that utilize natural hydrologic processes. Sometimes, however, federal and state agencies want to alter the hydrology and other physical characteristics of rivers and their watersheds. The debate on such issues ranges down many river corridors.

In order for the youth of our country to become informed participants in the political process, they must have a solid background in environmental issues. The school systems must, therefore, educate students about the nature of the environment. Through the study of rivers, not only does a concern for water become important to the students, but other issues begin to gain this same importance. And for our country, and our world, this can only be one giant step forward.

The Rivers Project curriculum is the end product of four years of environmental commitment by hundreds of high-school teachers in the United States and Canada. Because of the growing importance of environmental issues, teachers through whose towns a river or stream flows have sought to integrate water and river studies into their traditional content courses.

USING THE RIVERS CURRICULUM

When students visit a river or stream and become actively involved in observing, measuring, testing, and writing about that waterway, they quickly develop a sense of ownership toward that river or stream. They also tend to develop a broader understanding of the value of the academic discipline that has brought them to the water's edge. Toward these goals, the Rivers Project units were developed by teachers for use in science (chemistry, biology, earth science), geography, language arts, and mathematics classes. The Rivers Project curriculum prepares students to perform field investigations, with the primary laboratory being a local river or stream. Some activities are to be used in the classroom, focusing on preparation for the field experience, which may be one long trip or several shorter ones. Extensions of the curriculum units encourage teachers to make use of other kinds of field trips, to invite guest speakers to the school, and to make contact with local, state, and federal agencies for outside resources.

In a number of states, governmental agencies are using in their monitoring processes data collected by Rivers Project students. Such contact with state agencies is a vital component of the recommended scientific activities stated in the curricula for these units. As students experience hands-on learning activities that result in river data of real scientific or cultural value, affecting real-world issues they care about, they are motivated to learn even more.

The Rivers Project curriculum is not intended to be used as a textbook, but as a set of supplementary materials designed to enhance your existing program or to establish a basis for river study in your school. The materials involve students in a natural environment—the river—through a series of hands-on activities conducted through field-based study.

When using these units, let your imagination and your creativity run wild. The materials can prove a valuable addition to your traditional teaching. *Remember, what your students feel and touch as part of their river experiences will stay with them for the rest of their lives. Make it memorable!*

Rivers Project Curriculum Units

The river is the common strand weaving the units together into the interdisciplinary curricula you are about to use. This brief synopsis and the underlying connection of each curriculum unit to the other will aid in understanding how the Rivers Project units may be taught. You may use these units independently of each other, or you may combine them in an interdisciplinary approach, especially a team-teaching venture.

Rivers Chemistry defines water quality and guides students in basic data collection. Water-quality kits, which are readily available and easy to use, make conducting the tests a relatively uncomplicated task.

Rivers Biology focuses on stream-monitoring programs and the study of benthic macroinvertebrates. Living organisms in a river, stream, or lake are easily captured or documented. Their existence and numbers provide data for comparison with those of the chemical unit. Biological diversity for a water environment may change as the water quality improves or decreases.

Rivers Earth Science evaluates the physical features of a river system that provide clues to understanding the historical development within a local area. Students better understand the impact of the river drainage system on water quality when their study also factors in soil, slope, and flow. As scholars in the twenty-first century study the effects of agriculture, development, and transportation on the river and water resources, they will view the geology of an area with increasing attentiveness.

Rivers Geography enables students to develop a sense of the environmental impact of people occupying and organizing themselves along rivers. Study of the geography of the river as it relates to location, place, movement, region, and human-environment interactions along its banks gives form and reason to human migration and development. The river becomes a lab for an ever-changing society.

Rivers Language Arts focuses on the skills students will use as they investigate and write about their study of the river. Lessons include technical writing for scientific reporting, interviewing, research techniques for exploring local history, political letter writing, poetry and other forms of creative writing. Samples of, and references to, exemplary fiction and nonfiction written about rivers are included. Teachers of every discipline can use this unit to give voices to the discoveries and ideas garnered by their students through river study.

Rivers Mathematics provides real-life application of mathematical processes and skills, using data gathered during field studies and from reference sources. Topics range from measurement and working with percentages to standard deviations. This material specifically teaches the mathematical skills required for the science units in the Rivers Project curriculum.

Scheduling and Team Teaching Options

Each science unit, and the geography unit, can be used as a freestanding unit involving about one month of consistent focus. Alternatively, any of these units can be integrated into the regular activities of the class throughout a longer period. The language arts and mathematics units can be used in language arts or mathematics classes to support and expand river activities being done in the science classes. Science and environmental education teachers who wish to broaden student experience in other areas, or to add an interdisciplinary dimension to their curriculum, can also use these units as support material.

Because each unit can stand alone, a few units do have some duplication of topics. For example, because of its importance, analysis of fecal coliform is included in both the chemistry and the biology units. If teachers in both disciplines are using the Rivers Project curriculum, such testing may be performed in just the biology class, with the results shared with the chemistry class.

A single teacher in a school may use a Rivers Project unit, or several teachers may work as a multidisciplinary team. In many schools, what began as a single unit has grown over the course of several years into a schoolwide project as more teachers and students have become involved and the school has acquired more materials and equipment for river study.

Using Your River or Stream in This Curriculum

Teachers and students can use the Rivers Project units on any river or stream anywhere in the world. The constants are the water tests and educational studies that student perform on the river. Each river or stream presents a unique set of parameters for collecting and studying. Investigators approach bigger rivers very differently from smaller streams or shallow rivers. A cold mountain river displays vastly different flora and fauna from the slow, sluggish coastal river. Factors such as population density, natural and modified drainage patterns, and climate vary not only from river to river but from one point along a river to another. The study of each river and its corresponding watershed, therefore, has special attributes that cannot be dealt with in generic materials such as these.

You and your students will want to build a library of handbooks, field guides, and other support material appropriate to your specific area. The best sources for this information are local agencies that monitor and study the waterway. Soil and water conservation district offices, state and local conservation departments, environmental protection or water agencies, and local universities are good places to begin. Most state agencies have a number of relevant free publications. While building the library, locate a person who can advise the class in the field. Many schools have found locally based state employees who are willing to provide content support, sometimes equipment, and even to join the class on water-monitoring days. Once your class has a mentor, river study often becomes easier and more meaningful for you and your students. More than likely, the data collected by the students will also be important to the mentor.

ABOUT THE RIVERS PROJECT

The Rivers Project curriculum in these six units started with teachers who loved teaching and loved the rivers in their communities. They banded together to spread their enthusiasm, knowledge, and learning tools among students and other teachers.

History of the Rivers Project

The Rivers Project began as the Illinois Rivers Project in February 1990 as a pilot program involving eight high schools along the Mississippi and lower Illinois Rivers. With scientific literacy as the ultimate goal of the Project, students collected and analyzed water samples from test sites along both rivers. The study of the rivers was extended to include historical, social, and economic implications of the state of the rivers, thus involving students from classes across the curricular areas of science, social studies, and English.

SOILED NET, a telecommunication network linking the participating schools with each other and with Project headquarters, provided a technological framework for many of the Project's activities.

In December 1991, the Illinois Rivers Project received a grant from the National Science Foundation to develop a formal Rivers Project curriculum. The resultant units, in chemistry, biology, earth science, geography, language arts, and mathematics are applicable to any river in the world. To further the Rivers Project, Southern Illinois University at Edwardsville hosts a training session each summer. At these programs, teachers who use Rivers Project materials serve as mentors for participating teachers in classroom and field-study sessions.

Goals of the Rivers Project Curriculum

The three principle goals of the Rivers Project curriculum are:

1. to increase students' knowledge and understanding of important issues and concepts related to the river.

2. to prepare students with the necessary skills to properly investigate and report relevant information regarding the river.

3. to inspire students to take action to resolve problems that contribute to the overall deterioration of the natural beauty and functions of the river.

Project Funding

The Rivers Project began with funding from the Illinois State Board of Education through a Scientific Literacy Grant. Subsequent funding for Illinois teacher training was obtained from the Illinois Board of Higher Education, Dwight D. Eisenhower Title II funds. A grant from the U.S. Fish and Wildlife Service allowed Midwestern schools in Iowa, Minnesota, and Wisconsin to participate. The National Science Foundation, under its Materials Development Program, provided funds for the final development and testing of the Rivers Project curriculum units. Along the way, many others in the academic and business community, as well as numerous local, state, and federal agencies provided support.

TELECOMMUNICATIONS

A key component of the Rivers Project is the sharing of water-quality data and student writings among schools in the project. Though schools can communicate by mail, use of the computer networks associated with the Rivers Project provides for faster, more responsive, more directly accessible exchange. Students using these networks can not only contribute their data but also quickly access the data, writings, and queries of students at other Rivers Project schools, most notably students exploring the same river watershed.

The Rivers Project utilizes two telecommunications systems, e-mail and the World Wide Web. Either requires a computer and a modem. Because telecommunications is evolving rapidly, the telecommunications technology, data-handling, and data availability for the Rivers Project will undoubtedly also change. For the most current information on how to contact the Rivers Project, telephone Southern Illinois University at Edwardsville (SIUE) at (618) 692-3788 or (618) 692-3065.

E-Mail

Students using a computer that has a user account can send writings to the Rivers Project via e-mail using the address "rivers@siue.edu." Other students may read these on the World Wide Web. The Rivers Project also periodically publishes collections of student writings it has received.

World Wide Web

The Rivers Project is also available via the World Wide Web. This requires web browser software and access to the Internet. The URL (Uniform Resource Locator) is "http://www.siue.edu/OSME/river." This home page contains a searchable database of all water-quality data sent in to date and also a form that can be filled out online to report water-quality results. Selected student writings are also available via this home page. The Rivers Project home page contains a link to the e-mail address.

THE RIVERS CHEMISTRY UNIT

In *Rivers Chemistry,* students will learn what variables comprise and determine water quality. They will practice testing some factors in the laboratory and do one or more field trips to a local waterway to collect and test water samples. Finally, they will analyze their test results, determine overall water quality, and share their information with other schools using computer telecommunications.

CHEMISTRY AND THE RIVER

The National Sanitation Foundation has established nine parameters as indicators of water quality. These nine factors include both physical measurements and chemical tests:

1. pH refers to the acidity, alkalinity, or neutrality of water.

2. Temperature refers to the measured temperature of water

3. Turbidity refers to the clarity of water.

4. Total solids refers to the number of milligrams of solids (dissolved, suspended, or either) per liter of water.

5. Dissolved oxygen refers to the number of milligrams of oxygen gas dissolved in 1 liter of water.

6. Biochemical oxygen demand refers to the amount of dissolved oxygen lost in a sample of water over a five-day period due to organic matter.

7. Phosphate refers to the number of milligrams of phosphate ion per liter of water.

8. Nitrate refers to the number of milligrams of nitrate ion per liter of water.

9. Fecal coliform refers to the number of fecal coli present per 100 mL of water.

For each of these parameters, *Rivers Chemistry* gives students background information, supporting

activities, and instructions on analyzing data collected. Teacher Notes for each lesson contain additional information and suggestions for the instructor. Informational laboratory activities support specific science-related skills, such as using statistics, standards, and a spectrophotometer. A variety of assessment strategies support the lessons.

OUTCOMES FOR RIVERS CHEMISTRY

In this unit, students will learn how to analyze river water regarding (1) dissolved oxygen (2) fecal coliform (3) pH (4) biochemical oxygen demand (5) temperature (6) phosphate (7) nitrate (8) turbidity (9) total solids. Using these nine tests, students can determine if their water is excellent, good, medium, bad, or very bad. Involvement with local river quality should help students become more environmentally aware and concerned about our endangered planet.

ADVANCED PREPARATION

Before starting *Rivers Chemistry,* each teacher will need to gather numerous materials, become familiar with topics included in the unit, do preliminary planning for field trips, and assess student readiness for the project.

Student Preparation

This unit has been written for high school and middle school students in physical science and chemistry classes. Middle school students may require more instructional time per lesson than older students. Though students who have had algebra usually perform more comfortably in this unit, students without an algebra background have completed *Rivers Chemistry* successfully.

Teacher Preparation

Prior to introducing the *Rivers Chemistry* unit to your class, you should prepare by doing the following:

1. Read the entire unit.

2. Brush up on concepts used in this material.

3. Coordinate activities and curriculum with teachers considering doing other units of the Rivers curriculum.

4. Develop timeline for placing *Rivers Chemistry* in your yearlong instructional schedule. Times noted in each activity are approximations; allow some flexibility.

5. Discuss the curriculum with your school administration and secure permission for the field trips and the acquisition of materials.

6. Find and visit an appropriate field site. Select a site with suitability for the activities, easy accessibility, and minimal safety hazards. Obtain all necessary permissions from the landowner for students to visit the site.

7. As appropriate for your situation, send note to parents informing them that students will be involved in river or stream field trips, as well as safe handling of river water. Ask for signature if appropriate.

8. Schedule field trips and prepare field-trip permission forms. Secure field-trip transportation. (See discussion of Field Trip Management later in this section.)

9. Collect all necessary materials and equipment.

10. Make sure your laboratory is equipped with common safety devices, such as eyewash fountain, fire extinguisher, material safety data sheets (MSDS) for materials to be used, and first-aid kit.

11. Obtain maps of your site from the U.S. Geological Survey. Other sources include local or state agencies. For source information, contact your local Cooperative Extension Service. Global Positioning System (GPS) devices can be used to obtain latitude and longitude rather than maps. These are available through sporting supply stores or catalogs. Often, a local hunter, boater, or fish enthusiast will have one.

12. Enlist the aid of an expert (such as a conservation officer, planning commission member, Army Corps of Engineers employee, or public employee) who works with river- and stream-related concerns and who will be willing to address your students or lead them on a field trip.

13. Duplicate all materials to be distributed to students (including Student Information, Student Activity, and Assessment pages from this unit), punch holes for three-ring binders, and place in labeled files.

14. Several water-quality tests require special kits. Because of the ever-increasing variety of test kits, this unit does not include specific instructions for kit use. Become familiar with operation of the test kits you will use; prepare student instructions for those kits. Laminating the instructions will protect them from spills in the laboratory and in the field.

15. Generally, one waste container can be used for all the tests included in *Rivers Chemistry*. If your state or other jurisdiction requires separate containers for different types of chemical wastes at the levels produced in these lessons, prepare and label separate containers.

16. Get excited. Your enthusiasm will be contagious.

FIELD TRIP MANAGEMENT

Field trips, particularly field trips around a body of water, require careful planning and management. Here are steps to make *Rivers Chemistry* field trips safe and successful. Adapt this list to fit your own circumstances and preferences.

Before the Field Trip

___ Visit and select an appropriate field-trip site.

___ Secure school administration permission for field trip.

___ Secure permission from landowner.

___ Contact expert for help and content assistance.

___ Publicize the event with local newspaper, television, and radio

___ Arrange for field-trip transportation.

___ Arrange for appropriate adult supervision on trip.

___ Prepare directions for field-trip drivers.

___ Develop an activity plan for the field-trip day.

___ Arrange for lunches or snacks, drinking water, and rest rooms.

___ Tell students what activities they will perform at the field site.

___ Distribute field-trip permission forms to students, and receive signed forms. (Permission forms should include request for information about student allergies and other medical needs.)

___ Give instruction on field-day clothing and personal items (journal, handouts, pencil, sunscreen, insect repellent, lunch, drinks, medications for individual allergies and other needs).

Day Before the Field Trip

___ Make sure all student permissions have been turned in.

___ Review activities that will take place during field trip, including extra activities, such as writing and litter pickup.

___ Review safety procedures.

___ Each group assembles and prepares materials and equipment for their specific test or tests to be done at the river. This is often Part A of the field-trip-based activity.

___ Pack all field-trip materials and equipment.

___ Assign students to complete reading of field-trip activity sheets.

Field-Trip Day

___ Distribute directions to field-trip drivers.

___ Assign students to load equipment and materials for transportation to field site.

___ Assign responsibilities to supervising adults.

___ Distribute safety and field equipment and materials.

___ Students do assigned testing and sampling activities.

___ Secure all water samples to be transported.

___ If students have completed assigned activities, have them help other groups, do riverside cleanup, or write in their journals.

After the Field Trip

___ Students complete lab work.

___ Wash and store all equipment.

___ Students complete calculations for their water-quality activity.

SPECIAL MATERIALS AND EQUIPMENT NEEDED

Each lesson and each assessment includes a list of the specific equipment and materials it requires. Appendix F lists suppliers of chemical and other scientific items approved by the Environmental Protection Agency (EPA). Here is some essential equipment not found in most school physical science or chemistry laboratories:

- EPA-approved test kits for dissolved oxygen, phosphate, nitrates. Ideally, each class should have at least three of each kit, but a procedure by which an entire class can use one set of test kits is described later in this introduction.

- Turbidity test kit or Secchi disk. The Secchi disk can be easily fabricated in a school industrial arts department using the description in Student Information 4.2: How Can Turbidity Be Measured?

- Waste containers for liquids and solids, safety goggles, aprons, gloves, eyewash, and a first-aid kit available while testing at the field site

- Alcohol-filled thermometers equipped with metal jackets

- Life jacket and lifeline (rope) for each student if the waterway is not a small shallow stream

- Water-sampling device, purchased or constructed, if your class will obtain samples while standing on shore or in the water. At the end of a 3–4 meter pole is a test-tube type clamp to which a glass or plastic bottle can be affixed. An extension pole for paint rollers makes a good pole. If students are assigned to design the device, some trial-and-error models in the lab will help. For example, one- and two-liter soda bottles are easier to submerge when attached to the end of a long pole than are gallon milk jugs; glass (though breakable) is easier to submerge than light plastic. Telescoping poles are easy to transport but must be strong enough to submerge the sampling container. The bottles for the dissolved oxygen and fecal coliform test should be used to collect samples directly.

River field trips are integral to *Rivers Chemistry*. The minimum number is one, but two trips, even short ones, really make *Rivers Chemistry* more valuable. Students gain increased understanding of the factors that influence the health of the river environment. The more field trips, the better your students' experience will be. The number of times you sample the river and involve students in river testing will depend on your school's curriculum and your commitment to the project.

Most lessons contain a field-trip activity. You may complete several lessons up to the field trip activity, then do the field-trip-based activities for several lessons during one outing.

In *Rivers Chemistry*, each water-quality test is preceded by one more student information or activity session. These can usually be combined or spread out over several periods as needed. Each water-quality test, however, has specific time requirements. In planning lab and field-trip time, therefore, take into account the time students will need in order to perform the assigned tests.

- Weighted rope with a clamp attached, purchased or constructed, if your class will collect water samples while standing on a bridge or dock. Most commercial samplers consist of a one-liter acrylic cylinder attached to a nylon line. A metal collar assures rapid descent and minimizes drift. A brass messenger triggers a release mechanism to seal the cylinder at the desired sampling depth. The cylinder has an outlet for removing water samples in order to minimize possible contamination.

- Bacteria culture equipment for fecal coliform test

- A computer with modem and telephone hookup so students can exchange data with other schools electronically

SUGGESTED SCHEDULE

The *Rivers Chemistry* unit is flexible: you can plan to do some of the lessons or all. Within a particular lesson, you can choose which of the activities suit your purposes. You can concentrate exclusively on *Rivers Chemistry* as a self-contained unit within your school year, or you can do a few lessons at a time, spread over a semester or more. Many teachers devote three weeks to *Rivers Chemistry* at the beginning of the year, continuing after that to spread the rest throughout the school year. Plan to do at least three to four water-quality tests in order to get significant benefit from *Rivers Chemistry*.

Lesson	Water-Quality Test	Average Student Time Required
2	pH	20–25 min in lab
3	Temperature	20–30 min in field
3	Flow *	35–45 min in field
4	Turbidity	20–30 min in field
5	Total Solids	35–45 min in lab
6	Dissolved Oxygen	25–35 min in field
7	Biochemical Oxygen Demand	5-day incubation period, plus 25–35 min in lab
8	Phosphates	20–30 min in lab or field
9	Nitrates	20–30 min in lab or field
10	Fecal Coliform	30–45 min, plus 24-hr incubation

* Flow rate is not one of the nine tests used to determine water quality; it is, however, incorporated into the curriculum.

USING ONE SET OF TEST KITS FOR AN ENTIRE CLASS

Ideally, during laboratory and field trip sessions each *Rivers Chemistry* class should be divided into at least three groups and each group should have its own test kit for each test performed. To keep costs down, however, an entire class can use one set of test kits to conduct all nine tests on a single trip to the river, using the steps following. (Teachers who use this method will need to make minor adaptations in testing and data-table procedures.) Over the course of the project, groups can be rotated so all students get experience doing all tests.

Day One: One Class Period of 40–50 Minutes

1. Divide the students into six groups.

2. Demonstrate the operational procedure for each test.

Day Two: One Class Period of 40–50 Minutes

Students can practice in lab becoming familiar with the equipment and the instructions for their individual topic(s).

Day Three: Field Trip at the River or Stream

Group 1: measures temperature and flow rate (each at least three times) and collects at least 1 liter of sample water to do the pH test at the school lab.

Group 2: does the turbidity test at least three times and collects 8 to 9 liters of water sample to take back to the school lab.

Group 3: does the dissolved oxygen test at least three times and prepares at least 3 water samples for biochemical oxygen demand.

Group 4: does the phosphate test at least three times.

Group 5: does the nitrate test at least three times.

Group 6: prepares at least three water samples to do the fecal coliform test at the school lab.

After Return to the School Lab

Group 1: completes the pH test and finishes data table for temperature and flow rate.

Group 2: finishes data table for turbidity.

Group 3: places the water samples they prepared at the river in a setting that will allow for the temperature-controlled five-day incubation period required for the biochemical oxygen demand analysis. Finishes data table for dissolved oxygen.

Group 4: finishes data table for phosphate.

Group 5: finishes data table for nitrate.

Group 6: prepares at least three samples for the 24-hour incubation period required for the fecal coliform test.

Day Four: One Class Period of 40–50 Minutes

All groups do total solids test, using the 8 to 9 liters of water sample collected by Group 2. Group 6 finishes fecal coliform test.

Day Five: One Class Period of 40–50 Minutes

At the end of the five-day incubation period, Group 3 demonstrates how biochemical oxygen demand is determined. Students now have all needed data to obtain an overall water quality value.

Day Six: One Class Period of 40–50 Minutes

Transmit data via computer modem.

SAFETY CONSIDERATIONS

While doing *Rivers Chemistry,* the teacher must take responsibility for and teach the students about safety in the chemistry lab and at the field site.

Every state has governmental agencies responsible for the protection and monitoring of the environment. Persons involved in water quality should become familiar with their state and local environmental agencies. Information can generally be obtained by contacting the environmental agency at the state capital. Such agencies often have regional offices throughout the state.

The U.S. Department of Labor's Occupational Safety and Health Administration (OSHA) is responsible for enforcing federal laws dealing with safety and hazards in the workplace. Specifically, federal regulation (29CFR1910.1200) requires "Hazard Communication Standards" to ensure that the hazards of all chemicals produced or imported are evaluated, and that information concerning their hazards is transmitted to teachers. This transmittal of information must be comprehensive and include container labeling and material safety data sheets (MSDS). In *Rivers Chemistry,* therefore, it is assumed that when you receive laboratory chemicals you also receive the material safety data sheets.

Commercially available water test kits (See listing in Appendix F for HACH Company, LaMotte Company, and CHEMetrics, Inc.) are relatively safe for the students and the environment. Chemical waste should be disposed of properly, however. Even though the volume and concentrations of wastes are insignificant compared with a large river's volume, good environmental practices require that waste chemicals from these test kits NOT BE POURED OR DUMPED INTO THE RIVER. Specifically, the nitrate, phosphate, and dissolved oxygen test generally contain trace metals of cadmium, molybdenum, and manganese. The chemical waste from these tests should be stored in a container labeled "Waste." If the waste container is placed under an exhaust hood for several days, the water will evaporate and leave only a small volume of residue.

Safe collection of river samples and running of chemical tests outdoors requires special considerations. Your site may require that the person taking samples wear a life jacket and a tow line. If the water is likely to contain hazardous materials, then protective gloves should be worn. Safety goggles must be worn.

An example of a student guide on laboratory and field safety rules is included in Lesson 1. Students are asked to sign on the bottom of the page to verify that they have received and read the rules.

ASSESSMENT

Assessment is the opportunity for students to demonstrate what they have learned and to exhibit their ability to apply that knowledge in a meaningful way. The instructor has the responsibility to provide instruments that give students the opportunity to best show their knowledge and skills. *Rivers Chemistry* provides a wide array of types of assessment tools. Just as so many other aspects of this unit are flexible, so, too, are teachers welcome to select which assessment tools suit their preferences and circumstances.

Traditional assessment tools assess student knowledge of a subject in terms of how well the student has learned and can reproduce the facts provided in the lessons. In *Rivers Chemistry,* many of the short-answer questions at the end of Student Information Sheets and Student Activity Sheets are designed to meet these objectives. Teachers use these as in-class assignments and as homework. Samples answers for these sheets, which also include short writing assignments, are included in Appendix C. Teachers may use their own performance criteria and scoring rubric for such standard components of science classes as data handling, graphing, and lab performance.

Educators increasingly realize the importance of assessing the extent to which the student can apply the instructional information to problem-solving situations; in other words, teachers want to know whether their students can really use what they've learned. Alternative assessment, often referred to as authentic assessment, attempts to determine if the student's knowledge is "usable." Instead of multiple-choice or other paper-and-pencil tests, the Rivers Project curriculum emphasizes authentic assessments tools. Authentic assessment assignments usually do not have a single answer, and students must employ critical thinking skills and creativity. Two of the more popular forms of authentic assessment are performance assessments and portfolio assessments. In both, students demonstrate how they use the classroom instruction to find a logical solution to a problem.

Performance Assessment

Performance assessment requires students to actively demonstrate their ability to apply the information presented in the curriculum. Individual students or groups of students work cooperatively to demonstrate the extent of their understanding. This unit includes lab-based and research-oriented assessments for many of the lessons. Teacher Notes and student handouts for each assessment that pertains to a specific lesson are in Appendix B. Appendix A includes Teacher Notes and Student Information Sheets for assessment tools that apply throughout the unit, specifically collage and science notebook.

Portfolio Assessment

An academic portfolio is not an accumulation of all the assignments and tests of a grading period; rather, it is a collection of selected documents organized as evidence of a student's cumulative learning. Like an artist's or model's portfolio, the academic portfolio is an opportunity for the students to demonstrate the depth and breadth of their learning. The student takes responsibility for selecting what to include in the portfolio and how to organize it. Students must feel a sense of ownership for their portfolio. The goal of the portfolio process is that the student reflects on his or her personal learning process and recognizes learning as a process that extends beyond textbooks and lectures. Teacher Notes and Student Information on portfolios are included in Appendix A.

Guidelines for Investigating River or Stream Water Quality

Focus

Students will learn safety guidelines and techniques for labwork and field-work, how a journal can be used, become acquainted with the method for determining water quality, and learn various statistical methods.

Learner Outcomes

Students will:

1. learn how to keep a journal for personal and class work.
2. learn safety cautions in preparation for labwork and fieldwork.
3. learn techniques in preparation for labwork and fieldwork.
4. start to become familiar with the method used to evaluate water quality.
5. learn statistical techniques for measuring the precision and accuracy of data.

Time

Three to four class periods of 40–50 minutes per period. Students whose math level is low may require extra time for Student Information 1.5 and 1.6.

DAY 1: Student Information 1.1: Journal Writing
Student Information 1.2: Safety Guidelines and Contract

DAY 2: Student Information 1.3: Lab and Field Techniques
Student Information 1.4: The Quality of Your River or Stream

DAY 3: Student Information 1.5: Accuracy and Precision of Data
Student Information 1.6: Should All Data Be Used?

Advance Preparation

Prepare to supply students with Student Information 1.1 through 1.6. If desired, prepare two copies of Student Information 1.2 per student, so that each student may keep one copy and turn in one signed copy. If appropriate, add parental signature line.

Gather all necessary materials for this lesson. Make arrangements for each student to have a journal and a calculator with a square-root function for the entire unit. Decide whether to include project-long assessment tools presented in Appendix A, such as portfolios, science notebooks, or collages. If so, prepare to supply students with Student Information sheets about the selected assessments. If desired, distribute a copy of the Glossary for *Rivers Chemistry* to each student for reference throughout the unit.

Before beginning Student Information 1.4, become familiar with the method used for determining water-quality index (WQI). Refer to local water agencies and to resources in Appendix F as needed. Locate the page number in this book for the Q-value chart for each of the nine tests; make overheads or photocopies to share some of these charts with students.

Safety and Waste Disposal

Before having students handle materials in Student Information 1.3, make sure they are familiar with the safety procedures covered in Student Information 1.2.

Materials

Student Information 1.1: Journal Writing
Per student
journal with bound pages

Student Information 1.3: Lab and Field Techniques
For teacher demonstration (or per group)
200 mL distilled water
100 mL HCl, 12 *M*
glass beaker, 250 mL in size
soap
drying rack, oven, or recloseable plastic bag
30–40 mL standard solution
water-sampling pole, with clamp
sampling bottle
bucket or tub of water

Student Information 1.5: Accuracy and Precision of Data
Per student
calculator with square-root function

Vocabulary

accuracy
acid wash
deviation
distill wash
material safety data sheet (MSDS)
overall Water-Quality Index (WQI)
percent error
precision

Q-value percent
quotient test
reported value
standard deviation
standard solution
standard wash
statistics
weighting factor

Background Information for the Teacher

For Student Information 1.2, you may need to alter the safety guidelines for labwork and fieldwork, and the student contract, to fit your particular situation.

Introducing the Lesson	1. Have the students recall what the weather was one week ago. Emphasize that, in science, keeping a journal is important so investigators can recall past information readily.
	2. Ask students if they have ever heard of someone being injured at work or home while performing a specific task. Have them discuss what could have prevented the accident.
	3. Read the following passage to the class.

"Kristin, I have some bad news", the doctor said. "The lab report came back this morning. From all indications, you have a disease that is going to require your confinement at home for a long period of time." The doctor then gave Kristin all the particulars of the lab report. When Kristin arrived back home from the appointment, she had to sit down for fear of falling. That night, she couldn't sleep well, imagining the terrible ordeal ahead.

About 10 A.M. the phone rang. "Kristin, this is Dr. Sternberg. I want you to come to my office as soon as possible. The lab report may not be correct, and I want to have another set of tests performed." Kristin rushed to the doctor's office and had more labwork done. When the results came, they showed that the first report was erroneous; she was perfectly healthy.

"What happened on the first test?," she asked. The doctor replied, "It appears that the person in charge of the test did two things. First, that person did not use proper lab techniques when performing the test. Second, the tests seemed to have been run with instruments that were not cleaned properly."

4. Ask the students if they know of a parallel situation. How would they feel if it happened to them? Emphasize the importance of proper technique and cleanliness when performing a scientific test.

Developing the Lesson	1. Make sure each student has a journal. Have students read, discuss, answer questions, and prepare their journal as described in Student Information 1.1: Journal Writing. For specific teaching activities on journal writing, see *Rivers Language Arts*. (Answers and solutions for Student Information and Activity Sheets are in Appendix C.)
	2. If students will do science notebooks as well as journals, hand out and discuss Student Assessment: Keeping a Science Notebook. This sheet, as well as related Teacher Notes, is found in Appendix A.
	3. Have students read, discuss, and answer questions on Student Information 1.2: Safety Guidelines and Contract. Show students the location and use of safety devices. Emphasize the necessity for safety cautions in lab and in the field. Have students sign and return to you the safety contract.
	4. Have students read, and discuss Student Information 1.3: Lab and Field Techniques. Demonstrate or supervise a student demonstration of the acid wash and distill wash procedures. (If desired, during this lesson, and dur-

ing each succeeding lesson, have students look up the definition of new terms in the Glossary. Discuss the vocabulary with the class.)

5. Using a bucket or tub of water and the water sampling device, demonstrate or supervise a student demonstration of the water-sample collection technique students will use at their field site. Have students answer questions on Student Information 1.3.

6. Have students read, discuss, and answer questions on Student Information 1.4: The Quality of Your River or Stream. Discuss the importance of monitoring the quality of our waterways. Provide students with an overview of the Rivers Project. Explain that in this curriculum, all the information students are asked to learn relates directly to the local river or stream they are going to study. Using photocopies or overhead projection, show students examples of the Q-value charts in *Rivers Chemistry* lessons.

7. With the students, read and discuss Student Information 1.5: Accuracy and Precision of Data. Have students solve the problems. For additional specific teaching activities on statistical methods, see *Rivers Mathematics*.

8. With students, read and discuss Student Information 1.6: Should All Data Be Used? Have students solve the problems.

Concluding the Lesson

1. Hand out and discuss Student Information sheets about other project-long assessment tools you will be using, such as portfolios or collages. (For more Teacher Notes and sample student sheets on these assessment tools, see Appendix A.)

2. Have students read out loud one or two journal entries they feel are important regarding Lesson 1.

3. Have students note in their journals (or science notebooks) their predictions for the water quality of the river or stream they will be testing. Tell them that they will be referring to these predictions again after they have completed the water-quality testing and analyses.

4. Have students note advertising on television, on radio, or in newspapers that uses statistical methods. Example: "Sixty-five percent of doctors recommend Brand X."

Assessing the Lesson

1. Have students write in their journal a short story, poem, or paragraph that summarizes Lesson 1.

2. If students will be doing water-quality collages, have them start collecting materials.

Extending the Lesson

1. Arrange a field trip to a hospital or industrial lab or invite a laboratory technician to visit the class to discuss safety and laboratory techniques.

2. Arrange a field trip to a water testing lab or invite a water-quality technician to visit the class to discuss the performance and reporting of the nine tests of water quality.

3. Have students start a newsletter or bulletin board that informs others in their school about the local river or stream, periodically updating information as the project progresses. For specific teaching activities about writing newspaper articles, see *Rivers Language Arts*.

Journal Writing

Can you recall exactly what you did or observed several days ago?
Probably not. Because human memory is often faulty or incomplete, during
Rivers Chemistry, keep a written journal in which you record your thoughts
and activities about your river study.

Keeping a Journal

Your journal will be your own private record of your progress during this
course of study. Journal entries should focus on data collection as well as on
personal impressions of classwork, labwork, and fieldwork.

The journal should be bound so that pages cannot be removed or inserted.
When you receive your journal, write your name in the front, along with
"Rivers Chemistry." Then number all the pages consecutively. Label pages 1
and 2 as "Contents."

Beginning on page 3, place the following entries on each page:

Date:

Time:

Location:

Purpose:

Bring your journal to every class meeting and take it into the field as well.
Make an entry in your journal for each day class meets (more times if
desired), reflecting on each day's activities and relating what you have
learned to any information you have already acquired. At the end of each
activity, you will find suggestions for journal entries.

Include in your journal any equations and other information discussed in
class that are not part of the student information or student activity sheets.
After completing an activity, write a summary that includes analyses of
experimental data and your conclusions. If you are in the field, record the
weather conditions, wind velocity (mild, gusty, and so forth), approximate
water depth, plants and animals at the site, and any other observations you
feel are significant.

Write all journal entries legibly in ink. Do not erase or completely obliterate
any entry. If you want to make a change or revision, do so on a separate page
or draw a line through an unwanted entry and write in your correction. Add
the date and your initials to indicate you are the person making the correction.

© SIU, published by Addison Wesley Longman, Inc.

Include more than just data or scientific observations in your journal. Also record your personal impressions or reactions; summaries or critiques of class activities; assigned or independent study topics; and anecdotal information from your labwork or fieldwork. Write about special happenings, triumphs, and projects that didn't work out as you planned or expected.

The purpose of your journal is to help you see the broader meaning of your river study and reflect on its importance. Your journal is not only for scientific analysis but also for your thoughts, reflections, and inspirations. The journal is your personal repository for information you may want to retrieve in the future.

Questions

Read the following passage.

Only two more days remained until Cindy's mother's birthday. Cindy had already bought her mother a gift, but she still needed the right card. "Maybe I could write my own card," she thought, "But what could I say? How can I start?"

As she thought about her mother, Cindy remembered that a few days ago she had written in her journal some of her thoughts while she was with her class doing river work. She reviewed her journal entries and composed a card she felt was just perfect for her mother's birthday.

People often write, and draw, in journals thoughts, impressions, and facts that become valuable later. Many composers, writers, and artists find inspiration for their songs, stories, poems, books, and other creations this way.

1. List as many song titles as you can that involve water.
2. List as many book and poem titles as you can that involve water.

© SIU, published by Addison Wesley Longman, Inc.

Safety Guidelines and Contract

Labwork and fieldwork require specific, and different, kinds of safety precautions. By following the instructions in this material, you will be able to work safely in either type of setting. Once you have reviewed these materials, signify your agreement to follow these safety guidelines by signing your name to the Safety Contract.

Laboratory Safety Guidelines

1. Never perform an experiment in the laboratory without the permission and supervision of your teacher.
2. Never eat food or drink beverages in the laboratory.
3. Before performing any laboratory procedure, read the instructions and review the safety cautions.
4. Always wear safety goggles in the laboratory. Ordinary prescription glasses do not provide adequate protection from fumes or splashed chemicals.
5. Never allow chemicals or any hazardous material to come in contact with your skin. Wear protective gloves when handling chemicals or water that may be contaminated.
6. Shoes, not sandals, should be worn in the laboratory to protect your feet in the event of a spill or breakage.
7. If working with an open flame, tie back long hair and loose clothing. Make sure no flammable materials or vapors are nearby. Use tongs or insulated gloves to pick up equipment that has been heated recently.
8. Know the location of material safety data sheets (MSDS), portable eye-wash fountain, fire extinguisher, and first-aid kit and how to use each properly. **MSDS sheets** describe the proper safety precautions to observe when using specific chemicals.
9. Use a spatula for transferring solids, and use appropriate glassware for transferring liquids.
10. Never use dirty, cracked, or chipped glassware.
11. Never pick up broken glassware with your bare hands. Sweep broken glass into a dustpan and place in a waste container provided by your teacher.
12. If your skin comes in contact with acid, immediately wash with soap and rinse the area thoroughly with water.
13. If acid spills in your work area, inform your teacher immediately.
14. Dispose of excess chemicals or wastes as directed by your teacher.
15. Never return excess chemicals or reagents to their original containers.
16. At the end of each lab period, clean up your lab area and wash your hands with soap and water thoroughly.

© SIU, published by Addison Wesley Longman, Inc.

Field Safety Guidelines

1. Stay within the area directed by your teacher. Do not cross private property without the teacher's permission.
2. Always stay with your group, and do all sampling and analyses under the supervision of a teacher or your teacher's authorized aide.
3. Never engage in horseplay or distracting activities.
4. Wear safety goggles and protective gloves. Wear insect repellent and sunscreen if the conditions warrant.
5. Make sure you know the location of the first-aid kit and portable eyewash station. If you have any outdoor allergies, bring along any special medication that may be necessary in case of an allergy attack.
6. If working on a waterway bigger than a small, shallow stream, wear a life jacket and tow line.
7. Avoid walking on unstable or slippery ground, rocks, or wood.
8. Never drink from or wash food in a waterway. Bring water from the lab for washing and drinking.
9. Place all wastes in containers provided by your teacher, and take the wastes back to your school for proper disposal. Do not leave waste at the field site; do not dump waste into a waterway.
10. After you have completed your fieldwork, wash your hands with soap and potable water.

Safety Contract

I have read and understand all the laboratory and field safety rules, and I agree to follow these rules. If I fail to follow these rules, I will not be allowed to do the activities.

_____
Student's Signature

Questions

Read the following paragraph.

Judy finished her lab before the rest of the class. She put away her safety goggles and noticed that she had some leftover chemical. She wondered what would happen if the leftover was placed in acid. She picked up some of the chemical with her hand and placed it in a bottle of acid that was nearby. The acid turned to a dark color. She quickly dumped the contents into the sink, hoping her teacher had not noticed. In the process, she cracked the acid bottle and some spilled onto her sandal and the floor. She placed the rest of the chemical back into its original bottle, saying to herself, "Waste not, want not." She looked at her wristwatch; only one minute until bell time. She knew if she took time to clean her lab area and wash herself up, she wouldn't have

© SIU, published by Addison Wesley Longman, Inc.

much time to talk with Ginny in the hallway, so, as soon as the bell rang, out the door she scampered.

1. Make a list of lab safety cautions Judy did not follow.
2. Describe at least one negative impact that could have resulted from each broken safety caution.

Read the following paragraph.

Jack thought it was great being outside instead of sitting in class. As he looked around, he noticed a glittering metal object. "I think that's a silver dollar," he said to himself. Jack slowed his walking pace until his teacher and classmates were about 25 meters ahead of him. He quickly left the path, climbed the fence, and picked up the object. Sure thing—it was a silver dollar. He hopped back over the fence, ran to catch up, and rejoined his classmates just as they got to the water, thinking, "Today's my lucky day."

3. Make a list of field safety cautions Jack ignored.
4. What could have happened to make it Jack's unlucky day?

© STU, published by Addison Wesley Longman, Inc.

Lab and Field Techniques

In science, obtaining accurate results requires learning and practicing various lab and field techniques. Here are techniques you will use in several lessons in *Rivers Chemistry*.

Laboratory Techniques

Clean glassware helps insure accurate results. To clean glassware, use the following procedures.

1. Wash glassware with soap and water. Rinse thoroughly with tap water.
2. From your teacher, obtain a bottle of acid wash solution. **Acid wash** refers to rinsing with a dilute solution of hydrochloric acid (HCl). This solution is prepared by obtaining concentrated hydrochloric acid (12 *M*) and diluting it by half with distilled water. Example: Place 100 mL of distilled water in a beaker. Slowly and gently add 100 mL of concentrated hydrochloric acid. ALWAYS POUR ACID INTO WATER; never pour water into acid. If water is poured into acid, the acid may splatter out of the acid container and harm you, other students, or nearby equipment.
3. Turn on tap water so that you obtain a small gentle flow.
4. Over the sink, but out of line of the flowing tap water, carefully pour 5 to 10 mL of acid wash into the glassware. Holding the glassware over the sink, and out of line of the flowing tap water, slightly tilt and slowly rotate the glassware so the acid comes in contact with all the inner surface of the beaker. Slowly rotate the glassware several times.
5. Carefully, gently, slowly but still rotating the glassware, pour the acid from the glassware into the sink so that the tap water thoroughly flushes the acid wash down the drain. Allow the tap water to run for several minutes. Turn off the tap water.
6. This process, called "acid washing," will remove any matter that was not removed by soap and water in Step 1 above.
7. At this point, the acid inside your glassware must be removed. Obtain a bottle of distilled water.
8. Over the sink, pour 5 to 10 mL of distilled water into the glassware. Holding the glassware over the sink, slightly tilt and slowly rotate it so the distilled water comes in contact with all the inner surface of the glassware. While still rotating the glassware, pour the distilled water into the sink. This process is called **distill wash.**
9. Repeat Step 8 two more times. At this point, all acid wash will be removed from the glassware.

© SIU, published by Addison Wesley Longman, Inc.

10. Invert the glassware on a drying rack or place it right-side up in a drying oven. Do not dry the glassware with toweling, as small pieces of toweling may remain in the glassware.

11. If a drying rack or oven is not available, place the glassware in a resealable plastic bag until you are ready to use it.

   In several activities in *Rivers Chemistry,* you will be directed to do a standard wash after doing a distill wash. A **standard wash** refers to rinsing with a solution of known concentration or acidity, known as a standard solution. A **standard solution** is usually used to provide a true value for testing the accuracy of equipment or procedures.

12. A standard wash can be done on glassware after completing Step 9 of the distill-wash process, or after glassware has dried in Step 10.

13. Obtain from your teacher a bottle of standard solution. Over the sink, pour 5–10 mL of the standard solution into the glassware. Holding the glassware over the sink, slightly tilt and slowly rotate it so the standard solution comes in contact with all the inner surface of the glassware. While still rotating the glassware, pour the standard solution into the sink.

14. Repeat Step 13 two more times. Glassware is then ready for use.

Field Techniques

When doing analytical work in the lab or in the field, take extra care to insure that no clean container becomes contaminated with foreign matter from you or other sources. In fact, gloves not only protect you from the possible harmful pollutants in the water but also protect the water from you.

Water near the surface of a river or stream may be quite different from water at half depth or near the bottom. Surface water near the bank may differ from surface water halfway across the waterway. In order to obtain data that best represents the waterway, water samples should be taken halfway across a river or stream and at one-half its depth.

To reach a point from which you can take such a sample, you may be able to walk safely, if your waterway is small and shallow. In most other cases, you will need a pole in order to get as close to the middle as you can. If you do not have a commercial water-sample pole, an extension pole used by painters to attach a paint roller is ideal. It can be collapsed for easy transport or extended to various lengths. A test-tube type clamp can be fastened to the end to accommodate containers of various sizes. If a pole is used:

1. Attach a clean sampling bottle to the pole.
2. Extend the pole straight out over the water.
3. Rotate the pole so the mouth of the container faces down. Gently lower the container vertically into the water until it is at half-depth. If you lower the bottle right-side up, it will fill up with surface water before it reaches the halfway point of the waterway's depth. If you cannot see the bottom, lower

© SIU, published by Addison Wesley Longman, Inc.

the container until it is 10–20 cm below the surface. Avoid having either the container or the pole touch or otherwise disturb the bottom of the river or stream. If the bottom is disturbed, silt, mud, and so forth may get inside the bottle, preventing you from obtaining a true sample of water.

4. Slowly rotate the pole 90 degrees until the mouth of the container faces the current. Leave the container in this position for 30–60 seconds. This will allow water to flow into the container. If you rotated the bottle so the mouth faced away from the current, water would come in contact with the outside of the bottle before it reached the inside. This could contaminate the sample before it reaches the inside. (The bottle's inside surface, at this point, is most likely cleaner than its outside.) Continue to slowly rotate the pole until the container is right-side up (mouth facing upward).

5. Gently raise the container out of the water, and pour the water back into the river downstream. This first sample is discarded because you want the river water to wet the inside of the container.

6. Repeat Steps 2–5 one more time to ensure the inside is thoroughly wet by the water.

7. Repeat Steps 2–4. Gently raise the container out of the water and detach the bottle from the pole. This third sample will be used for analysis.

If you have a small, shallow stream you may need to modify these procedures. If your waterway is very large, you will need to take your sample from a bridge or dock, and you may need to attach weights to offset the force of the current. Whatever your circumstances and equipment, use techniques that will ensure you of obtaining accurate data from a sample that best represents your water.

Questions

1. Describe how an acid wash solution is prepared.
2. Why should glassware be:
   a. acid washed after it has been cleaned with soap and water?
   b. distill washed after it has been acid washed?
3. Why should you not disturb the bottom of a waterway when collecting a water sample?
4. After obtaining a bottle of water the first time, why should you dump it out?
5. Explain why you should lower the sampling bottle into the water upside down instead of right-side up.
6. Give two reasons why gloves should be worn when collecting a water sample.

© SIU, published by Addison Wesley Longman, Inc.

The Quality of Your River or Stream

Scientists, environmentalists, water-management agency representatives, industrial specialists, and other professionals often refer to the water quality of a river or stream. When they do so, they are referring to quantitative results of specific tests and analyses. In the course of the *Rivers Chemistry* unit, you will find out what determines water quality, and you will determine the water quality of your chosen waterway.

Identifying and Weighting Various Water-Quality Tests

In order for you to get a final grade in a school subject, you often take several exams and quizzes. The instructor then averages your grades from those tests in order to determine your final grade. The same is true when a waterway is graded. It undergoes numerous tests; evaluators then average the test results and award a final grade that indicates how good or bad the water is.

The National Sanitation Foundation uses nine tests to determine water quality: dissolved oxygen, fecal coliform, pH, biochemical oxygen demand, temperature change, phosphates, nitrates, turbidity, and total solids. In later lessons in *Rivers Chemistry,* you will learn the definitions, significance, and procedures for each of these tests.

Just as exams count more than quizzes, some of the nine water-quality tests count more than others. How much a single test counts when computing the overall value of a series of tests is called its weighting factor. Some tests have a higher weighting factor than others. Table 1-1 lists the nine tests and their individual weighting factors. Dissolved oxygen has the highest weighting factor of 0.17, while total solids has the lowest, 0.07. The weighting factor is actually the decimal equivalent of its percent. For example, dissolved oxygen's **weighting factor** of 0.17 is equivalent to 17 percent of the total grade; total solids count 7 percent of the final grade. If you add the weighting factors for all nine water-quality tests, they equal 1.00, or 100 percent. Try it, using Table 1-1.

© SIU, published by Addison Wesley Longman, Inc.

TABLE 1-1

Units and Weighting Factors for the Nine Water-Quality Tests

Test	Units	Weighting Factor	Percent	Total (%)
1. Dissolved oxygen	% Sat	0.17	= 17%	
2. Fecal coliform	colonies/100 mL	0.16	= 16%	
3. pH	units	0.11	= 11%	
4. BOD	mg/L	0.11	= 11%	
5. Temperature change	°C	0.10	= 10%	
6. Phosphate	mg/L	0.10	= 10%	
7. Nitrate	mg/L	0.10	= 10%	
8. Turbidity	meters or JTU	0.08	= 08%	
9. Total solids	mg/L	0.07	= 07%	

Converting Test Results to Common Values

Running each of these nine water-quality tests gives investigators data, but data for different tests are in different units. For instance, the unit for fecal coliform is colonies/100 mL, but the unit for temperature is degrees Celsius. The unit for each type of test is shown in Table 1-1. So how do investigators add up the results of all these tests if the results are in different units?

If you add 5 oranges and 6 apples, you do not get 11 oranges, nor do you get 11 apples. You get 11 fruits. In other words, you must convert the 5 oranges and 6 apples into a unit that is common for both; in this case, the common unit is fruit. Water quality experts have developed a unit that is common to all nine tests. It is called **Q-value percent.** Determining water quality requires converting results from each of the nine tests to the common Q-value. Each test for water quality has its own Q-value chart that facilitates this conversion. You will find and use these graphs in later lessons as you progress through *Rivers Chemistry*. An example of such a graph is Figure 1-1.

Here's how to do such a conversion. Assume you analyzed a sample of water and found 300 mg/L of total solids. Now you need to convert total solids from mg/L to Q-value percent. Find 300 mg/L on the horizontal axis of Figure 1-1. The 300 mg/L line intersects the curve at 60 percent. Therefore, the Q-value for 300 mg/L of total solids is 60 percent.

Determining Overall Water Quality

After converting each test result to its Q-value, multiply each Q-value by its corresponding weighting factor. This will give you a decimal score

© SIU, published by Addison Wesley Longman, Inc.

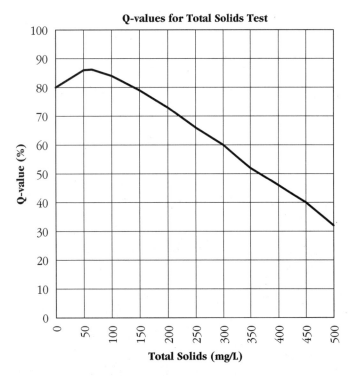

Figure 1-1: Graph for Converting Total Solids from mg/L to Q-value

(or percent, if you use the percent values instead of the decimal values). Adding all the scores (or percent values) for the nine tests yields the final grade. This final grade for water is called **overall water quality index** (WQI). Finally, to convert the water quality index into a term that describes the quality of the water—how good or bad it is—use the table in Table 1-2.

TABLE 1-2

Quality of Water

Overall Water Quality Index	Quality of Water
90–100%	Excellent
70–89%	Good
50–69%	Medium
25–49%	Bad
0–24%	Very Bad

After completing the *Rivers Chemistry* unit, you will be able to:
1. do all nine water-quality tests.
2. convert each test to its Q-value percent.
3. calculate the total percent for each test.
4. determine WQI.

© SIU, published by Addison Wesley Longman, Inc.

Questions

1. Define weighting factor.
2. Why is the Q-value used?
3. How is the WQI obtained?
4. A sample of river water was analyzed and the following information was obtained. Duplicate this chart on your own paper.

Test	Units	Q-value (%)	Weighting Factor	Total (%)
1. Dissolved oxygen	46% Sat	38	0.17	
2. Fecal coliform	16,000 colonies/100 mL	8.0	0.16	
3. pH	7.7 units	91	0.11	
4. BOD	4.39 mg/L	63	0.11	
5. Temperature change	0.1°C	93	0.10	
6. Phosphate	0.63 mg/L	51	0.10	
7. Nitrate	10.37 mg/L	48	0.10	
8. Turbidity	0.30 meters	5.0	0.08	
9. Total solids	475 mg/L	36	0.07	

WQI = _____

Quality of Water = _____

a. Determine the total percentage for each of the nine tests, and place your answers in the blank column. (Some of the chart has already been filled in.)
b. Determine the WQI.
c. Determine the quality of water.

5. Another river sample was tested, and the Q-value for total solids must be calculated. Duplicate the chart below on your paper.

Test	Units	Q-value (%)	Weighting Factor	Total (%)
Total Solids	150 mg/L		0.07	

a. Using Table 2-1, find the Q-value for total solids if total solids = 150 mg/L. Place your result in the chart.
b. Find the total percent for total solids. Place your result in the chart.

© SIU, published by Addison Wesley Longman, Inc.

Accuracy and Precision of Data

In everyday speech, people may use the terms *accuracy* and *precision* interchangeably, but in scientific work, they have different meanings, representing essential concepts in scientific data gathering and analysis. **Accuracy** refers to closeness to the truth. Assume a jar had 1,000 beans, and you guessed it had 900. If a friend guessed it had 800, your guess would be more accurate than your friend's because your guess is closer to the true value of 1,000.

Precision refers to the closeness of several readings to one another. In Figure 1-2, the arrows are close together; therefore the person who shot the arrows has good precision.

A   B

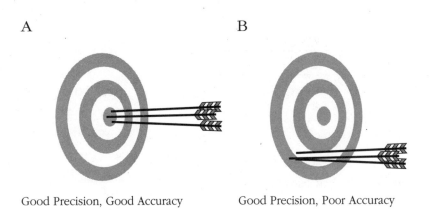

Good Precision, Good Accuracy   Good Precision, Poor Accuracy

Figure 1-2: Accuracy versus Precision

The arrows on Target A in the figure are close together and are also inside the center. The person who shot the arrows has good accuracy (the center represents the truth), and the person also has good precision (the arrows are close together). The arrows on Target B are close together but are far from the center. This represents good precision but poor accuracy.

In analyzing water, often no one knows the truth. No person knows exactly how much bacteria is in the Mississippi River. If the truth is not known, only precision can be found. On the other hand, if the truth is known, both accuracy and precision can be determined. **Statistics** is the branch of mathematics that deals with the collection, analysis, interpretation, and presentation of data. In these materials, you will learn several statistical procedures that scientists and mathematicians use to determine accuracy, precision, or both.

© SIU, published by Addison Wesley Longman, Inc.

Percent Error

In circumstances in which truth is known, investigators can calculate the degree of inaccuracy of data gathered, known as the **percent error.**

$$\text{Percent error} = \frac{|\text{True Value} - \text{Experimental Value}|}{\text{True Value}} \times 100\%$$

Example: You made a standard nitrate solution that had 1.0 mg nitrate/L. The concentration of this standard is then a known truth. Your friend then tested the solution and determined it had 0.9 mg/L of nitrate. Your friend's percent error is 10%.

$$\text{Percent error} = \frac{|1.0 - 0.9|}{1.0} \times 100\% = 10\%$$

When more than one set of data is gathered, the results are averaged, and that average is then used in calculating percent error. The average is called **mean.** In water-quality analysis, for instance, any of the nine tests performed must be done at least three times, to increase the usefulness of the results.

Example: You made a standard nitrate solution that had 1.0 mg/L. One student tested the solution and reported 0.7 mg/L; another student tested the solution and reported 0.9 mg/L; a third tested and reported 1.2 mg/L. To find the percent error, first find the mean of the reported values:

$$\text{Average} = \frac{0.7 \text{ mg/L} + 0.9 \text{ mg/L} + 1.2 \text{ mg/L}}{3} = 0.9 \text{ mg/L}$$

$$\text{Percent error} = \frac{|1.0 - 0.9|}{1.0} \times 100\% = 10\%$$

Problems

1. A 1.0 mg/L nitrate standard solution was made. Four tests were made on the solution, and the following results were obtained: 0.8 mg/L, 0.8 mg/L, 1.0 mg/L, and 1.0 mg/L. Calculate the percent error.
2. Using a 5.0 mg/L phosphate standard solution, three tests were run. The tests showed 4.8 mg/L, 5.1 mg/L, and 5.4 mg/L. Calculate the percent error.

Deviation and Standard Deviation

To determine how precise your data are, you need to find the **deviation,** or difference, between each measured value and the average, or mean, value. Once the deviation is known, you can do a more sophisticated calculation, known as standard deviation, which gives a more detailed indication of how much variation among the values exists.

Finding the deviation for each value is the first step in finding the standard deviation for the overall results. To find the standard deviation, perform the following steps:

© STU, published by Addison Wesley Longman, Inc.

Step 1: Find the mean (m) of the test results.

$$m = \frac{result_1 + result_2 + \ldots + result_n}{n}$$

Step 2: Find the deviation (d_x) for each result by subtracting the mean (m) from each result (x) and using the absolute value.

$$d_x = |x - m|$$

Step 3: Square each deviation found in Step 2.

$$|(x - m)|^2 = (d_x)^2$$

Step 4: Find the sum of the squared results, and divide the sum by one less than the number of results.

$$\frac{(d_1^2 + d_2^2 + d_n^2)}{n-1}$$

Step 5: Calculate the standard deviation, d_s, by taking the square root of the quotient found in Step 4.

$$d_s = \frac{(d_1^2 + d_2^2 + \ldots + d_n^2)}{n-1}$$

Example: A sample of river water taken from a particular location was tested three times for nitrate, and the following results were obtained: 1.50 mg/L, 1.20 mg/L, and 1.70 mg/L.

Step 1: Find the mean (m).

$$m = \frac{1.50 \text{ mg/L} + 1.20 \text{ mg/L} + 1.70 \text{ mg/L}}{3} = 1.50 \text{ mg/L}$$

Step 2: Find the deviation for each result.

deviation for 1st test (d_1) = $|1.50 - 1.50|$ = 0.00
deviation for 2nd test (d_2) = $|1.20 - 1.50|$ = 0.30
deviation for 3rd test (d_3) = $|1.70 - 1.50|$ = 0.20

Step 3: Square each deviation.

$(d_1)^2 = (0.00)^2 = 0.00$
$(d_2)^2 = (0.30)^2 = 0.09$
$(d_3)^2 = (0.20)^2 = 0.04$

Step 4: Sum the squared numbers, and divide by one less than number of results.

$$\frac{0.00 + 0.09 + 0.04}{3 - 1} = 0.065$$

Step 5: Find standard deviation (d_s) by taking the square root of the answer from Step 4.

$$d_s = 0.065 = \pm\ 0.25$$

© SIU, published by Addison Wesley Longman, Inc.

Reported Value

The **reported value** is the mean of the individual tests together with the standard deviation. So, the reported value in the example would be 1.50 ± 0.25 mg/L. This means that your data show that the water at your location has 1.50 mg of nitrate per liter, ± 0.25. In other words, you are stating that the amount of nitrate could be as high as 1.75 mg/L or as low as 1.25 mg/L.

Example: A sample of river water taken from a particular location was tested four times for pH, and the following results were obtained: 6.74 units, 7.23 units, 6.85 units, and 7.28 units.

Step 1. Find the mean (m).

$$m = \frac{6.74 + 7.23 + 6.85 + 7.28}{4} = \frac{28.1}{4} = 7.03 \text{ units}$$

Step 2: Find the deviation for each result.

$$d_1 = |\,6.74 - 7.03\,| = 0.29$$
$$d_2 = |\,7.23 - 7.03\,| = 0.20$$
$$d_3 = |\,6.85 - 7.03\,| = 0.18$$
$$d_4 = |\,7.28 - 7.03\,| = 0.25$$

Step 3: Square each deviation.

$$(d_1)^2 = (0.29)^2 = 0.084$$
$$(d_2)^2 = (0.20)^2 = 0.040$$
$$(d_3)^2 = (0.18)^2 = 0.032$$
$$(d_4)^2 = (0.25)^2 = 0.063$$

Step 4: Sum the squared numbers, and divide the sum by one less than the number of results.

$$\frac{0.0084 + 0.040 + 0.032 + 0.063}{4 - 1} = 0.073$$

Step 5: Find the standard deviation by taking the square root of the answer from Step 4.

$$d_s = \sqrt{0.073} = \pm 0.27 \text{ units} = \text{standard deviation}$$

Therefore, the reported value is

$$7.03 \pm 0.27 \text{ units.}$$

DRIFTWOOD

The American writer Mark Twain (1835–1910), an avid river watcher, often cited a comment made by the British politician Benjamin Disraeli (1804–1881) on the subject of statistics: "There are three kinds of lies: lies, damned lies, and statistics."

Problems

1. A sample of river water was collected at a test site and tested 5 times for fecal coliform. The following results were obtained.

© SIU, published by Addison Wesley Longman, Inc.

Observations	Colonies/100 mL
1	950
2	760
3	1213
4	894
5	1116

    a. Determine the mean of the 5 tests.

    b. Calculate the standard deviation.

    c. What value should be reported?

2. A sample of water was analyzed for dissolved oxygen 3 times, and the following data were collected: 18.6 mg/L, 17.5 mg/L, and 19.2 mg/L.

    a. Determine the mean of the tests.

    b. Calculate the standard deviation.

    c. What value should be reported?

© SIU, published by Addison Wesley Longman, Inc.

Should All Data Be Used?

When you run a particular test several times on a sample of water, some of the data may differ quite a bit from most of the other results. For instance, assume that when you ran 6 tests to determine the phosphate concentration, you obtained the following data: 2.5 mg/L, 3.2 mg/L, 2.7 mg/L, 4.3 mg/L, and 2.3 mg/L.

As you look at the data, the 4.3 mg/L result seems rather far from the other data. So, when determining the reported value for phosphate concentration, should you use this 4.3 mg/L result or not? Is it too far from the other data or not?

Quotient Test

In order to determine whether to reject a piece of data that seems quite different, a test has been developed called a **quotient test.** This test involves the following steps, illustrated using the data in the preceding example.

Step 1: Arrange the data in decreasing order.

$$4.3 \text{ mg/L}, 3.2 \text{ mg/L}, 2.7 \text{ mg/L}, 2.5 \text{ mg/L}, 2.3 \text{ mg/L}$$

Step 2: Subtract the smallest number from the largest number. The different between the two is called **range.**

$$\text{range} = 4.3 \text{ mg/L} - 2.3 \text{ mg/L} = 2.0 \text{ mg/L}$$

Step 3: Find the difference between the questionable data and its closest neighbor. (In this example, the closest neighbor to 4.3 mg/L is 3.2 mg/L.)

$$4.3 \text{ mg/L} - 3.2 \text{ mg/L} = 1.1 \text{ mg/L}$$

Step 4: Find the quotient of the difference obtained in Step 3 and the range.

$$\text{Quotient} = \frac{\text{difference}}{\text{range}} = \frac{1.1 \text{ mg/L}}{2.0 \text{ mg/L}} = 0.55$$

Step 5: In the Number of Observations column of Table 1-3, find the number of tests that were run. In the Quotient column of this table, find the number that corresponds to the number of observations.

5 tests (number of observations) corresponds to a quotient of 0.64.

Step 6: Compare the quotient calculated in Step 4 with the quotient obtained in Step 5. If the Step-4 quotient is less than the Step-5 quotient, then retain the questionable data. If the Step-4 quotient is greater than or equal to the Step-5 quotient, then reject the questionable data. Because 0.55 is less than 0.64, 4.3 mg/L is retained.

© SIU, published by Addison Wesley Longman, Inc.

TABLE 1-3

Typical Rejection Quotient

Number of Observations	Quotient *
3	0.94
4	0.76
5	0.64
6	0.56
7	0.51
8	0.47
9	0.44
10 or greater	0.40

* when values are accurate 90 percent of the time

Problems

1. Assume the following concentrations of calcium carbonate were obtained from an analysis of river water. Should the 214 mg/L result be rejected? Why or why not? Show your calculations.

Test Number	Results (mg/L)
1	203
2	204
3	207
4	214

2. Assume the total solids in three water samples were measured at 810 mg/L, 900 mg/L, and 2520 mg/L.
   a. Should the largest number be rejected? Why or why not? Show your calculations.
   b. Should the smallest number be rejected? Why or why not? Show your calculations.

3. The water temperature at a test site was measured, and the following data were collected: 27°C, 28°C, 29°C, 26°C, 31°C, and 28°C.
   a. Should the highest reading be rejected? Why or why not? Show your calculations.
   b. Should the lowest reading be rejected? Why or why not? Show your calculations.

© SIU, published by Addison Wesley Longman, Inc.

LESSON 2

The pH of River or Stream Water

Focus	Students will study the concepts of acids, bases, salts, and neutralization. Acid rain and other ecological implications are discussed. Students will use indicators to obtain pH values of various common substances and to measure the pH of a river or stream; they will then use standard methods to determine the quality value of the water for pH.

Learner Outcomes

Students will:
1. learn the definitions of acid and base.
2. learn how to distinguish between an acid and base.
3. learn the meaning of neutralization and be able to give applications.
4. know how to use various indicators to determine the pH of a solution.
5. learn various natural and human causes that affect the pH of a waterway.
6. monitor the pH of a river or stream.

Time

Three to four class periods of 40–50 minutes per period and a field trip to a river or stream

DAY 1:   Student Information 2.1: What Are Acids and Bases?
Student Information 2.2: What Is pH?

DAY 2:   Student Activity 2.3: Finding the pH of Some Common Liquids

DAY 3:   Student Information 2.4: The pH of Rivers and Streams

FIELD TRIP: Student Activity 2.5: Measuring the pH of a River or Stream

Advanced Preparation

Prepare to supply students with Student Information 2.1, 2.2, and 2.4 and Student Activity 2.3 and 2.5. In Student Activity 2.5, at least three samples of water need to be analyzed. Written material assumes three groups each collect and analyze one water sample. If you do not use three groups, adjust procedures accordingly.

Gather all necessary materials for this lesson. Student Activity 2.3 requires 10 clean test tubes per group. To insure the tubes are clean, either use new tubes, or use the glassware cleaning procedures covered in Student Information 1.3. This may be a good time for the students to perform these lab techniques.

To prepare red cabbage juice for Student Activity 2.3, submerge raw red cabbage leaves in distilled water in a 250–500 mL beaker; gently simmer the solution for 15 to 30 minutes. Then decant or filter the juice. Refrigerate to retard spoilage.

Any instrument used to obtain data must be calibrated against a standard. Before students use pH paper in Student Activity 2.3, obtain a pH = 7 buffer or distilled water, and check to see if the paper gives a reading of approximately pH = 7. If not, obtain new pH paper. If students will use a pH meter or probe, calibrate it following manufacturer's directions. This may be an appropriate time to show students how to calibrate an instrument or to allow them to do so under your direction and supervision.

Review Lesson 1 regarding water sampling equipment and technique. Review information in the unit introduction on field trip management.

Safety and Waste Disposal

Follow all laboratory and field safety procedures presented in Lesson 1. All solid and liquid waste used in Student Activities 2.3 and 2.5 can be rinsed down the drain.

Materials

Student Activity 2.3: Finding the pH of Some Common Liquids

Per student
safety goggles
lab apron
safety gloves

Per group
10 test tubes
labeling tape or marker
2–6 mL of each of the following solutions (as colorless as possible):

vinegar	distilled water
household ammonia	tap water
clear noncola carbonated soda	apple juice
liquid antacid	grapefruit juice
liquid dish detergent	

20-30 mL red cabbage juice
roll of pH paper with its pH color chart (range of 0 to 14)
tweezers
medicine droppers or pipettes

Optional
pH meter
buffer solution (pH = 7) for standardizing

Student Activity 2.5: Measuring the pH of a River or Stream

Per student
safety goggles
lab apron
safety gloves

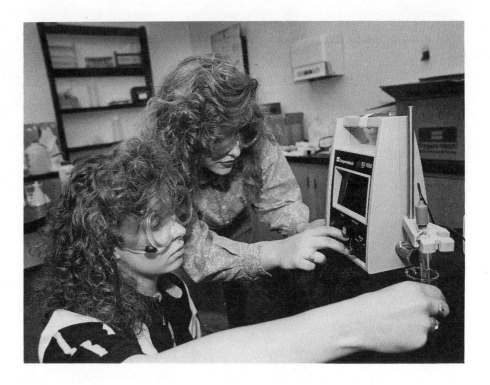

life jacket and tow line (for deeper-water sites)
rubber waders or boots (for shallower-water sites)
calculator with square-root function
Per group
100 mL distilled water
sampling bottle, with lid, at least 100-mL
30 mL HCl solution, 6 *M*
wax marking pencil
water-sampling pole with clamp
pH-measuring device: roll of pH paper with its pH color chart (range of 0 to
14); pH test kit; or pH meter with 1-m cord

Vocabulary

acid	indicator
acid rain	neutral
alkaline	neutralization
base	pH
buffer	salt
hydronium ion	

**Background
For the Teacher**

A solution's temperature directly affects its pH. If a meter has been calibrated in the lab, using it at a field site may create a source of error if the two locations differ in temperature. Under most circumstances, calibration does take place in the laboratory (at room temperature). Therefore, the procedures instruct students to return the water samples to the lab and allow them to reach room temperature before taking a pH reading.

Information on constructing a water-sampling pole are included in the introduction to the *Rivers Chemistry* unit.

Introducing the Lesson

1. Show students some common household materials and ask them to predict whether the materials are acids or bases. Use the ensuing discussion to assess how much students already know about acids and bases.
2. Ask students to give examples of how they have heard the terms acid or base used in everyday life.

Developing the Lesson

1. Have students read and discuss Student Information 2.1: What Are Acids and Bases? (Answers and solutions for Student Information and Student Activity sheets are in Appendix C.)
2. Have students read and discuss Student Information 2.2: What Is pH? Have students answer questions from Student Information 2.1 and 2.2.
3. Demonstrate how pH of a solution can be obtained. Discuss various methods that can be used, such as indicators and meters. You can demonstrate several different indicators (such as litmus, bromthymol blue, phenol red, goldenrod paper, and phenolphthalein) to show the variation in color changes.
4. Have students do Student Activity 2.3: Finding the pH of Some Common Liquids.

Concluding the Lesson

1. Have student read, discuss, and answer the questions for Student Information 2.4: The pH of Rivers and Streams.
2. Have students do Student Activity 2.5: Measuring the pH of a River or Stream, which involves a field trip. Three samples of water must be analyzed..
3. Discuss ways to reduce pollution in order to keep river and stream pH more neutral.

Assessing the Lesson

1. If students will do collages on river and stream water quality throughout the *Rivers Chemistry* unit, have them begin by assembling pictures, news articles, advertisements, and so forth that center around water or pH, such as references to *acid* or *base*. Student will add to them as they progress through other lessons in *Rivers Chemistry*. As the students continue through the remaining lesson, clippings can be added to the collage.
2. Have students develop a short poem that contains the words *pH, acid, base,* and *acid rain*. For specific teaching activities on writing poetry, see *Rivers Language Arts*.

3. Have students write a paragraph on one of the following questions:
   a. What is an acid?
   b. What is an indicator?
   c. Why does acid rain occur?
   d. Can rain be basic?
4. Have students do the lab-based student Assessment for Lesson 2: Dilution of an Acid, found in Appendix B.

Extending the Lesson

1. Have students experiment with making their own natural pH indicators. Most colored flowers, fruits, and vegetables will act as an acid-base indicator. Extract the colored matter by heating the material or pulverizing it in a blender. Red radishes, plums, grape juice, beets, and red onions are good indicators.
2. Encourage students to compare their pH data with the data of students at other field sites. Interschool communications may be done by letter, electronic mail, or the Internet.
3. Have students hypothesize how the pH of their river might change at different times of the year and why. If possible, monitor pH throughout the year to test their hypotheses.

What Are Acids and Bases?

To many people, the word *acid* brings to mind a substance that can dissolve metals or cause severe skin burns. Even the acid in your stomach is often portrayed negatively in television advertisements. Yet without stomach acid you could not digest food. Acids are a very important group of chemicals.

Acids

To a chemist, an **acid** is a substance that produces one or more **hydronium** (hi DROH nee uhm) **ion** (H_3O^+) in water. Hydronium ion is often called hydrogen ion. Nearly all fruits contain an acid. Acids generally have a sour taste. A lemon tastes sour because its juice is an acid. Both vinegar and sour milk contain an acid. In the following chart are a few common acids.

Some Common Acids

Name	Chemical Formula	Where Acid Is Found
Ascorbic acid	$C_6H_8O_6$	Vitamin C tablet
Acetylsalicylic acid	$C_9H_8O_4$	Aspirin
Carbonic acid	H_2CO_3	Carbonated drink
Sulfuric acid	H_2SO_4	Automobile battery
Formic acid	HCOOH	Bee, wasp, and ant stings
Hydrochloric acid	HCl	Human stomach

Bases

Most people are not as intimidated by the word *base* as they are by the word *acid*. Basic, or **alkaline** (AL kuh luhn) compounds, are found in products that range from deodorants to drain cleaners. Chemists define a **base** as any substance that produces hydroxide ions (OH^-) when dissolved in water. Bases feel slippery to the touch and generally have a bitter taste. As with acids, they are numerous. The following chart lists a few common bases.

© SIU, published by Addison Wesley Longman, Inc.

Some Common Bases

Name	Chemical Formula	Where Acid Is Found
Aluminum hydroxide	$Al(OH)_3$	Deodorant, antacid
Ammonium hydroxide	NH_4OH	Household ammonia cleaners
Magnesium hydroxide	$M_g(OH)_2$	Laxative, antacid
Sodium hydroxide	$NaOH$	Drain cleaner (lye)
Calcium hydroxide (lime)	$Ca(OH)_2$	Brick mortar, plaster of Paris

Neutralization

Acids and bases are usually studied together because they chemically react with each other. An acid-base reaction is called a **neutralization** (nyoo truh luh ZAY shuhn) reaction because one of the two products formed is water. Water generally is not thought of as being acid or alkaline, but **neutral.**

Acid + Base → Salt + Water

The other product formed in a neutralization reaction is called a **salt.** Because there are numerous acids and bases, there are numerous salts. Here are some examples.

	Acid	+	Base	→	Salt	+	Water
Example 1	$2HCl$	+	$Mg(OH)_2$	→	$MgCl_2$	+	$2H_2O$
Example 2	H_2SO_4	+	$2NaOH$	→	Na_2SO_4	+	$2H_2O$
Example 3	HCl	+	$NaOH$	→	$NaCl$	+	H_2O
Example 4	H_2SO_4	+	$Mg(OH)_2$	→	$MgSO_4$	+	H_2O

An example of a common neutralization reaction occurs when you take an antacid to relieve acid indigestion. Hydrochloric acid (HCl) is the acid in your stomach that helps digest food. If your stomach has a large amount of hydrochloric acid (which may occur after a large meal), you can get an upset stomach. So you may take an antacid to get relief. The antacid, which is a base, reacts with the stomach acid to produce a salt and water (neutralization), and you obtain relief. The preceding Example 1 is this type of neutralization, because many antacids contain magnesium hydroxide, $Mg(OH)_2$.

Neutralization reactions also are used by farmers whose farmland is too acidic. The soil may be acidic for many reasons, including acid rain or the natural breakdown of plant and animal materials. Many crops do not grow well if soil is very acidic. So farmers may place lime (CaO) on their farmland. When lime comes in contact with water in the soil, a base, calcium hydroxide, $Ca(OH)_2$, is formed. The calcium hydroxide (base) reacts with the acid in the soil to produce a salt and water (neutralization).

DRIFTWOOD

One reason why ocean water is salty is because over billions of years acids and bases have neutralized each other to form salt and water. By weight, ocean water is about three percent salt.

© SIU, published by Addison Wesley Longman, Inc.

Questions

1. In your own words, what is an acid?
2. Describe one physical characteristic of most acids.
3. In your own words, what is a base?
4. Describe two physical characteristics of most bases.
5. What is a neutralization reaction?
6. Give two examples of a neutralization reaction.

DRIFTWOOD

The lime used by farmers is a white powdery substance. Because lime is a soluble base, it also can be used to treat water that is too acidic.

© SIU, published by Addison Wesley Longman, Inc.

What Are Acids and Bases?

What Is pH?

Sometimes scientists need to how acidic or basic a liquid is. Your blood, for example, should always be slightly basic. If it becomes too basic, however, it cannot perform its functions well. The water in a swimming pool should be kept slightly basic for maximum comfort. The pH of a waterway affects the health of the organisms in it. This lesson will give you information on how to measure the acidity or alkalinity of a liquid.

pH

The letters pH stand for the Latin words *potentia hydrogenii,* meaning concentration of hydrogen ions. Therefore, the acidity and alkalinity of a liquid is a reflection of how many hydrogen ions are in the liquid. To express the concentration of hydronium ions in a liquid, scientists use a numbered scale called the pH scale. The scale generally varies from zero to fourteen, as shown in Figure 2-1. If a liquid has a pH number below 7, the liquid is acidic. If the pH number is greater than 7, the liquid is basic. If the pH number is exactly 7, it is not acid nor basic; it is neutral.

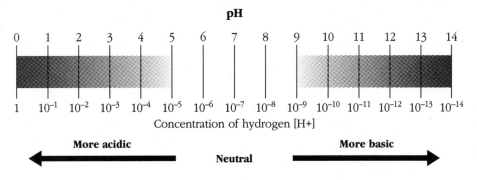

Figure 2-1: pH Scale

The lower the pH number, the more acidic is a liquid. Strong acids have a pH number of 0, 1, or 2. Stomach acid is a strong acid, because its pH number is generally between 1 and 2. Weak acids have pH numbers a little less than 7.

The higher the pH number, the more alkaline is a liquid. Strong bases have a pH number of 12, 13, or 14. Weak bases have pH numbers a little more than 7. Pure, unpolluted water should have a pH number of 7.

© SIU, published by Addison Wesley Longman, inc.

Acid-Base Indicators

One way to determine if a liquid is an acid or base is to use an **indicator,** a substance that can determine the presence or absence of a particular chemical. An acid-base indicator is a substance that changes color in response to the pH of the liquid it touches. A common pH indicator is litmus, which is extracted from lichens. Litmus indicator paper is manufactured by allowing strips of paper to absorb litmus. If red paper is used, then a red litmus indicator is produced. Likewise, if blue paper is used, blue litmus indicator is made. If a few drops of an acid are placed on blue litmus paper, the paper turns to a pink-red color. If an acid is placed on red litmus paper, the paper remains red. If a few drops of a base are placed on red litmus paper, the paper turns blue. If the base is placed on blue litmus paper, the paper remains blue.

Litmus paper cannot tell you the pH number of a liquid. It can only tell you if a liquid is an acid or base. However, by using both red and blue litmus paper, you can determine whether a liquid has a pH of 7 (neutral). Have each paper come in contact with the same liquid. If neither paper changes color (red litmus remains red and blue litmus remains blue), that liquid is neutral.

Many types of acid-base indicators have been developed. Some colored fruits, vegetable, and flowers can be used as indicators. Juice extracted from red cabbage, grapes, beets, or red roses turns different colors in acids or bases.

Other indicators can give you more information about the acidity or alkalinity of a liquid. Commercial pH indicator paper can give you a general pH number. Indicator paper is not exact, but it can give more information about pH than can litmus paper.

Electrical devices have been developed to find the pH of a liquid. Investigators use these devices, called pH meters, when they need more exact pH numbers. Like calculators, these meters have become small in size and easy to use.

Buffers

Sometimes maintaining a solution at a constant pH is important. For example, your blood needs to have a pH of (or very close to) 7.4. To keep the pH at this level, your blood contains a buffer. A **buffer** is a substance capable of maintaining a constant pH even when small amounts of acid or base are added to the solution.

© SIU, published by Addison Wesley Longman, Inc.

Questions

1. Explain the meaning of the numbers on the pH scale.
2. Define an acid in terms of pH.
3. Define a base in terms of pH.
4. What pH does a neutral liquid have?
5. What is one "drawback" of litmus paper?
6. What is a buffer?
7. Liquid A has a pH = 4.7. Liquid B has a pH = 2.3.
   a. Which liquid has more hydronium ions?
   b. Which liquid is more acidic?
8. Liquid A has a pH = 8.4. Liquid B has a pH = 10.7. Which liquid is more basic?

© SIU, published by Addison Wesley Longman, Inc.

Finding the pH of Some Common Liquids

Purpose

To determine the pH of some common liquids using various methods.

Background

Except for pure water, many liquids you come in contact with are either acidic or basic.

Safety and Waste Disposal

Review lab safety guidelines in Student Information 1.2. Although most of the liquids in this activity are harmless, you should not place any of them in your mouth or allow them to come in contact with your skin. One of the liquids used in this activity contains ammonia; avoid inhaling its fumes, as they can irritate your lungs and nasal passages.

All the liquids can be discharged down the drain by thoroughly flushing with tap water for several minutes.

Procedure

1. Put on your safety goggles and apron.
2. Label the test tubes 1 through 10, respectively.
3. Pour 1–3 mL (no more than half of what is available) of each of the nine liquids listed in the Data Table into 9 test tubes so that each liquid is in the test tube whose number corresponds to the number of the liquid in the Data Table. Fill the tenth tube about ¾ full of red cabbage juice.
4. Obtain a piece of pH paper about 3 cm long. Holding one end of the paper with tweezers over the sink, allow 1–2 drops of liquid 1 to wet the unheld end of the paper. The pH paper will turn a certain color. Hold the pH chart near the newly colored pH paper, and find the matching color in order to determine the pH of liquid 1. Record the result in the Data Table in column labeled "pH (Indicator 1)."
5. Repeat Step 4 for test tubes 2–8, using a fresh piece of paper with each tube.
6. Thoroughly rinse each test tube in the sink with tap water.

Materials

Per student
- safety goggles
- lab apron
- safety gloves

Per group
- 10 test tubes
- labeling tape or marker
- 2–6 mL of each of the following solutions (as colorless as possible):
  vinegar
  household ammonia
  clear noncola carbonated soda
  liquid antacid
  liquid dish detergent

distilled water
tap water
apple juice
grapefruit juice
- 20–30 mL red cabbage juice
- roll of pH paper with its pH color chart (range of 0 to 14)
- tweezers
- medicine droppers or pipettes

Optional
- pH meter
- buffer solution (pH = 7) for standardizing

© SIU, published by Addison Wesley Longman, Inc.

7. Distill wash each test tube three times, and shake as much of the distilled water from each tube as you can.
8. Repeat Step 3, using the remainder of the nine liquids.
9. Record the color of the cabbage juice in the Data Table.

10. Add, drop by drop, cabbage juice to each of the 9 liquids until you see a color change. Record the color when a change occurs. Using Table 2-1, record the relative pH of each liquid.

11. Thoroughly rise each tube with tap water into the sink and put your equipment away.
12. Clean up your lab area and wash your hands.

Observations

DATA TABLE

Materials	pH (Indicator 1)	Cabbage Juice: Initial Color _____	
		Color	Relative pH
Vinegar			
Ammonia cleaner			
Clear noncola carbonated soda			
Liquid antacid			
Liquid dish detergent			
Distilled water			
Tap water			
Apple juice			
Grapefruit juice			

TABLE 2-1

Red Cabbage Juice Indicator

Color	Relative pH
Bright red	Strong acid
Red	Medium acid
Reddish purple	Weak acid
Purple	Neutral
Blue-green	Weak base
Green	Medium base
Yellow	Strong base

© SIU, published by Addison Wesley Longman, Inc.

Analyses and Conclusions

1. List all the liquids that tested acidic and all the liquids that tested basic in the pH-paper test.
2. List all the liquids that tested acidic and all the liquids that tested basic in the cabbage-juice test.
3. List all the liquids that tested neutral in each test.
4. How do the lists in 1 compare with the lists in 2? Mention discrepancies, if any occurred.
5. How do the results of the two methods compare in list 3? Mention discrepancies, if any occurred.
6. Compare your results with those of other students, taking notes of consistencies and discrepancies.
7. After checking with other students, hypothesize why discrepancies occurred, if any did.

Critical Thinking Questions

1. Some people treat stomach indigestion by taking a little baking soda mixed in water. What does this indicate about baking soda?
2. One way of treating an acid spill is to pour a small amount of base on it. Explain what this would do to the pH of the spill.
3. Based on the results of this activity, predict whether the following would be acidic or basic: window cleaner, orange juice, dill pickles, shampoo. Explain your reasoning.

Keeping Your Journal

1. Write a story about a visit to a grocery store, focusing on the pH of liquids displayed in various store aisles.
2. Note for one day the beverages you consume. Classify them into acids and bases. Of which did you consume more: acids or bases?

© SIU, published by Addison Wesley Longman, Inc.

The pH of Rivers and Streams

The pH of rivers and streams depends on various natural conditions and on pollutants entering the water. The pH of water is important to aquatic life. If the pH falls below 4 or rises above 9, many aquatic life-forms will die.

Acidic River Water

A river or stream can be acidic as the result of natural or human-made pollutants. In some regions of the country, a major cause of such acidity is acid precipitation—rain or snow—entering the waterway. Such precipitation, whose most well-known form is **acid rain,** has a pH less than 7.

You may be surprised to learn that rain is naturally slightly acidic. Here's the reason: when water comes in contact with carbon dioxide (CO_2), a gas in the air, the carbon dioxide dissolves in the water, forming carbonic acid (H_2CO_3).

$$CO_2 \quad + \quad H_2O \quad \rightarrow \quad H_2CO_3$$

Carbon dioxide   Water   Carbonic acid

Only a limited amount of carbon dioxide gas will dissolve in water, so the natural pH of rain is generally between 6.0 and 6.9.

The same chemical reaction also occurs when carbonated beverages are manufactured. Carbon dioxide gas, under pressure, dissolves in flavored water, producing carbonic acid. (That is why, in Activity 2.3, the clear noncola carbonated soda tested acidic.) When you open a carbonated soda, excess carbon dioxide gas is released.

Other gases besides carbon dioxide will dissolve in water. For instance, sulfur oxides dissolve in water to produce sulfuric acid (H_2SO_4), and nitrogen oxides dissolve in water to produce nitric acid (HNO_3).

When rain, snow, or any other form of precipitation falls to earth though an atmosphere containing large amounts of any of these three gases, the precipitation's pH will be low. When such precipitation falls to earth, it can drastically drop the pH of any water with which it comes in contact.

When acid rain falls to earth, it may accumulate in rivers and streams. Unless the acidity of the waterway is neutralized by a basic substance, it will remain acidic. A river can be acidic and still be productive, provided its pH does not fall below 4.

© SIU, published by Addison Wesley Longman, Inc.

How Do Excess Pollutants Get Into the Atmosphere?

Carbon dioxide gas, sulfur dioxide gas, and nitrogen dioxide gas are produced when fossil fuels such as gasoline, diesel, kerosene, coal, and oil are burned. At the present time, the main methods of transportation use fossil fuels such as gasoline and diesel. A large proportion of our electricity comes from power plants that burn coal and oil. The more humans burn these fuels, the more acid rain results.

Waterways Can Be Basic, Acid, or Neutral

With acid precipitation falling regularly, you might think that all rivers and streams would have a low pH value. This is not always so. Calcium carbonate $(CaCO_3)$ occurs abundantly in nature in the form of chalk, limestone, and shells. When calcium carbonate dissolves in water, a base, calcium hydroxide, $Ca(OH)_2$, is formed. So, when acid rain falls or comes in contact with basic calcium carbonate, a neutralization reaction occurs, which keeps waterways from being highly acidic.

Some waterways may not receive acid rain but may have bases reaching them. In this case, the river water has a pH greater than 7. Rivers with a pH of 8 to 9 can still support aquatic life.

A waterway that does not receive a sufficient amount of base, or into which humans dump acidic substances, can have a low pH. Dumping a large amount of acid can overload a river or stream with acid and drastically reduce its pH. This is one reason you were instructed in Lab and Field Techniques in Lesson 1 to dispose of excess chemicals and other waste as directed by your teacher, and why you were also instructed to allow tap water to run for several minutes when acid-washing glassware.

Because acids and bases are abundant in nature, neutralization reactions occur continuously. If a waterway has a balance of both acids and bases feeding into it, its pH will remain near the 7 mark.

Controlling pH

What can be done to improve and control the pH of waterways? Acid rain can be controlled by limiting the amount of pollutants released into the air. Government-enforced restraints on automobile, power-plant, and industrial emissions of pollutants would help. Anyone who burns trash or leaves contributes to the acid rain problem, because these materials contain nitrogen and sulfur. Finally, tougher standards for the release of acid-producing pollutants from farming, mining, and lawn care would also help.

© SIU, published by Addison Wesley Longman, Inc.

Questions

1. Suppose an area receives a large amount of rainfall that is high in sulfur dioxide and nitrogen dioxide. This area has many limestone cliffs, as well as soil having crushed limestone. Predict the pH for rivers and streams that flow through this area. Explain your reasoning.

2. Discuss two reasons why a waterway may have a low pH.

© SIU, published by Addison Wesley Longman, Inc.

Measuring the pH of a River or Stream

Purpose

To measure the pH of a river or stream and assess the impact of pH on water quality.

Background

You will obtain a sample of water from your site and return to the lab for its pH analysis. You will convert your pH data into its Q-value percent. The Q-value will help you determine if the water at your site is good or bad regarding pH.

Safety and Waste Disposal

Follow all laboratory and field safety procedures discussed in Lesson 1. All liquid waste can be rinsed down the drain with running water.

Procedure

PART A. Before Going to the Field Site

1. Obtain a sampling bottle (and lid) of at least 100 mL.
2. Clean the bottle and cap with soap and water, rinse thoroughly with tap water, acid wash, and distill wash them, following procedures from Student Information 1.3, Lab and Field Techniques. Cap the bottle.
3. Label the bottle with your group name or number.

PART B. At the Field Site

4. Record the date, time, location, and weather conditions at the field site.
5. Describe your field site. Example: Are rock formations nearby? Do ditches or drains empty into your river or stream? Do you see signs of humans having disposed of litter or other waste in or near the water?
6. Put on safety goggles, apron, and gloves.
7. Obtain a sample of river or stream water, using the procedures in Student Information 1.3, Lab and Field Techniques. Cap the bottle and return to the lab.

PART C. In the Laboratory

8. Allow the sample bottle to set for 5–10 minutes, so it can reach room temperature.
9. Measure the pH of the water sample, and record in your Data Table.
10. Obtain and record the pH results from the other groups in your class.

Materials

Per student

- safety goggles
- lab apron
- safety gloves
- life jacket and tow line (for deeper-water sites)
- rubber waders or boots (for shallower-water sites)
- calculator with square-root function

Per group

- 100 mL distilled water
- sampling bottle, with lid, at least 100 mL
- 30 mL HCl solution, 6 *M*
- wax marking pencil
- water-sampling pole with clamp
- pH-measuring device: roll of pH paper with its pH color chart (range of 0 to 14); pH test kit; or pH meter with 1-m cord

© SIU, published by Addison Wesley Longman, Inc.

Observations

Date _____   Location _____

Time _____   Weather Conditions _____

Site Description _____

_____

DATA TABLE

Group	pH Reading

Average pH = _____

Standard Deviation = _____

Reported Value = _____ ± _____

Q-value = _____

Calculations

11. Using your result and the results from the other groups, calculate and record the average pH.
12. Calculate and record the standard deviation.
13. Record the reported value.
14. Convert the average pH value into its equivalent Q-value using Figure 2-2. Record the Q-value.

Analyses and Conclusions

Q-value for pH	Quality of Water
90–100%	Excellent
70–89%	Good
50–69%	Medium
25–49%	Bad
0–24%	Very bad

1. Using your pH Q-value and the preceding table, rate your river or stream from excellent to very bad.
2. Using your descriptions of the field site, describe the factors you think contribute to the pH of the water.
3. What might be done to improve the pH level at your field site?

© SIU, published by Addison Wesley Longman, Inc.

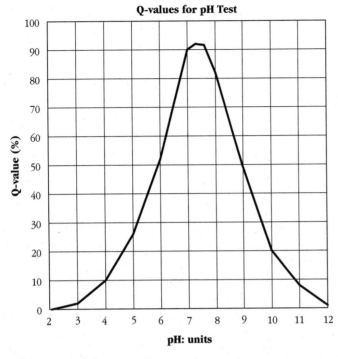

Figure 2-2: Graph for Converting pH to Q-value

Critical Thinking Questions

1. Explain how the pH of your field site might affect the organisms living in or near that waterway.
2. Predict how the pH at your field site might vary at different times of the year. Explain your reasoning.

Keeping Your Journal

1. Would you like the pH of your test site to change? Why?

LESSON 3 — *Temperature and Flow Rate of a River or Stream*

Focus

Students will study various natural and human factors that affect the temperature and flow rate of a waterway, as well as impacts each factor has on a waterway. They will measure the temperature and flow rate of a waterway and use their data to determine the water quality of the waterway.

Learner Outcomes

Students will:

1. Learn how natural and human factors influence the temperature of a waterway.
2. Learn how temperature affects the amount of dissolved oxygen in water.
3. Learn how temperature affects various forms of aquatic life.
4. Learn the relationship between flow rate and water temperature.
5. Determine the temperature change and flow rate of a waterway and evaluate the results using standard measures of water quality.

Time

Two class periods of 40–50 minutes per period and a field trip to a river or stream

DAY 1: Student Information 3.1: Causes and Effects of Temperature Change in a River or Stream

DAY 2: Student Information 3.2: How to Determine Temperature Change and Flow Rate

FIELD TRIP: Student Activity 3.3: Measuring Temperature Change and Flow Rate of a River or Stream

Advanced Preparation

Prepare to supply students with Student Information 3.1 and 3.2 and with Student Activity 3.3. Gather all necessary materials and equipment. In Student Activity 3.3, three sets of temperatures need to be collected. Written material assumes three groups each collect and analyze one set of temperature readings. If you do not use three groups, adjust procedures accordingly.

For Student Activity 3.3, locate a relatively straight section of moving water on your waterway approximately 1.6 km long such that students can measure flow rate along a straight stretch of 20–100 meters. If the class will use oranges in Student Activity 3.3, make arrangements to retrieve them (if possible). If a cork is used, make arrangements to retrieve it. Review information in the unit introduction on field trip management.

Safety	Follow all field safety procedures presented in Lesson 1. Arrange for adult supervision at both the upstream and the downstream field sites.

Materials	**Student Activity 3.3: Measuring Temperature Change and Flow Rate of a River or Stream** *Per student* safety goggles lab apron safety gloves life jacket and tow line (for deeper-water sites) rubber waders or boots (for shallower-water sites) calculator with square-root function *Per group* Celsius thermometer, alcohol-filled with a metal jacket or electronic; or temperature probe 25–50 cm of light chord (1 per temperature-measuring device) orange or brightly colored cork *Per class* measuring tape, 50–100 meters 2 stopwatches or watches with second hand

Vocabulary	aerobic microorganism	flow rate
	anaerobic microorganism	temperature
	Celsius thermometer	thermal water pollution
	flow	

Background for the Teacher	Flow rate data are not used to determine the Water-Quality Index. However, this information may help students make meaningful comparisons of tests taken at different times.

Introducing the Lesson	Have students read and discuss Student Information 3.1: Causes and Effects of Temperature Change in a River or Stream and Student Information 3.2: How to Determine Temperature Change and Flow Rate. Are there industries or power plants in the area that use the waterway as a coolant? Are there dams, diversions, or irrigation structures nearby? Has any student ever observed a sample of water under a microscope to view microorganisms? If so, what was its appearance?

Developing the Lesson	1. Have students discuss and answer questions on Student Information 3.1 and 3.2. (Answers and solutions for student sheets are in Appendix C.)

Bring out the positive and negative effects of thermal change on aquatic life, and emphasize the importance of controlling thermal exchanges in waterways and monitoring water temperatures to check for possible problems.

2. Explore with students how fossil-fuel or nuclear power plants located near a river can affect the temperature of the waterway. Compare the water-temperature impacts of these types of power plants with the effects of hydroelectric plants and other energy sources.

3. Have students read and discuss Student Activity 3.3: Measuring Temperature Change and Flow Rate of a River or Stream. Assign students to specific tasks.

4. Review field safety procedures.

5. Have students do Student Activity 3.3, which involves both an upstream and a downstream field site.

Concluding the Lesson

1. If a temperature change occurred in Student Activity 3.3, have students discuss whether the change is significant. If they think it is significant, have them develop a hypothesis for its cause. Discuss what could be done, such as governmental controls at local, state, or federal levels. Should they give their information to the school or local paper? Should they compose a letter to an authority? For specific teaching activities on writing political action letters, see *Rivers Language Arts*.

Lesson 3: Temperature and Flow Rate of a River or Stream

Assessing the Lesson

1. Have students add to their water-quality collages.
2. Have students write a poem regarding any experience they have had that involves temperature or flow of a waterway (such as swimming in very cold water, fishing in cool pools, watching sticks float by).
3. Introduce the scenario described in Assessment for Lesson 3: More Than One Answer—Evaluating Change (located in Appendix B). Divide students into special-interest groups and have them role-play the situation. Conclude with a general discussion in which groups share their concerns and different points of view.

Extending the Lesson

1. Have students research whether any nearby industries use river water for cooling purposes. If so, have students interview industry officials to determine the temperature of water that is taken in by the plant and the temperature of the water that is released back into the river. For specific teaching activities on nonfiction research and on interviewing, see *Rivers Language Arts*.
2. Arrange a field trip to a power plant or other source of thermal pollution. Invite an official of a power plant to visit the class so that students can ask questions regarding the issues in this lesson.
3. If issues about local development along waterways are discussed at open meetings, encourage students to attend. Are environmental concerns addressed at the meetings?
4. Arrange for students to view aquatic microorganisms using a microscope. Invite a biology teacher to visit the class.
5. Have students use flow rate to determine the volume of water (flow) pa ing a given point per time, if a cross-sectional area of the waterway is known. For specific teaching activities on determining cross-sectional ar and on determining flow, see *Rivers Earth Science*.

Causes and Effects of Temperature Change in a River or Stream

When your skin is exposed to the summer sun, it feels warmer. The sun's rays increase the temperature of your skin. The temperature of any object, including water, increases when exposed to sunlight or any other heat source. **Temperature** is a measure of how hot or cold an object is.

What Natural Factors Affect a Waterway's Temperature?

The temperature of a river or stream varies naturally with such factors as its water source, the seasons, and the amount of rainfall. Rivers and streams fed by melting glaciers and snow (which have temperatures near 0°C) are colder than those fed by underground springs (which often have temperatures near 13°C). Rivers receiving ground runoff water are colder in winter than in summer. If rainfall increases, the amount of water a waterway receives increases; this increase in volume (also called **flow**) lowers water temperature. Generally, too, an increase in the speed, or current, of the water is also associated with a decrease in water temperature. The speed of the water is also called its **flow rate** [expressed in meters per second (m/s)].

Natural properties of water itself also tend to keep the temperature of rivers and streams from fluctuating too greatly. For instance, water absorbs a lot of heat before it changes temperature, so the temperature of river or stream water rises slowly as it is warmed by the sun, and it cools slowly after the sun sets. Second, water frozen into ice is less dense than liquid water, so ice will float on top of a river, insulating the water below. Though floods or drought may cause drastic changes in waterway temperature, these changes are almost always temporary. Permanent change usually occurs gradually over long periods of time.

What Human Factors Affect a Waterway's Temperature?

Human factors may greatly upset the natural processes that keep water temperature stable over time. Industries that provide electricity need large amounts of water, so they are often located near a river, lake, or ocean. Fossil-fuel and nuclear power plants generally pump water from a waterway, heat it until it becomes steam, then use the steam to operate an electric generator. After being run through a turbine, the steam cools and converts back to liquid water. If the power plant places that high-temperature water back into the waterway, the temperature of the river, stream, or bay will increase.

© SIU, published by Addison Wesley Longman, Inc.

Some industries use water as a coolant to absorb heat that is produced during a chemical or mechanical process. If the heated water is returned to the waterway, it can produce a noticeable rise in the river's temperature. Thermal **water pollution** is the deliberate dumping of high-temperature water into rivers, lakes, and oceans.

Trees and other forms of vegetation along a waterway help shield water from sunlight. Private and public entities may remove vegetation along a waterway in order to provide for urban development, irrigation, and industrial and agricultural expansion. This removal of vegetation subjects the water to more sunlight, which may increase its temperature drastically.

Dams, dikes, and agricultural diversions built along many waterways act to slow the flow of waterways. For instance, the Mississippi River has many dams and locks to facilitate transportation by ship and barge. In arid areas, dams are used to store water that accumulates during wet seasons for use in dry seasons. Dams are also used for hydroelectric power production, flood control, and wetlands modification for agricultural and recreational use. Agricultural diversions take water from a river to use for irrigation. Dams, dikes, and agricultural diversions have many benefits, but they may reduce flow and flow rate so drastically that water temperature rises to harmful levels.

What Happens When the Temperature of a Waterway Rises?

As the temperature of water increases, the amount of oxygen dissolved in that water decreases. This affects the aquatic life in that waterway.

Microscopic organisms (microorganisms) are present in all natural waterways. Microorganisms are of two types: aerobic (ayr OH bik) and anaerobic (an uh ROH bik). **Aerobic microorganisms** require oxygen in order to live; **anaerobic microorganisms** do not.

Generally, the populations of microorganisms are held in check by natural processes in the water, but an increase in temperature may trigger increases in microorganism populations. Because aerobic organisms require oxygen for life, an increase in this population reduces the amount of dissolved oxygen in water.

An increase in the population of anaerobic organisms does not itself reduce the amount of dissolved oxygen in water, because anaerobic organisms do not require oxygen for life. When any aquatic life large or microscopic dies, the remains decay. The natural decay process utilizes oxygen. So, if water contains large amounts of microorganisms, large amounts will die and decay; their decay uses up large amounts of oxygen in the water.

So a rise in the temperature of a waterway will lead to a lack of oxygen in the water. This creates adverse conditions for aquatic life, such as fish, that depend on the oxygen for life.

© SIU, published by Addison Wesley Longman, Inc.

Can Excess Heat in Water Have Any Positive Effects?

In most circumstances, thermal changes have negative environmental consequences, but, in some circumstances, change may result in conditions that improve the aquatic environment and allow for improved plant and animal growth. For instance, some studies are underway that explore using waste heat to extend or improve agricultural and aquatic production. In fact, artificially warmed waters have enhanced commercial catfish and oyster farming.

Questions

1. Name four natural processes that may cause temperature change in a river or stream.
2. Describe one source of thermal pollution.
3. Discuss the pros and cons of dams and other structures that control the flow of river and stream water.
4. What are some negative ecological effects of thermal pollution on natural water systems?
5. Discuss positive uses of excess thermal energy in water systems.

DRIFTWOOD

If you find a temperature change of several degrees between a sampling site and an upstream site along a river or stream, you might want to investigate the area further. Look at factors such as the amount of sunlight reaching the sampling area, the streams that flow into area, and human sources of thermal pollution.

© SIU, published by Addison Wesley Longman, Inc.

How to Determine Temperature Change and Flow Rate

Thermal pollution is indicated by a change in temperature from one location along a waterway to another. Therefore, to determine if a river or stream is thermally polluted, you must take a temperature reading at two different locations. To determine the temperature, a temperature measuring device, such as a thermometer marked off in degree units, is used. There are different temperature scales; however, the temperature scale you will use is the Celsius scale. A **Celsius thermometer** is an instrument that measures temperature on a scale such that 0 degrees is the temperature at which water freezes and 100 degrees is the temperature at which water boils.

How To Measure Temperature Change

to measure temperature change in a river or stream, select two locations along the waterway that are as identical as possible. The sites should have a similar flow rate, depth, width, and exposure to sunlight. The two sites should be approximately 1.6 kilometers apart. For best accuracy, use the same temperature-measuring device at both sites. The times at which the two measurements are made should also be as close as possible, so that the variable of exposure to sunlight will not be a contributing factor to any temperature difference.

Use either an alcohol-filled glass thermometer fitted with a protective metal jacket, an electronic thermometer, or a temperature probe. Do not use mercury-filled thermometers, because an accidentally broken thermometer could release mercury into the environment. Mercury compounds can be toxic to humans and aquatic life.

Subtract the lower temperature reading from the higher one to determine the change in temperature. A large difference in temperature (2°C or greater) indicates the possibility of thermal pollution. If there is no change or very little change (less than 2°C), you can assume no thermal pollution exists for the section of the river or stream between the two sites.

How Is Flow Rate Determined?

To determine flow rate, you will measure the time it takes a floating object to be carried by the current from one point to another. The distance (in meters) from one point to another is divided by the time (in seconds). In a river, an

© SIU, published by Addison Wesley Longman, Inc.

orange works well as the floating object because it is highly visible and biodegradable (if accidentally lost). Retrieve the orange if possible. In a stream, you can use a smaller object, such as a brightly colored cork. Definitely retrieve the cork. Do not use any object that can harm aquatic life or pollute the river.

Measure a distance of 20 to 100 meters along the shore. One timekeeper should stand at the "starting point," while a second timekeeper stands at the "stopping point." Toss the floating object into the river or stream upstream from the starting point. As soon as the object floats by the starting point, both timekeepers start their stopwatches. As the object floats by the downstream timekeeper, the timekeepers stop their watches and record the time in seconds. If the two stopwatches indicated different elapsed times, calculate the average. The timekeepers can communicate with each other with hand signals, voice, or two-way radios. If the flow rate is fairly slow, only one timekeeper is required, because the timekeeper can move from the starting point to the stopping point more quickly than can the object. To calculate the rate of flow in meters per second, divide the distance in meters by the time in seconds.

Questions

1. Describe the procedure and data needed in order to determine temperature change in a river or stream.
2. Why are mercury-filled thermometers not recommended for use in the field?
3. Describe the procedure for measuring the flow rate of a river or stream.

© SIU, published by Addison Wesley Longman, Inc.

Measuring Temperature Change and Flow Rate of a River or Stream

Purpose

To measure temperature change and flow rate of a river or stream and to assess the impact of temperature change on water quality.

Background

In this activity, you will determine if water temperature changes along a section of a river or stream. To identify any temperature difference, you will record the temperature of the waterway at two different locations. If the temperatures readings at the two sites differ significantly, then you can assume that heat has been added or removed from the water. If heat has been added, the temperature change indicates thermal pollution.

Because weather conditions affect the temperature of river and stream water, you will also record air temperature, as well as other variables, such as how much sunshine, cloud cover, precipitation, or wind is present at the site.

Flow rate is not a measure of water quality. It does, however, influence water temperature, so you should measure it whenever you measure the temperature of a waterway. Also, if you record water temperature on more than one date, the flow-rate measurements will help you compare your results more accurately.

Safety

Observe all field safety procedures presented in Lesson 1.

Procedure

PART A. Measuring Temperature Change

1. Before going to the field site, attach a cord to the temperature-measuring device so that it can be easily retrieved if accidentally dropped.

2. At the field site record the date, air temperature, weather conditions, time, and location in the Data Table.

3. Put on safety gear. Attach one end of the cord used in Step 1 to your hand.

4. Lower the temperature-measuring device until the end or bulb is approximately 10 cm beneath the surface of the water. Hold the device in this position for 2–3 minutes. If possible, read the temperature while the device remains in the water; otherwise, remove it and read the temperature quickly. Record the temperature in the Data Table.

Materials

Per student
- safety goggles
- lab apron
- gloves
- life jacket and tow line (for deeper-water sites)
- rubber waders or boots (for shallower-water sites)
- calculator with square-root function

Per group
- Celsius thermometer, alcohol-filled with a metal jacket, or electronic; or temperature probe
- 25–50 cm of light chord (1 per temperature-measuring device)
- orange or brightly colored cork

Per class
- measuring tape, 50–100 meters
- 2 stopwatches or watches with second hand

© SIU, published by Addison Wesley Longman, Inc.

5. Move upstream to the second site and repeat Step 4.

PART B. Measuring Flow Rate

6. Mark off a distance of 20 to 100 meters along the shore of the waterway. Record the distance (meters) you are using. Post two student observers with stopwatches, one at the starting point and one at the stopping point.

7. Toss the floating marker into the current several meters upstream from the starting point. As soon as the marker reaches a point directly across from the starting point, the observers should start their watches. They should stop their watches when the marker reaches a point directly across from the stopping point. Record the time, in seconds, it took the floating marker to go from the starting point to the stopping point.

© SIU, published by Addison Wesley Longman, Inc.

Observations

Date _____   Air Temperature (°C) _____

Time _____   Weather Conditions _____

Location of upstream Field Site _____

Location of downstream Field Site _____

DATA TABLE 1: Water Temperature at Sampling Site

Water temperature at upstream field site: _____ °C

Water temperature at downstream field site: _____ °C

                                     Δ Temperature: _____ °C

Group	Δ Temperature (°C)

Average pH = _____

Average Δ Temperature = _____ (°C)

Standard Deviation = _____

Reported Value = _____ °C ± ____

Q-value = _____ %

DATA TABLE 2: Flow Rate

Location of Starting Point _____

Location of Stopping Point _____

Distance from starting point to stopping point = _____ m

Time object required to travel from starting point to stopping point = _____ sec

Flow rate = _____ m/sec

Group	Flow rate (m/sec)

Average Flow Rate = _____ (m/sec)

Standard Deviation = _____

Reported Value = _____ m/sec ± ____

© SIU, published by Addison Wesley Longman, Inc.

Calculations

8. Find the temperature difference between the two sites and record the difference in the Data Table.
9. Obtain and record the temperature change from the other groups.
10. Using your result and the results from the other groups, calculate and record the average temperature change.
11. Calculate and record the standard deviation.
12. Record the reported value.
13. Using the average temperature change, find its equivalent Q-value using Figure 3-1. Record the Q-value.
14. To find flow rate, divide the distance by the time in seconds. Record your flow rate in meters per second.
15. Obtain and record the flow rate from the other groups.
16. Using your result and the results from the other groups, calculate and record the average flow rate.
17. Calculate and record the standard deviation.
18. Record the reported value.

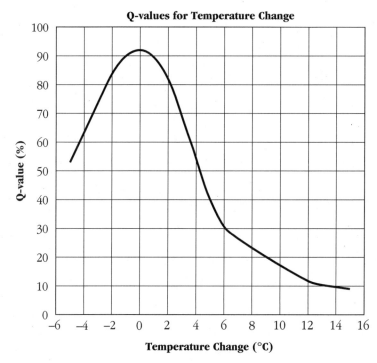

Figure 3-1: Graph for Converting Temperature Change Values to Q-Value

Analyses and Conclusions

Q-value for Temperature	Quality of Water
90–100%	Excellent
70–89%	Good
50–69%	Medium
25–49%	Bad
0–24%	Very bad

1. Using your Q-value for temperature and the information given in the preceding chart, rate your river or stream water from excellent to very bad.
2. Describe the section of river or stream that is between the two sampling sites. Are there ditches or drains that empty into the waterway? Are farms, homes, industries, or power plants nearby? What sort of material flows into this section of the waterway from the surrounding area?
3. What factors do you think contributed to the water temperature in this section? If the temperatures at the two samplings sites were significantly different, what could cause the difference?
4. Do you think the flow rate in the middle of the waterway is the same, smaller, or larger compared to the flow rate you found? Why?

Critical Thinking Questions

1. Suppose you found that the temperature of a river was 22.3°C at a test site and 25.8°C upstream. In traveling between the two sites, you observe two farms with buildings at least 0.4 km (¼ mile) from the river. You also see two smaller streams flowing into the river between the two sites.
   a. Calculate the change in water temperature, and determine the Q-value using Figure 3-1.
   b. Rate the quality of the water for change in temperature.
   c. Give two possible explanations of why temperature is lower at the test site than at the upstream site.

Keeping Your Journal

1. How do you respond to warm sunny days? What effect do warm, sunny days have on a waterway? Write a short story emphasizing the similarities between your response to the sun and the river's response.
2. As you travel between the two test sites, sketch the environment along the way. Include any buildings, streams, hills, and roads you see. Does the river pass through woods, wetlands, fields, hills, or areas inhabited by people? Label possible sources of thermal pollution and conditions such as soil erosion, manufacturing plants, urban development, or landfills that might pollute the river in other ways.

© SIU, published by Addison Wesley Longman, Inc.

Turbidity in River or Stream Water

Focus	Students will study the concept of turbidity. They will discover the causes of turbidity and become aware of various practices that help reduce turbidity. They will simulate how a water treatment plant clarifies water. Finally, they will measure the turbidity of a river or stream and use standards to determine the quality of the water.

Learner Outcomes

Students will:

1. Understand the term *turbidity* and how it is related to water quality.
2. Learn causes and effects of turbidity and be able to suggest ways of reducing turbidity.
3. Learn how to measure turbidity.
4. Learn how a water treatment plant reduces turbidity.
5. Determine the turbidity of a river or stream and use turbidity data to determine water quality.

Time

Three class periods of 40–50 minutes per period plus a field trip to a river or stream

DAY 1:   Student Information 4.1: What Is Turbidity?

DAY 2:   Student Information 4.2: How Can Turbidity Be Measured?

DAY 3:   Student Information 4.3: How Does a Water Treatment Plant Handle Turbidity?

Student Activity 4.4: Reducing Turbidity in Water

FIELD TRIP: Student Activity 4.5: Measuring the Turbidity of a River or Stream

Advanced Preparation

Prepare to supply students with Student Information 4.1, 4.2, and 4.3 and with Student Activity 4.4 and 4.5. Obtain all necessary material and equipment.

If you plan to test a river of high turbidity, obtain a Secchi disk. Make sure it is properly weighted so it will sink into the water vertically. If students will use a turbidimeter or turbidity kit, learn its operational procedures. Review information in the unit introduction on field trip management.

Safety and Waste Disposal   Follow all lab and field safety procedures presented in Lesson 1. In Student Activity 4.4, students should decant the liquids into the sink and collect the solids into a waste container in order to avoid clogging laboratory drains. If students use a turbidity test kit in Student Activity 4.5, follow the chemical-disposal instructions in its instructional manual, if available. If the kit does not include disposal instructions, collect all liquid and solid waste into a waste container. Then place the waste container under a laboratory hood, or simply expose it to the air. The water will evaporate, leaving a small amount of solid waste. Unless a large number of tests are run, it will take many years before any sizable amount accumulates.

Materials

Student Activity 4.4 Reducing Turbidity in Water

Per student

safety goggles, lab apron, and gloves

Per group

3–4 L muddy river or stream water

3 Imhoff cones, graduated cylinders, or transparent soda bottles; 1 L each

labels or labeling markers

laboratory balance

weighing paper

spatula

5 g aluminum sulfate (alum)

2.5 g iron (II) chloride

2.5 g calcium oxide (lime)

waste container

Student Activity 4.5 Measuring the Turbidity of a River or Stream

Per student

safety goggles, lab apron, and gloves

life jacket and tow line (for deeper-water sites)

rubber waders or boots (for shallower-water sites)

calculator with square-root function

Per group

Secchi disk (calibrated), turbidity kit, or turbidimeter

extra steel weights (if using Secchi disk)

waste container (if using turbidity kit)

water-sampling pole, with clamp (if using turbidity kit)

sampling bottle, with lid, of correct size to match turbidity-kit requirements (if using turbidity kit)

binoculars (if disk will be viewed from a bridge)

Vocabulary	erosion	Secchi disk
	floc	sedimentation
	flocculation	suspension
	Jackson Turbidity Unit (JTU)	turbidimeter
	nephelometer	turbidity
	Nephelometric Turbidity Unit (NTU)	

Background for the Teacher

Turbidity can be measured using a Secchi disk, a turbidity test kit, or a turbidimeter. Your equipment choice depends on the body of water you select and on available funds. The Secchi disk can be fabricated easily with little expense, but it does not work on shallow streams or very clear waterways. Test kits are relatively inexpensive; on highly turbid water, however, students may find them difficult to use at first. Electronic turbidimeters can be used on any body of water, but they are expensive. Graphs are included in Student Activity 4.5 to accommodate your choice of instrument.

Introducing the Lesson

1. Have students read and discuss Student Information 4.1: What Is Turbidity? Emphasize that water can have some degree of turbidity naturally, but many human activities increase turbidity in water.

Developing the Lesson

1. Have students answer questions on Student Information 4.1. (Answers and solutions for student sheets are in Appendix C.)
2. Have students read, discuss and answer questions on Student Information 4.2: How Can Turbidity Be Measured? If students will be using a Secchi disk at the field site, emphasize how it is fabricated and used. If students will use a turbidity meter or kit, detail procedures for its operation.
3. Have students read, discuss, and answer questions on Student Information 4.3: How Does a Water Treatment Plan Handle Turbidity?
4. Have students carry out Student Activity 4.4. For best results, let the containers stand overnight and have students observe them the next day.
5. Have students prepare equipment for Student Activity 4.5, then carry out procedures and the field site.

Concluding the Lesson

1. Have students complete calculations and answer questions for Student Activity 4.5. As a class, discuss the turbidity of the field site.
2. Have students develop a list of causes of turbidity and suggest ways to minimize these sources of pollution. Have construction projects in your community caused erosion problems? Have students been involved in activities that may have increased turbidity in a waterway? Are they familiar with farming practices that reduce land erosion by water and wind? How does turbidity affect water recreational activities?

Assessing the Lesson

1. Have student do lab-based Assessment for Lesson 4: The Turbidity of Milk (located in Appendix B).
2. Have students add to their water-quality collages.
3. Have students compose a fictional short story, written in the first person, from the point of view of a piece of suspended matter in river or stream water. (For specific teaching activities on creative writing, see *Rivers Language Arts.*) The following is an excerpt taken from a story written by a high school student involved in the Rivers Project:

"I arrived at the river on (student's birthday or other notable date) after traveling several months from Chester, Illinois, where my family and I resided. We had a comfortable home, not extravagant but cozy, adjacent to the taproot of a large oak tree. Each day we helped supply nutrients and water to the tree. I can still remember when that tiny acorn fell in our midst, took root, and matured. The tree grew tall and stately and I took pride in its grandeur.

"At 7:00 P.M., 24 days ago, my world was drastically changed. A careless human started a fire that swept through the entire forest. By noon, the oak tree was dead and later fell crashing to the ground. I and my family, for the first time in eons, were exposed to the wind and rain of the outside world.

"Being tiny pieces of soil with no place to live, my family and I were soon separated from one another by the raging waters that flowed across the eroding land. I have not seen my family for such a long time.

"I was tossed to and fro by the flowing water until I arrived at the river. Now I am a piece of suspended matter in a vast river. Harmful microorganisms live on my body, and I keep sunlight from reaching aquatic plants beneath me."

Extending the Lesson

1. Have students develop a plan of action for themselves and their families to reduce turbidity. In what ways would plans differ for rural families, urban dwellers, and suburban dwellers?

2. Invite a professional farmer or lawn-care person to speak to the class. Have students develop questions to ask regarding the agricultural methods the speaker uses to reduce turbidity. For specific teaching activities on interviewing, see *Rivers Language Arts*.

3. Tour a local water treatment plant or have one of its officers visit the class. What is the source of the water? How does the treatment plant handle turbidity?

What Is Turbidity?

If you visited the Mississippi River in Illinois or states further south, you would be able to see only about 20 to 38 centimeters beneath the water's surface. On the other hand, if you visited some lakes in Alaska, you would be able to see 30 to 37 meters below the surface. The degree to which a body is not clear is called **turbidity** (ter BIHD ih tee). The Mississippi River is very turbid, but those Alaskan lakes have low turbidity.

What Causes Turbidity?

Turbidity is a measure of how much material is suspended in water. A **suspension** (suh spehn chuhn) is produced when solid matter is dispersed throughout a liquid. All bodies of water are turbid to some degree, even those Alaskan lakes, though suspended particles are sometimes too small or too few in number for humans to notice. Common types of matter suspended in water include small pieces of soil, sewage, industrial waste, and microorganisms.

Any natural or artificial process that places suspended matter in water is a cause of turbidity. Plant root systems normally keep soil from being blown or washed into a river or stream. When forest fires and poor agricultural practices destroy or remove plants from the soil, erosion of the land may result. **Erosion** (ih ROH Zhuhn) is the tearing down and transporting of solid matter by wind, water, or ice. By the process of erosion, soil may be washed or blown into a river or stream. Tornadoes, earthquakes, and floods also can place suspended matter in water.

Living organisms such as plants and animals do add suspended matter to waterways. For example, small portions of decomposing leaves and body waste from birds and animals may wind up in the water.

Many human activities around waterways increase turbidity. People sometimes use waterways to dump garbage and to dispose of waste from sewage systems. River traffic, both commercial and recreational, may erode the banks of the river and agitate the sediments on the river bottom. Dredging waterways to maintain a proper water depth for barges and ships increases turbidity.

Is Turbidity in Water Good or Bad?

There is no single answer to the question of whether turbidity is good or bad. Some aquatic species survive well in highly turbid water. The Mississippi

© SIU, published by Addison Wesley Longman, Inc.

River is very turbid, yet its waters hold abundant life. Some forms of aquatic life can survive only in water with low turbidity.

Generally, humans prefer less turbid water. For aesthetic, recreational, and health reasons, most of us like water sparkling clear. This preference for clear water has undoubtedly helped humans survive, because turbidity can mean that harmful contaminants are present in the water.

High turbidity can be an indicator of poor water quality. Suspended solids in drinking water can indicate and support the growth of harmful microorganisms. Suspended solids also can interfere with chemical testing and purification of water.

At high levels of turbidity, water loses its ability to support aquatic life. The suspended solids prevent sunlight from reaching aquatic plants. Without light, photosynthesis cannot take place. When photosynthesis is curtailed, green plants cannot produce oxygen; this reduces the concentration of dissolved oxygen in the water. Dissolved oxygen is necessary for fish survival and other aquatic life.

Turbidity changes may disturb bottom-dwelling species, such as clams. Increased turbidity causes more solids to settle to the bottom of a river or stream, especially where the flow rate is slow. As solid matter settles, it may cover bottom-dwelling plants and animals, reducing their ability to survive and reproduce. The clamming industry in the Mississippi River has decreased because solids have covered many of the clam beds.

DRIFTWOOD

Recently a group of students planted willow seedlings along the eroded bank of a midwestern river hoping that some of the seedlings would take root and grow, thus keeping the river bank from eroding further.

What Can Be Done to Reduce Turbidity?

Many of the causes of high turbidity can be reduced by people initiating better environmental practices. For example, people can practice good agricultural techniques and good forest fire prevention so that soil erosion is kept to a minimum. People can replenish plants and trees that have been destroyed by forest fires, tornadoes, or floods. People can become more careful with the disposal of their wastes. These are but a few examples that can reduce turbidity. Perhaps you can think of more controls and practices that could be instituted to decrease turbidity.

Questions

1. Describe in your own words what is meant by turbidity.
2. Check the definitions of *turbidity* in a dictionary. Do any of these definitions correspond to the way the word is used in discussing water quality? Explain.
3. High turbidity in a river or stream is not very attractive. What are some additional adverse effects on the environment and on aquatic life?

© SIU, published by Addison Wesley Longman, Inc.

4. List one natural and one human-related cause of increased turbidity of river or stream water.

For Further Research

1. Relate turbidity to the types of aquatic life that can develop and live in a river or stream.
2. Find out how turbidity levels in a waterway can vary with changes in season.

© SIU, published by Addison Wesley Longman, Inc.

How Can Turbidity Be Measured?

Turbidity is measured by determining the amount of light transmitted through water. As the number of particles of solid matter in water increases, less light passes through, so the maximum depth at which you can see objects beneath the water's surface decreases.

Jackson Candle Turbidimeter

Early attempts to quantify turbidity were described in 1900 by G.C. Whipple and D.D. Jackson. Jackson developed standard suspensions using measured amount of microscopic solid matter mixed with distilled water. Using a candle and a flat-bottomed glass, he determined the turbidity of water samples by measuring the length of a column of sample needed in order for a candle flame to disappear from view. The apparatus, shown in Figure 4-1, is called the Jackson Candle **Turbidimeter** (ter bih DIHM ih ter). A more turbid sample ("A" in the figure) needs only a short column of sample for the candle flame to disappear, while a less turbid sample ("E" in the figure) requires a longer column of sample. The turbidity results using this method are reported in **Jackson Turbidity Units** (JTU).

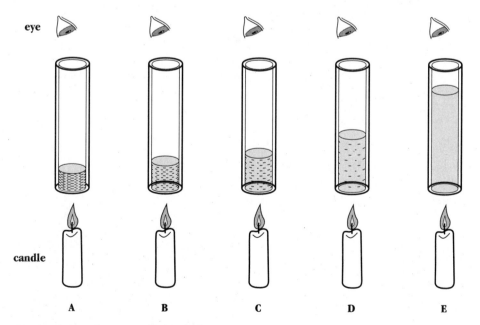

Figure 4-1: Jackson Candle Turbidimeter

© SIU, published by Addison Wesley Longman, Inc.

Scientists found the Jackson Candle Turbidimeter difficult to use, so they developed other methods to measure turbidity; however, JTU units are still used. Another unit, **Nephelometric** (NEHF uh luh meh trik) **Turbidity Unit,** (NTU), is also used. The two units are equivalent, meaning 1 JTU equals 1 NTU.

Turbidimeter

Turbidimeters, such as a **nephelometer** (nehf uh LAHM ih ter), are electronic devices that measure how clear a liquid is by measuring the amount of transmitted light. A water sample is placed in a tube or cup and inserted into the meter. Light is passed through the sample. A totally transparent sample transmits all the light; turbid samples do not. The amount of light transmitted is then measured and read directly from the meter. Most turbidimeters are calibrated to give readings in JTUs or NTUs.

Turbidity Test Kit

Some commercial turbidity test kits function like the Jackson Candle Turbidimeter. Instead of the light from a candle, however, the kits use a black-and-white "X" or other figure. Using natural light, a sample of river water is compared with a standard. For example, if a standard is rated 20 JTU and if the river water sample appears to be as turbid as the standard, then the river water is rated 20 JTU.

Secchi Disk

A **Secchi** (SEHK ee) **disk** is another device for measuring turbidity. A circular disk, 20 cm in diameter, is divided into four quarters that are alternately painted black and white (as shown in Figure 4-2). A cord, chain, or dowel is attached to the disk so the disk may be lowered vertically into the water. The cord is calibrated, usually into one-inch (2.54 cm) intervals, so that the depth can be measured. The disk is slowly lowered into the water until it disappears from view; the depth is recorded. The disk is lowered a few centimeters more and then slowly raised until it is just visible; the depth is recorded again. The average of the two depth values is used. Because the Secchi disk must be lowered until it is not visible, this device cannot be used in shallow water or in water of low turbidity.

© SIU, published by Addison Wesley Longman, Inc.

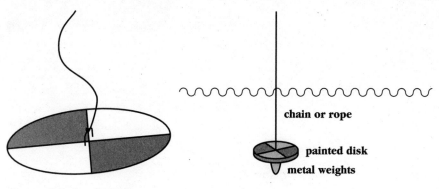

Figure 4-2: Secchi Disk

Questions

1. Turbidity can be measured using various instruments. All such devices, however, measure not the actual amount of suspended material itself in water but one particular effect of that suspended matter. What effect is that?

© SIU, published by Addison Wesley Longman, Inc.

How Does a Water Treatment Plant Handle Turbidity?

One of the first steps in making water safe to drink is to remove any suspended matter from the water. Because most suspended matter settles to the bottom if water is allowed to set undisturbed, a water treatment plant places water in holding areas for several hours. Some of the suspended matter settles to the bottom, allowing the top portion of water to become less turbid. This process is called **sedimentation** (sehd uh muhn TAY shuhn).

Small suspended matter does not settle to the bottom even if water is allowed to sit for several days. In order to remove small matter, water treatment plants use a process called **flocculation** (FLAHK yuh lay shuhn). The plant adds chemicals such as aluminum sulfate (alum) or a mixture of iron (II) chloride and CaO (lime) to the water. These chemicals, called flocculation agents, form a gelatinous or fluffy solid called **floc** (flahk). As the floc forms and sinks to the bottom, small matter, including microscopic matter, adheres to or is entrapped by the floc. Once the floc and its captured matter arrives at the bottom, the top portion of water in the holding area is less turbid.

Water treatment plants may use either or both processes. Neither process harms drinking water; however, the treatment plant must properly dispose of the solid matter that settles to the bottom of the holding tanks.

Questions

1. In a water treatment plant, what is floc?
2. What is the difference between flocculation and sedimentation?

For Further Investigation

1. Find out what further treatments are given to drinking water in your area and how treatments may vary according to the time of year.
2. Research how sewage water is treated before being released into the environment. Compare treatment of sewage water with that of drinking water.

© SIU, published by Addison Wesley Longman, Inc.

Reducing Turbidity in Water

Purpose

To use sedimentation and flocculation to clarify water.

Background

In this activity, you will model how a water treatment plant clarifies turbid water. You will use two different flocculation agents: aluminum sulfate and a mixture of iron (II) chloride and calcium oxide.

An untreated water sample will serve as the control. The control will enable you to compare the effectiveness of sedimentation and flocculation.

Safety and Waste Disposal

Follow all lab safety procedures presented in Lesson 1. You will use raw river or stream water that may contain harmful contaminants; therefore, wear safety goggles, apron, and gloves while doing this activity. At the end of the activity, dispose of waste as directed by your teacher.

Procedure

1. Put on your safety goggles, lab apron, and gloves.
2. Obtain three, 1-liter volume containers or Imhoff cones. Label one container *alum:* a second container *iron (II) chloride + lime:* the third *control*.
3. Measure 5 g alum onto a piece of paper, and place it next to the container labeled *alum*. Measure 2.5 g iron (II) chloride onto a piece of paper. Measure 2.5 g lime onto a piece of paper. Thoroughly mix the iron (II) chloride and lime, and place the mixture next to the container labeled *iron (II) chloride + lime*.
4. Obtain 3 liters of raw, muddy river or stream water. Mix the water thoroughly to make sure the suspended matter is distributed evenly. Pour 1 liter of water into each labeled container. Add the alum to its container and the mixture of iron(II) chloride and lime to its container.
5. Allow the containers to set undistarbed for 30 minutes.
6. Place a white sheet of paper behind each container. View the top portion of water in each container, and rank the containers from least turbid to most turbid. Record your results in the Data Table.
7. If possible, let the containers stand overnight, and repeat Step 6 the next day.
8. Dispose of the contents of the containers as instructed by your teacher, clean your lab area, and wash your hands with soap and water.

Materials

Per student
- safety goggles, lab apron, and gloves

Per group
- 3–4 L muddy river or stream water
- 3 Imhoff cones, graduated cylinders, or transparent soda bottles; 1 L each

- labels or labeling markers
- laboratory balance
- weighing paper
- spatula
- 5 g aluminum sulfate (alum)
- 2.5 g iron (II) chloride
- 2.5 g calcium oxide (lime)
- waste container

© SIU, published by Addison Wesley Longman, Inc.

Observations

DATA TABLE

River or Stream Water	Change in 30 Minutes	Change Overnight
with alum		
with iron(II) chloride and lime		
control		

Analyses and Conclusions

1. Which treatment produced clearer water?
2. To what extent did letting the water samples sit longer affect the results?

Critical Thinking Questions

1. Which method of turbidity reduction would you recommend for use by a water treatment plant ? Why?
2. Why would it be dangerous for someone to drink untreated river water even though it has low turbidity?
3. Explain why flocculation agents normally would not be used to clarify water in a natural aquatic environment such as a river or lake.

Keeping Your Journal

1. Write a story about a journey of a drop of water from being a raindrop to being in a glass of drinking water.

© SIU, published by Addison Wesley Longman, Inc.

Measuring the Turbidity of a River or Stream

Purpose

To measure the turbidity of a river or stream and assess the impact of turbidity on water quality.

Background

In this activity you will measure the turbidity of a river or stream by using a Secchi disk, turbidimeter, or turbidity test kit. If the body of water is a shallow stream, do not use the Secchi disk.

Safety

Follow all field safety procedures presented in Lesson 1. Because hazardous materials may be present in the river, be sure to wear safety goggles and gloves. Be sure to wear a life jacket and a tow line if you are testing water that is deep or has a fast current. Exert extra caution to avoid slipping or falling into the water. Dispose of waste as directed by your teacher.

Procedure

PART A. Before Going to the Field Site (if using a Secchi disk)

1. Calibrate the rope by marking off one-inch (2.54 cm) or two-cm increments.
2. If the disk is made of plastic or wood, add steel weights to the disk, so it will sink vertically in the water.

PART B. At the Field Site

3. If possible, take your readings from the middle of the river or stream. A dock or small bridge may be available; otherwise stand on the bank.
4. Put on safety goggles, gloves, life jacket, and tow line; wear rubber wading boots if appropriate.
5. Slowly lower the Secchi disk vertically into the water until you cannot see it. (If the disk cannot be lowered vertically but "sways out" due to the current, add more steel weights. (Lead weights should not be used, because they are environmentally harmful). Record the depth in Data Table 1 as Trial 1, Depth A.
6. Lower the disk a few centimeters more, then slowly raise it until it first becomes visible. Record the depth in as Trial 1, Depth B.
7. Repeat steps 5 and 6 two more times, as Trials 2 and 3.

If you are using a turbidimeter or test kit, only Steps 3 and 4 apply. Follow the operating instructions for your meter or kit, and record the results for three trials in Data Table 2.

Materials

Per student
- safety goggles, lab apron, and gloves
- life jacket and tow line (for deeper-water sites)
- rubber waders or boots (for shallower-water sites)
- calculator with square-root function

Per group
- Secchi disk (calibrated), turbidity kit, or turbidimeter

- extra steel weights (if using Secchi disk)
- water-sampling pole, with clamp (if using turbidity kit)
- sampling bottle, with lid, of correct size to match turbidity-kit requirements (if using turbidity kit)
- waste container (if using turbidity kit)
- binoculars (if disk will be viewed from a bridge)

© SIU, published by Addison Wesley Longman, Inc.

Observations

Date _____   Location _____

Time _____   Weather Conditions _____

DATA TABLE 1: Secchi Disk Readings

	(A) Depth at Which Secchi Disk Disappears (m)	(B) Depth at Which Secchi Disk Reappears (m)	$\dfrac{A + B \, (m)}{2}$
Trial 1			
Trial 2			
Trial 3			

Average = _____

Standard Deviation = _____

Reported Value = _____ m ± ____

Q-Value = _____%

DATA TABLE 2: Turbidimeter or Turbidity Kit Readings (JTU)

	Turbidity (JTU)
Trial 1	
Trial 2	
Trial 3	

Average = _____ JTU

Standard Deviation = _____

Reported Value = _____ JTU ± ____

Q-value = _____ %

Calculations

8. If you used a Secchi disk, for each trial, add the depth when the disk disappeared to the depth when it reappeared. Divide this sum by 2, and record the result for Trial 1 in the far-right column of Data Table 1. Repeat for Trials 2 and 3.
9. Calculate and record the average of the results of the three trials.
10. Calculate and record the standard deviation.
11. Record the reported value.
12. Convert your average turbidity value (obtained in Step 9) into its equivalent Q-value, using either Figure 4-3 or 4-4. Record the Q-value.

© SIU, published by Addison Wesley Longman, Inc.

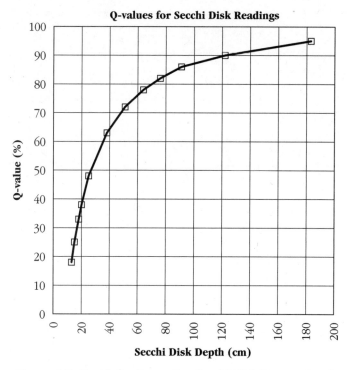

Figure 4-3: Graph for Converting Secchi Disk Data to Q-value

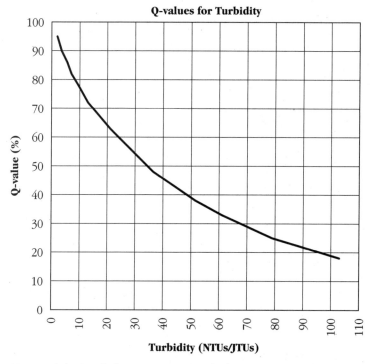

Figure 4-4: Graph for Converting Turbidimeter or Kit Data to Q-value

© SIU, published by Addison Wesley Longman, Inc.

Measuring the Turbidity of a River or Stream   **75**

Analyses and Conclusions

Q-value for Turbidity	Quality of Water
90–100%	Excellent
70–89%	Good
50–69%	Medium
25–49%	Bad
0–24%	Very bad

1. Using your average turbidity value and its corresponding Q-value, rate your river or stream water from excellent to very bad.
2. Describe your field site. Do streams, ditches, or drains feed into your site? Is there new construction or bare soil that might easily erode? Which features contribute to the turbidity of the water?
3. What would improve the clarity of the water at your field site?

Critical Thinking Questions

1. Explain how the turbidity of your field site might affect the aquatic organisms living in the river or stream.
2. Predict how the turbidity might vary at your test site at different times of the year. Explain your reasoning.

Keeping Your Journal

1. Write your impressions or feelings about your field site. Do you think it is ugly or pleasing? How might it be improved? What could you do to improve the site?
2. Write a few descriptive phrases about the river or stream that you might later develop into a poem or story about your site. Sketch any unusual or interesting features of the site.

© SIU, published by Addison Wesley Longman, Inc.

LESSON 5 — Total Solids in River or Stream Water

Focus	Students will study the total amount of solid matter that is dissolved or suspended in a river or stream. They will discover what is meant by hard and soft water, and learn what differentiates unsaturated, saturated, and supersaturated solutions. They will measure the total solids in a waterway and use standard methods to determine the quality of the water.
Learner Outcomes	Students will: 1. Distinguish between turbidity and total solids in a river or stream. 2. Learn the causes and effects of hard water. 3. Learn how to test water to determine if it is hard or soft. 4. Learn what differentiates unsaturated, saturated, and supersaturated solutions. 5. Determine the amount of total solids in a river or stream and use their data to determine water quality.
Time	Three class periods of 40–50 minutes per period and a field trip to a river or stream

DAY 1:	Student Information 5.1: What is Meant by Total Solids? Student Information 5.2: What Is Meant by Hard and Soft Water?
DAY 2:	Student Activity 5.3: Determining the Hardness of Water Student Activity 5.4: Measuring Total Solids in a River or Stream, Part A
FIELD TRIP:	Student Activity 5.4: Measuring Total Solids in a River or Stream, Part B
DAY 3:	Student Activity 5.4: Measuring Total Solids in a River or Stream, Part C

Advanced Preparation	Prepare to supply students with Student Information 5.1 and 5.2 and with Student Activity 5.3 and 5.4. Gather all necessary equipment and materials. Learn the operational procedures for the water-hardness test kit or strips the class will use. In Student Activity 5.4, at least three samples of water need to be analyzed. Written material assumes three groups each collect and analyze one water sample. If you do not use three groups, adjust procedures accordingly.

If the water in your area is very soft, it may contain insufficient amounts of calcium to run Student Activity 5.3. To make soft water hard, add one gram of powdered calcium carbonate, $CaCO_3$, per liter of water and shake. Allow to stand for 24 hours. Decant the clear solution from any powder remaining, and test for hardness.

The materials list for Student Activity 5.4 includes one 500-mL beaker and one 250-mL graduated cylinder per group, but a smaller beaker and graduated cylinder may be used. Make sure your laboratory balance will accommodate the size beaker you plan to use.

Review Lesson 1 regarding water sampling equipment and technique. Review information in the unit introduction on field trip management.

Safety and Waste Disposal

Follow all laboratory and field safety procedures presented in Lesson 1. In Student Activity 5.3, hydrochloric acid is used. Review laboratory cautions for acid use as well as acid spills. Chemicals used in Student Activity 5.3 and 5.4 can be flushed down the sink.

Materials

Student Activity 5.3: Determining the Hardness of Water

Per student
safety goggles, lab apron, and gloves

Per group
3 beakers, 250-mL each
300 mL of hard water
labels or labeling marker
water-hardness test kit or paper test strips

Student Activity 5.4: Measuring Total Solids in a River or Stream

Per student
safety goggles, lab apron, and gloves
life jacket and tow line (for deeper-water sites)
rubber waders or boots (for shallower-water sites)
calculator with square-root function

Per group
laboratory balance
beaker, 500-mL
10–20 mL of dilute HCl (6 *M*)
1-L sampling bottle, with lid
ringstand, ring, wire gauze, and heat supply (hot plate, Bunsen burner, or lab oven)
labeling tape or marker
sealable plastic bag (large enough to hold a 500-mL beaker)
tongs
water-sampling pole, with clamp
graduated cylinder, 250-mL

Vocabulary

dissolved solid	solute
hard water	solution
precipitate	solvent
saturated solution	supersaturated solution
scale	total solids
soft water	unsaturated solution
solubility	

Background for the Teacher

Highly turbid water has large amounts of suspended matter, but it may have a low amount of dissolved solids. A Rocky Mountain stream has low turbidity, but it may have large amounts of dissolved solids. Just because a body of water lacks turbidity does not mean it has high water quality. In fact, turbid water with low total solids could have a higher water quality than clear water with high total solids.

Some water-hardness test kits and test strips determine the hardness of water by measuring only the calcium-ion content. If you use such a test kit, remember that other ions (such as magnesium and iron) may also be present in your river or stream. Student Activity 5.3: Determining The Hardness of Water considers only the calcium ion.

Introducing the Lesson

1. Have students read and discuss Student Information 5.1: What Is Meant by Total Solids? They can record definitions of *total solids, dissolve,* and *suspend.* Discuss the relationship among the terms. How are they different? Discuss the difference between turbidity and total solids.

Developing the Lesson

1. Have students answer questions on Student Information 5.1. (Answers and solutions for student sheets are in Appendix C.)
2. Have students read, discuss, and answer questions on Student Information 5.2: What is Meant by Hard and Soft Water? This information will prepare them for Student Activity 5.3: Determining the Hardness of Water.
3. Show students how to use a water-hardness test kit or test strips.
4. Have Students do Activity 5.3: Determining the Hardness of Water. This activity allows students to explore the degree of hardness of local water.
5. Have students discuss Student Activity 5.4: Measuring Total Solids in a River or Stream. Review laboratory and field safety cautions. Discuss the procedure for the activity. Have students do Part A of Student Activity 5.4 in the laboratory.
6. Have students do Part B of Student Activity 5.4 at the field site, then Part C in the laboratory.

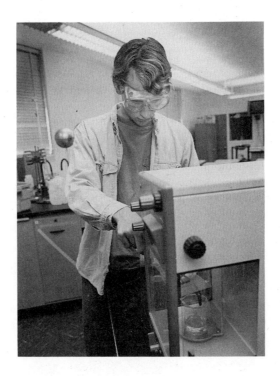

Concluding the Lesson

1. Discuss ways to keep total solids in waterways at low levels.

Assessing the Lesson

1. Have students add to their water-quality collages.
2. Obtain water samples from other areas or other water sources, such as farm wells, and have students test them for hardness and for total solids.

Extending the Lesson

1. Have students conduct a survey to determine how many homes in your community have water softeners and calculate the percentage of homes with softeners. For specific teaching activities on percentage and on statistics, see *Rivers Mathematics*.
2. Have a water softener company representative visit the class. Discuss the cost, advantages, and disadvantages of having a water softener.
3. Have students do research on caves such as Mammoth Cave in Kentucky, Carlsbad Caverns in New Mexico, Luray Caverns in Virginia, Howe Caverns in New York, and Oregon Caves in Oregon. Students can use pushpins to indicate the location of the caves on a map. For specific teaching activities on doing nonfiction research, see *Rivers Language Arts*. For specific teaching activities on mapping, see *Rivers Geography*.

What Is Meant by Total Solids?

The term **total solids** refers to all solid matter that is either suspended or dissolved in water. Turbidity is the result of only suspended solids; it does not include dissolved solids.

How are dissolved solids different from matter that causes turbidity? Dissolved particles are mixed with the water evenly, so every part of the solution has the same composition. **Dissolved solids** cannot be separated from water by sedimentation or flocculation. Examples of solutions include table sugar or salt dissolved in water. A solid that has dissolved in water is not visible even with the aid of a microscope.

How Do Dissolved Solids Get into a Body of Water?

Solubility (sahl yuh BIL uht ee) refers to the ability of a substance to dissolve in another substance. A large number of chemicals are soluble (dissolve) in water. Nitrates, for example, are very soluble. If sodium nitrate or potassium nitrate are in the soil, rain will dissolve them. The water will carry the dissolved nitrates into nearby waterways. In the same manner, dissolved chlorates, chlorides, and sulfates may also be washed into a river or stream.

How Are Total Solids Measured?

The amount of total solids is determined by evaporating a measured quantity of water to dryness and then weighing the residue. The residue is composed of both the dissolved and the suspended matter. The quantity of total solids in water may be reported in grams per liter (g/L) or milligrams per liter (mg/L). Mg/L is often referred to as parts per million (ppm).

Example: 1L of river water is allowed to evaporate, leaving 4 grams of residue. The amount of total solids would be 4 g/L or 4000 mg/L or 4000 ppm.

The Effect of High Levels of Total Solids

Drinking water should have no more than 0.5 grams of total solids per liter. Drinking water with higher levels tends to have an unpleasant taste, may induce health problems, and is unfit for many household and industrial uses. A high level of total solids in water may also adversely affect aquatic plans and animals, depending on what the solids are.

© SIU, published by Addison Wesley Longman, Inc.

Questions

1. What is the major difference between turbidity and total solids?
2. Describe how the amount of total solids in water is determined.
3. What units are used to measure total solids?
4. What maximum level of total solids is acceptable in drinking water?

Problems

1. When 1.00 liter of water from a stream near your school was evaporated, 0.75 grams of total solids remained. Express the amount of total solids in the water in mg/L and ppm.
2. While running a total solids test, students found that only 0.8 L of water had been collected. When the water was evaporated, 0.65 g of residue remained. Express the amount of total solids in the water in mg/L and in ppm.

© SIU, published by Addison Wesley Longman, Inc.

What Is Meant by Total Solids?

What Is Meant by Hard and Soft Water?

If your household water is hard water, you probably have noticed a ring around your bathtub after bathing, or you might have noticed that soap does not lather easily. The "ring-around-the-tub" and the lack of lather are results of various kinds of dissolved solids in the water.

What Is Hard Water?

Hard water is water that contains large quantities of calcium (Ca^{2+}), magnesium (Mg^{2+}), or iron (Fe^{2+}) ions. These three metal ions prevent or make it "hard" for most soaps and detergents to form a soapy lather. Soft water is water that contains few or no calcium, magnesium, or iron ions. Water can be classified as soft, moderately hard, hard, or very hard according to the amount of dissolved calcium carbonate.

Is Hard Water Undesirable?

From a natural perspective, hard water creates geological wonders such as the Carlsbad Caverns and the rock terraces around mineral-laden hot springs. Aquatic life do not appear to be adversely affected by water containing high levels of calcium, iron, and magnesium ions.

From a human-use perspective, hard water is definitely undesirable. The metal ions in hard water can give the water an unpleasant taste and can stain laundry. Hard water leaves deposits, called **scale,** in water pipes, water heaters, steam irons, and other appliances. Hard water requires more soap for cleaning. It reacts with soap to produce unsightly scum on laundry, washing machines, and bathtubs.

Many homeowners purchase and maintain special water equipment that converts hard water to soft water. This conversion adds to the cost of providing water for home use.

What Is a Solution?

When a substance, such as table salt, dissolves in another substance, such as water, the result is a **solution.** The substance that is dissolved is the **solute** (SAHL yoot). The substance dissolving the solute is the **solvent** (SAHL vuhnt).

There are nine types of solutions, depending on whether the solute and the solvent are in gas, liquid, or solid form. For instance, one type of solution

© SIU, published by Addison Wesley Longman, Inc.

results when a solid solute, such as table salt, dissolves in a liquid solvent, such as water. A second type of solution results when a gas, such as carbon dioxide, dissolves in a liquid, such as water. Another type of solution results when a liquid, such as antifreeze (ethylene glycol), dissolves in another liquid, such as water. This type of solution is used in automobile radiators. Of the nine types of solutions, shown in the following table, some types are rare or not generally thought of as a solution.

The Nine Types of Solutions

Solute	Solvent	Example
gas	gas	air
gas	liquid	oxygen in water
gas	solid	hydrogen in platinum
liquid	gas	water vapor in air
liquid	liquid	antifreeze in water
liquid	solid	mercury in copper
solid	gas	sulfur in air
solid	liquid	table salt in water
solid	solid	copper in nickel

How Much Solute Can Dissolve in a Solvent?

Under normal conditions, a solvent can dissolve only a certain amount of solute. For example, 100 g of water at 20°C can dissolve only about 35 g of table salt (NaCl). If a solvent dissolves the maximum amount of solute, it forms a **saturated solution.** If the solvent has not dissolved the maximum amount of solute, the results is an **unsaturated solution.** Under unusual circumstances, it is possible for a solvent to dissolve more than the maximum amount of solute. If this occurs, then the results is a **supersaturated solution.** A supersaturated solution is usually unstable and the extra solute is unlikely to stay in solution for very long. The slightest disturbance of a supersaturated solution usually will cause the excess solute to reform as an insoluble solid called **precipitate** (pri SIP uh tayt).

Generally, the hotter the liquid solvent, the more solid solute it can dissolve. This is the reason hot water spewing from the earth will have more dissolved solid solute than a cold mountain spring. At 90°C, 100 g of water can dissolve approximately 40 g of table salt, which is 5 g more than at 20°C.

In some cases, the hotter the liquid solvent, the less solid solute it can dissolve. For example, the amount of cesium sulfate, $Ce_2(SO_4)_3$, that dissolves in 100 g of water decreases as the temperature of the water increases.

© SIU, published by Addison Wesley Longman, Inc.

When the solute is a gas, the hotter the liquid solvent, the less gas will dissolve. Thus, less oxygen gas will dissolve in hot water than in an equal amount of cold water. For this reason, river and stream water usually contains less dissolved oxygen in the summer than in the winter. On a hot summer's day, few fish are likely to be near the surface of a river because the fish have sought deeper, colder water for a sufficient supply of dissolved oxygen.

How is Hard Water Formed?

Any soluble compound containing calcium, magnesium, or iron may produce hard water. Calcium carbonate (and limestone, which contains it) is plentiful in nature. After water falls to the earth as rain or snow, it may come into contact with calcium carbonate and other minerals that contain calcium, magnesium, or iron. Some of these minerals dissolve, releasing metal ions into the water, producing hard water.

Other factors besides temperature, which has already been mentioned, affect how much solute will dissolve in a solvent. For example, calcium carbonate dissolves more readily in slightly acidic water than in nonacidic water. You can see this effect if you stroll through an old cemetery in an area affected by acid rain. The writing and decorations on old tombstones made of limestone or marble (both of which contain calcium carbonate) will most likely be almost totally dissolved by the acid rain.

Mammoth Cave in Kentucky and Carlsbad Caverns in New Mexico were once solid calcium carbonate. Over a long period of time, the calcium carbonate developed cracks and fissures into which water seeped, slowly dissolving the calcium carbonate to form the magnificent caverns. As the water dripped down from cavern walls and ceilings, some of the dissolved calcium carbonate was redeposited as icicle-like stalactites or as stalagmites projecting up from the cavern floor. The water traveled to other areas, sometimes leaving new deposits of calcium carbonate. Some of the calcium carbonate remained dissolved in the water and reached nearby waterways, producing hard water.

Questions

1. What is the difference between hard and soft water?
2. How are limestone caves formed?
3. State three practical problems that can be caused by hard water.
4. a. When adding sugar to tea, what is the solvent and what is the solute?
   b. How could you determine if a solution was unsaturated or saturated?
   c. How could you test the effect of temperature regarding the solubility of sugar in tea?
5. Why is acid rain particularly damaging to structures made of limestone or marble?

© SIU, published by Addison Wesley Longman, Inc.

What Is Meant by Hard and Soft Water?

Determining the Hardness of Water

Purpose

To determine if water samples are soft, moderately hard, hard, or very hard.

Background

In this activity, you will measure the amount of calcium carbonate in three water samples using a water-hardness kit or paper test strips. Then you will classify the water samples as very hard, hard, moderately hard, or soft.

Safety and Waste Disposal

Follow all lab safety procedures presented in Lesson 1. Wear safety goggles, apron, and gloves. Dispose of all test materials as advised by your teacher.

Procedure

1. Put on safety goggles and apron. If you are testing raw river or stream water, put on safety gloves.
2. Label the beakers: "1," "2," and "3."

3. Obtain 300 mL of hard water as directed by your teacher, and pour 100 mL into each of the three beakers.
4. Using a water-hardness test kit or paper test strips, determine the amount of calcium carbonate in each sample, and record in the data table.

Calculations

5. Calculate the average mg/L of calcium carbonate for the three samples, and enter the average in the Data Table.

Materials

Per student
- safety goggles, lab apron, and gloves

Per group
- 3 beakers, 250-mL each
- labels or labeling marker
- 300 mL of hard water
- water-hardness test kit or paper test strips

© SIU, published by Addison Wesley Longman, Inc.

Observations

DATA TABLE

Trial	Calcium Carbonate (mg/L)
1	
2	
3	
Average of the three trials	

Analyses and Conclusions

Dissolved Calcium Carbonate (milligrams/liter)	Classification
0–74	soft
75–149	moderately hard
150–299	hard
300 or greater	very hard

1. Use the preceding table, classify the water sample as soft, moderately hard, hard, or very hard.
2. What problems, if any, might the sample water cause if you were to use this kind of water in your home?

Critical Thinking Questions

1. If you were purchasing a new home, why would you want to know whether the water supply is soft or hard?
2. In this activity, you were testing for calcium carbonate. Why might the results not reflect the total amount of metal ions in the water? What other metal ions might be present?

Keeping Your Journal

1. Discuss ways by which metal ions can get into the water supply.
2. Obtain a small bottle of mineral water that is for drinking. Taste it and describe how the flavor differs from tap water or plain bottled water. Read the label to see what minerals are present in the bottled mineral water, and record them in your journal. Did you find the taste of mineral water pleasant or not?
3. Find out how water softeners work, and describe the process in your journal.

© SIU, published by Addison Wesley Longman, Inc.

Measuring Total Solids in a River or Stream

Purpose

To measure the amount of total solids in river or stream water and assess the impact on water quality.

Background

Most people obtain their water from a water purification facility. The facility may be privately owned or maintained by a city. In order to provide you with water, the purification facility must receive water from a source, such as a river. The purification facility will pump water from the river, clean the water, and then deliver it to your home by underground pipes. If the river water has a large amount of total solids, then the facility will need more time and equipment to reduce the amount of solids before you can use the water. This additional treatment will cost more money. On the other hand, if the river has a low amount of total solids, then less time and equipment will be required and the water will be less costly to treat.

In this activity, you will go to a river or stream and obtain a water sample. Then, you will determine the amount of total solids in your sample.

Safety and Waste Disposal

Follow all lab and field safety procedures presented in Lesson 1. Be sure to wear both safety goggles and gloves. You cannot tell by its appearance whether glassware is hot or cool, so be sure to handle it with tongs. Pour unused river water into the sink.

Procedure

PART A. Before Going to the Field Site

1. Make sure your laboratory balance can accommodate a 500-mL beaker. If not, use the largest size beaker your balance can accommodate.
2. Put on your safety goggles, gloves, and apron.
3. Label sealable plastic bag with your group name or number.
4. Clean the beaker and the 1-L sampling bottle with soap and water, rinse thoroughly with tap water, acid wash, and distill wash them, following procedures from Student Information 1.3: Lab and Field Techniques.

Materials

Per student
- safety goggles, lab apron, and gloves
- life jacket and tow line (for deeper-water sites)
- rubber waders or boots (for shallower-water sites)
- calculator with square-root function

Per group
- laboratory balance
- beaker, 500-mL
- 10–20 mL of dilute HCl (6 *M*)

- 1-L sampling bottle, with lid
- ringstand, ring, wire gauze, and heat supply (hot plate, Bunsen burner, or lab oven)
- labeling tape or marker
- sealable plastic bag (large enough to hold a 500-mL beaker)
- tongs
- water-sampling pole, with clamp
- graduated cylinder, 250-mL

© SIU, published by Addison Wesley Longman, Inc.

5. Place the beaker on a ring-stand ring equipped with a wire gauze. Gently, with a low burner flame, heat the beaker until it is dry. Allow the beaker to cool to room temperature. From this point, do not handle the beaker with your bare hands because moisture and oil from your skin can alter the mass of the beakers.

6. Using tongs, place the beaker on a laboratory balance and record its mass. Place the beaker in a sealable plastic bag in order to keep it clean and dry.

PART B. At the Field Site

7. Record the date, location, time, and weather conditions. Record in your journal details of your field site.

8. Wearing gloves and goggles, use the water-sampling pole to collect 1 liter of river or stream water in the 1-L sampling bottle. If the sample contains any floating debris, such as small pieces of wood or leaves, discard the sample and collect a new sample. Cap the bottle.

PART C. In the Laboratory

9. In the remaining steps, each time a sample is to be transferred, it must be swirled and thoroughly mixed before being transferred; otherwise, some of the total solids may remain in the sample bottle, preventing an accurate measure of total solids.

10. Remove the beaker from its plastic bag.

11. Swirl the bottle of river water several times so the contents are thoroughly mixed. Using a graduated cylinder, measure 250 mL of sample. Swirl the graduated cylinder, and pour the river water into the beaker.

12. Swirl the bottle of river water several times, and measure another 250 mL of sample using a graduated cylinder.

13. Using tongs, place the beaker on a ringstand ring equipped with wire gauze. Bring the water to a gentle boil with your burner. As the water level in the beaker drops, swirl the second 250 mL of sample in the graduated cylinder, and add it to the beaker.

14. Repeat steps 11 and 12 until 1 L of river sample has been used. When you have used all but the last 10–15 mL of the sample, turn the burner heat to low until all the sample has been used. When most of the water has evaporated, total solids have a tendency to "splatter." If the heat under the beaker is too high, some residue may splatter out of the beaker and burn you. If residue splatters out, accurate results cannot be obtained. Also, if the beaker is heated too quickly, the beaker may crack and rupture.

15. Allow the beaker to cool to room temperature.

16. Using tongs, place the beaker on a laboratory balance and record its mass.

Measuring Total Solids in a River or Stream

© SIU, published by Addison Wesley Longman, Inc.

Observations

Date _____   Location _____

Time _____   Weather Conditions _____

DATA TABLE

Volume of water evaporated   _____ L

Mass of beaker and residue   _____ g

Mass of empty beaker   _____ g

Mass of residue   _____ g   _____ mg

Amount of total solids   _____ mg/L

Group	Total Solids (mg/L)

Average =   _____ mg/L

Standard Deviation =   _____

Reported Value =   _____ mg/L ± ____

Q-value =   _____%

Calculations

17. Calculate the grams of total dissolved solids by subtracting the mass of the empty beaker from the mass of the beaker plus residue. Convert grams of residue to milligrams.
18. Obtain and record the results from the other groups.
19. Using your result and the results from the other groups, calculate and record the average total solids in mg/L.
20. Calculate and record the standard deviation.
21. Record the reported value.
22. Convert the average total solids value into its equivalent Q-value using Figure 5-1. Record the Q-value.

© SIU, published by Addison Wesley Longman, Inc.

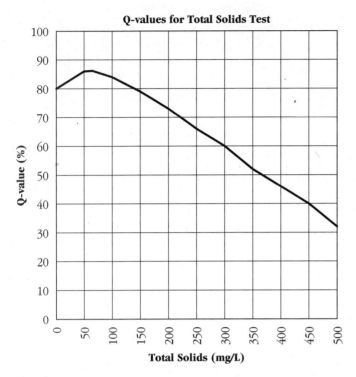

Figure 5-1: *Graph for Converting Total Solids (mg/L) to Q-value*

Analyses and Conclusions

Q-value for Total Solids	Quality of Water
90–100%	Excellent
70–89%	Good
50–69%	Medium
25–49%	Bad
0–24%	Very bad

1. Using your Q-value for total solids and the preceding table, rate your river or stream from excellent to very bad.
2. Describe your field site. Do you see rock formations nearby? Do ditches or drains empty into your river or stream? Is there new construction or bare soil that might easily erode? Are farms, homes, or industries nearby? Are there trees and plants that may drop leaves into the water? Do you see any organisms in or near the water. Do you see signs that humans have been disposing of litter or other waste in or near the water?
3. What factors do you think contribute to the amount of total solids present in the water?
4. What might be done to reduce the level of total solids in the water at your field site?

© SIU, published by Addison Wesley Longman, Inc.

Measuring Total Solids in a River or Stream

Critical Thinking Questions

1. Explain how the amount of total solids at your field site might affect the organisms living in the river or stream.
2. Predict how the level of total solids might vary at your test site at different times of the year. Explain your reasoning.
3. Explain the relationship between the total solids results you obtained in this lesson and the turbidity readings you made in Lesson 4.
4. What was the pH and water temperature at your field site. How might these two factors influence the amount of dissolved solids in the water?

Keeping Your Journal

1. How does the amount of total solids contribute to the uniqueness of your river or stream?
2. Would you like to see the amount of total solids in your river or stream reduced? Why or why not?

© SIU, published by Addison Wesley Longman, Inc.

LESSON 6   *Dissolved Oxygen in River or Stream Water*

Focus	Students will discover the importance of dissolved oxygen (DO) to aquatic life. They will learn how temperature and pressure affect the solubility of gases in water. They will develop an understanding of the ecological balance between oxygen enrichment and oxygen depletion in natural water systems. In the field, they will determine the concentration of dissolved oxygen in water samples and use standard methods to determine the quality of the water.
Learner Outcomes	Students will: 1. Learn the meaning of dissolved oxygen. 2. Learn that solubility of gases increases with increasing pressure and decreases with increasing temperature. 3. Understand the relationship between dissolved oxygen and aquatic life in a waterway. 4. Learn what factors may deplete the amount of dissolved oxygen in a waterway. 5. Determine the amount of dissolved oxygen of a river or stream and use dissolved oxygen data to determine water quality.
Time	Two to three class periods of 40–50 minutes per period and a field trip to a river or stream DAY 1: Student Information 6.1: What Is Dissolved Oxygen? DAY 2: Student Activity 6.2: Investigating the Solubility of Gases FIELD TRIP: Student Activity 6.3: Measuring Dissolved Oxygen in a River or Stream (Parts A and B at field site, Part C in lab)
Safety and Waste Disposal	Follow all lab and field safety procedures presented in Lesson 1. Chemicals used in Student Activity 6.2 can be flushed down the sink. In Student Activity 6.3, chemicals are to be placed in a waste container and allowed to evaporate.
Advanced Preparation	Prepare to supply students with Student Information 6.1 and with Student Activity 6.2 and 6.3. Gather all necessary equipment and materials. Learn the operational procedures for the dissolved-oxygen test kit your students will be using. (Some information is provided in Background for the Teacher.)

In Student Activity 6.3, at least three samples of water need to be analyzed. Written material assumes three groups each collect and analyze one water sample. If you do not use three groups, adjust procedures accordingly. Each test requires approximately 15 minutes. As part of this activity, the class will collect three samples of river water in DO bottles for use in Lesson 7. Test kits generally supply only one DO bottle; if your class has only one test kit with one DO bottle, obtain two additional DO bottles.

Review Lesson 1 regarding water sampling equipment and technique. Review information in the unit introduction on field trip management. After water collected in Lesson 6 has incubated for five days, students will perform Student Activity 7.2. Therefore, make certain the fifth day does not fall on a day that school is not in session. If you plan the field trip for Lesson 6 for a Thursday or Friday, Student Activity 7.2 can take place the following Tuesday or Wednesday.

Materials

Student Information 6.1: What Is Dissolved Oxygen?
For possible teacher demonstration
carbonated beverage, precooled
carbonated beverage, room temperature

Student Activity 6.2: Investigating the Solubility of Gases
Per student
safety goggles and lab apron
Per group
beaker, 500-mL
graduated cylinder, 100-mL
heat source (hot plate or Bunsen burner with ring stand, ring, and wire gauze)
laboratory balance that will accommodate the mass of a carbonated beverage
carbonated beverage, precooled
paper toweling
watch or classroom clock
Celsius thermometer

Student Activity 6.3: Measuring Dissolved Oxygen in a River or Stream
Per student
safety goggles, lab apron, and gloves
life jacket and tow line (for deeper-water sites)
rubber waders or boots (for shallower-water sites)
calculator with square-root function
Per group
Celsius thermometer, alcohol-filled with a metal jacket, or electronic
dissolved-oxygen test kit
dissolved-oxygen bottle with stopper (if not included in test kit)
water-sampling pole, with clamp

aluminum foil
labeling tape or marker
temperature-controlled lightproof incubator
waste container
plastic trash bag (for paper waste from test-kit packets)
straightedge or ruler

Vocabulary

atmosphere	percent saturation
dissolved oxygen	pressure

Background for the Teacher

For most classes, Student Activity 6.3 is the first field activity in which students use prepackaged solid chemicals at the field site. Students will discover that doing labwork at the site differs from working in a school lab where they have access to tables and other conveniences. Running a test while sitting on a river bank, and opening chemical packets while the wind is blowing, are often difficult. If your site has such conditions, advise your students to take extra caution. On the other hand, if your site is a small stream in a quiet woods or meadow, such difficulties may not be as pronounced.

Dissolved oxygen kits by different manufacturers use different sets of instructions, but they all work in a similar way. First, a chemical is added so that it can react with the oxygen that is dissolved in the water. This chemical reaction forms an insoluble colored precipitate. At this point, the oxygen is said to be "fixed." Up to this point, it is important to have no air bubbles in the DO bottle. After the oxygen has been fixed, air bubbles in the bottle are not as crucial, although it is still good laboratory technique to have no air bubbles.

If air bubbles are present before the oxygen is fixed, the test should be aborted and started over with a new sample. After the oxygen is fixed, other chemicals are added to dissolve the precipitate and produce a colorless solution and thus conclude the test. To determine the amount of dissolved oxygen in mg/L, the user counts the number of drops of added chemical used in the final step.

While running a dissolved oxygen analysis, the stopper is taken from the bottle so that chemicals can be added, then replaced in the bottle. This procedure occurs at least twice for most test kits. Students may have difficulty keeping air bubbles out of the bottle while performing these procedures. They can minimize this problem by placing the stopper in the bottle with moderate speed and gentleness. If the stopper is inserted too slow or fast, air bubbles have a greater tendency to form. When you obtain your test kit, take time to practice this procedure so you will become familiar with the problem and can model a technique that avoids this problem.

If a tiny air bubble is present before the oxygen is fixed, here is a technique that can avoid the necessity of aborting the test. Obtain small glass beads, or cut glass tubing into small lengths. Place the glass gently in the bottle, so no water splashes out; the small air bubble will be expelled. Continue the test. This method may produce slightly inaccurate results; if this is used on only one of the three samples, however, the inaccuracy will be further minimized when the average is calculated.

The temperature of the water sample that will be used in Lesson 7 may be colder than the recommended incubation temperature of 20°C. If the temperature of the sample rises above 20°C, however, dissolved oxygen will come out of solution. The ground glass stopper firmly placed in the DO bottle should form a tight seal so a closed system is present, preventing dissolved oxygen from escaping. If the system is not closed, dissolved oxygen will escape and will produce a BOD value greater than zero even if no organic matter is present. Therefore, if the water temperature is less than 20°C, as the difference between the water sample temperature and the incubator system increases, so does the inaccuracy of the test. If the water temperature is above 20°C, this problem will not exist. If possible, plan the timing and location of the field trip in Lesson 6 so that the water temperature is between 15°C and 20°C.

Introducing the Lesson

1. Have students read and discuss Student Information 6.1: What Is Dissolved Oxygen? Assess students' knowledge about the solubility of gases by opening two cans of carbonated drink, one cold and one at room temperature. Ask students to discuss how the two cans differ when they are opened. (One container emits more gas than the other. Then see if students can hypothesize why there is a difference. (A cold liquid holds more dissolved gas than a warm one.)

2. Ask students to recall from Lesson 3 how nuclear and fossil-fuel power plants can affect the temperature of a waterway. Discuss how seasonal temperatures affect the amount of dissolved oxygen in a river or stream.

Developing the Lesson

1. Have students answer questions on Student Information 6.1. Relate this information to the next water-quality test—biochemical oxygen demand—which the students will explore in Lesson 7. (Answers and solutions for student sheets are in Appendix C.)

2. Have students carry out Student Activity 6.2: Investigating the Solubility of Gases.

Concluding the Lesson

1. Have students carry out Student Activity 6.3: Measuring Dissolved Oxygen in a River or Stream.

2. Discuss with students ways to keep dissolved oxygen levels at a comfortable level for fish and other aquatic life. Consider seasonal changes, temperature, rainfall, and pollution from surrounding farms, industries, and residential developments.

Assessing the Lesson

1. Have students do lab-based Assessment for Lesson 6: How Much Oxygen in the Fish Tanks (located in Appendix B).

2. Have students add to their water-quality collages.

Extending the Lesson

1. Have students contact a local fishery or wildlife agency to find out how much dissolved oxygen various species of fish require. For specific teaching activities on doing nonfiction research, see *Rivers Language Arts*.

2. Invite a fishery or wildlife professional to visit the class so that students can ask questions regarding dissolved oxygen and other topics of student interest.

3. Have students write a short story about how a fish might react if its supply of dissolved oxygen were suddenly reduced or depleted. For specific teaching activities on creative writing, see *Rivers Language Arts*.

What Is Dissolved Oxygen?

In Lesson 5 you studied solutions. One type of solution that was mentioned had a gas solute and a liquid solvent. The study of dissolved oxygen refers to this type of solution. **Dissolved oxygen,** as the name implies, is oxygen gas dissolved in water.

Solubility of Gases in Water

All gases will dissolve in water to some extent, but some gases dissolve better than others. For example, carbon dioxide (CO_2) gas is about 200 times more soluble in water than oxygen (O_2) gas. Nitrogen (N_2) gas is only half as soluble as oxygen gas. Despite differing solubilities of gases, they all follow two basic laws, one in regard to temperature and the other in regard to pressure.

Effect of Temperature on Gas Solubility

Lesson 5 stated that solids generally dissolve better in water as the temperature increases. Gases, however, do just the opposite. As the temperature rises, less gas will dissolve in water.

Temperature of One Liter of Water (°C)	Amount of Oxygen That Will Dissolve (mg/L)
10	48
20	45
30	38
40	32
50	26

Using the preceding table, notice that oxygen gas is almost twice as soluble in water at 10°C than it is at 50°C. As shown in the table, if the water temperature is 10°C, 48 mg of oxygen gas will dissolve in 1 liter of water. Another way to communicate this information is to say that the solubility of oxygen gas at 10°C is 48 mg/L. The unit for dissolved oxygen is mg/L.

Effect of Pressure on Gas Solubility

Air has a mass. In fact, the air that surrounds the earth has enough mass that every square inch of the earth's surface has on it a force of 14.7 pounds. The

© SIU, published by Addison Wesley Longman, Inc.

amount of force exerted over a unit area is called **pressure.** Air pressure is often measured in pounds per square inch. Other units for air pressure are **atmosphere** (atm) and mm (or inches) of mercury. 1 atm equals 760 mm (29.92 inches) of mercury. In this lesson, the unit used for pressure will be atmosphere.

As pressure increases, more gas will dissolve in water. As shown in the following table, as pressure increases, the amount of oxygen that will dissolve in one liter of water increases.

Air Pressure on One Liter of Water (atm)	Approximate Amount of Dissolved Oxygen (mg/L)
1	46
2	88
3	129
4	170

What Other Factors Affect the Amount of Dissolved Oxygen in Water?

You learned in Lesson 3 that the decay process requires oxygen gas. Several types of circumstances often increase the amount of decaying material in a waterway. If a river or stream has a large amount of decaying vegetation such as leaves or aquatic microorganisms, then the amount of dissolved oxygen is reduced. Sometimes people dump raw sewage, garbage, grass, and other decayable substances in a river or stream. As these objects decay, the amount of dissolved oxygen falls.

Some natural processes act to increase the amount of dissolved oxygen. Aquatic plants produce oxygen gas if sufficient sunlight is available. The oxygen gas dissolves in the water, helping replenish oxygen that is removed. If the water has high turbidity, however, light may not reach aquatic plants.

Water that "splashes" into the air has more dissolved oxygen than water that does not. Water in a rapidly flowing mountain river or stream that splashes against rocks will have more dissolved oxygen than the water of a calm, slow-moving body of water.

As you have already learned, the seasons of the year, time of day, and water depth also affect the temperature of the water, and thus the amount of dissolved oxygen in the water. At lower depths, water is under greater pressure, which also increases the amount of dissolved oxygen the water at those depths can contain.

© STU, published by Addison Wesley Longman, Inc.

Dissolved Oxygen Requirements for Fish

Just as you need an adequate amount of oxygen gas in the air to live, so fish and other aquatic life need adequate amounts of oxygen gas to be dissolved in water. Different species of fish require differing amounts of dissolved oxygen. Trout and salmon need 8 to 15 mg/L of dissolved oxygen. Some Mississippi River fish—such as buffalo, carp, and catfish—require 4 to 8 mg/L of dissolved oxygen, so they will survive in waters in which trout or salmon would die.

Questions

1. Using your own words, describe what is meant by dissolved oxygen.
2. How is the solubility of gases in liquids affected by changes in temperature?
3. How is the solubility of gases in liquids affected by changes in pressure?
4. Describe one way that the level of dissolved oxygen can be decreased in a waterway other than by changing temperature or pressure.
5. Explain why daily and seasonal variations in levels of dissolved oxygen are common.
6. What might be done to help insure that a sufficient amount of dissolved oxygen is present in a waterway?

DRIFTWOOD

As a human being, you are unable to use oxygen that is dissolved in water. If you could, you would be able to breathe under water.

An underwater diver must use an oxygen tank. So far, no one has invented a device that can take dissolved oxygen out of the water in a way that humans can use that oxygen for breathing while underwater. Reflect on this. In the future, maybe you will invent such a device.

© SIU, published by Addison Wesley Longman, Inc.

Investigating the Solubility of Gases

Purpose

To observe the effect of pressure and temperature on dissolved carbon dioxide.

Background

In this activity, you will investigate the effect of pressure and temperature on the carbon dioxide dissolved in a can of carbonated soda. Carbonated beverages are canned or bottled under several atmospheres of pressure of carbon dioxide gas, so the liquid in each can will dissolve more carbon dioxide gas than it would at just one atmosphere. When you remove the tab or cap from a carbonated beverage, you can see and hear the excess carbon dioxide gas escaping. Carbon dioxide gas escapes from the beverage until it reaches its normal solubility level at one atmosphere of pressure.

Safety and Waste Disposal

Follow all laboratory safety procedures presented in Lesson 1. No substance used in the laboratory should be ingested. Therefore, do not drink any of the soda that you are testing in this activity. At the end of the activity, pour the soda down the drain. Rinse and recycle the empty beverage can.

Procedure

PART A. Pressure and Solubility

1. Put on your safety goggles and apron.
2. Using a graduated cylinder, measure 100 mL of water. Pour the water into a 500-mL beaker, and place the beaker on a heat source until its temperature reaches 50°C.

3. While the water is heating, dry (with toweling) the outside of a cooled, unopened can of soda.
4. Find the mass of the can of soda and record in Data Table 1.
5. Carefully open the can and allow the excess carbon dioxide gas to escape. (This will take about 3 minutes.)
6. Weigh the can and record its mass. Repeat this step every three minutes until 15 minutes have elapsed. Check the beaker of water periodically to make sure it has not overheated.

PART B. Temperature and Solubility

7. Measure the temperature of the opened soda can and record the temperature in Data Table 2. Measure the temperature of the heated water to make sure that it is 50°C.
8. Place the opened can in the 500-mL beaker that contains the heated water. Allow the can to warm for 10 minutes. Turn off your heat source.
9. Record the temperature of the liquid inside the can.
10. Remove the can from the hot water. Dry the outside of the can with toweling.
11. Find the mass of the can, and record its mass in Data Table 2.

Materials

Per student
- safety goggles and lab apron

Per group
- beaker, 500-mL
- graduated cylinder, 100-mL
- heat source (hot plate or Bunsen burner with ring stand, ring, and wire gauze.)
- laboratory balance that will accommodate the mass of a carbonated beverage
- carbonated beverage, precooled
- paper toweling
- watch or classroom clock
- Celsius thermometer

© SIU, published by Addison Wesley Longman, Inc.

Observations

DATA TABLE 1: Pressure and Solubility

Time (minutes)	Mass (g)
0	
3	
6	
9	
12	
15	

Amount of carbon dioxide lost = _____ g

DATA TABLE 2: Temperature and Solubility

Time	Temperature (°C)	Mass (g)
Initial time:		
After 10 minutes		

Amount of carbon dioxide lost = _____ g

Calculations

12. Calculate the grams of carbon dioxide lost from the heated, opened can and record in Data Table 1.
    (Initial mass of opened can – mass of can heated for 10 minutes = mass of carbon dioxide lost)

13. Calculate the number of grams of carbon dioxide lost after 15 minutes as the internal pressure of the can was reduced to atmospheric pressure. Record in Data Table 2.
    (Mass of unopened can – mass of opened can after 15 minutes = mass of carbon dioxide lost)

Analyses and Conclusions

1. Explain why the opened can of carbonated beverage weighed less after 15 minutes.
2. What do you think would happen if you let the opened can stand overnight?
3. What effect did a rise in temperature have on the mass of the carbonated beverage in the opened can? Explain this result.

© SIU, published by Addison Wesley Longman, Inc.

Critical Thinking Questions

1. One summer morning, some teenagers bought several cartons of soda to take to the beach. They put the soda in the truck of their car but then forgot to take it out until late afternoon. When they opened the truck, they found that the cans had burst and soda was everywhere. Propose a hypothesis for why this happened.

2. Marita and Joe went fishing one hot summer day. Marita let her fishing line hang several meters deeper in the river than Joe. Marita caught her limit of fish. Joe caught only one catfish. Offer a hypothesis as to why Marita caught more fish than Joe.

Keeping Your Journal

1. Write in your journal what you have learned about the effects of pressure and temperature on a can of soda and how you might apply this information to your daily life.

2. Think of an everyday situation in which temperature and pressure effect the solubility of a gas, and write a story about it. In your story explain how temperature and pressure had an impact on what happened.

© SIU, published by Addison Wesley Longman, Inc.

Investigating the Solubility of Gases

Measuring Dissolved Oxygen in a River or Stream

Purpose

To measure the amount of dissolved oxygen in a water sample taken from a river or stream and to use this information to assess water quality.

Background

When you collect your water sample, use only the dissolved oxygen (DO) bottle from your testing kit. Do not use any other kind of bottle and do not transfer water to the DO bottle from another container.

DO bottles are specifically designed for collecting water samples that are to be tested for dissolved oxygen. The neck of a DO bottle has a collection collar that surrounds the opening. To keep air bubbles from forming inside the DO bottle, make sure that the collection collar contains water when you insert the glass stopper. There should be no air bubbles inside the bottle.

Once you have determined the average dissolved oxygen concentration and the average temperature, you will use Figure 6-1 to obtain the percent saturation. **Percent saturation** is the percent of milligrams of oxygen gas dissolved in one liter of water at a given temperature compared with the maximum milligrams of oxygen gas that can dissolve in one liter of water at the same temperature.

Example: Assume the average temperature is 20°C and the average dissolved oxygen is 8.0 mg/L. Using Figure 6-1, locate 20 degrees on the Water Temperature scale and locate 8.0 mg/L on the Dissolved Oxygen Concentration scale. Using a ruler or straightedge, draw a line from 20 degrees to 8.0 mg/L. The drawn line will intersect the Dissolved Oxygen Saturation line at 85%.

To get accurate dissolved oxygen readings, complete Part A of the Procedure for this activity at the field site.

Materials

Per student
- safety goggles, lab apron, and gloves
- life jacket and tow line (for deeper-water sites)
- rubber waders or boots (for shallower-water sites)
- calculator with square-root function

Per group
- Celsius thermometer, alcohol-filled with metal jacket, or electronic
- dissolved-oxygen test kit

- dissolved-oxygen bottle with stopper (if not included in test kit)
- water-sampling pole, with clamp
- aluminum foil
- labeling tape or marker
- temperature-controlled lightproof incubator
- waste container
- plastic trash bag (for paper waste from test-kit packets)
- straightedge or ruler

Safety and Waste Disposal

Follow all laboratory and field safety procedures presented in Lesson 1. Wear safety goggles and gloves. Pour all waste into a waste container.

Procedure

PART A. Testing for Dissolved Oxygen

1. Record the date, location, time, air temperature, and weather conditions.

© SIU, published by Addison Wesley Longman, Inc.

2. Put on safety goggles, gloves, and other safety equipment for your site.

3. Measure and record the water temperature.

4. Rinse a DO bottle with river water two or three times.

5. Obtain a sample of river water in the DO bottle. Make sure there are no air bubbles inside. If bubbles are present, empty the bottle into the river a few meters downstream, and collect another sample, again making sure there are no air bubbles inside.

6. Immediately stopper the bottle. Firmly holding the stopper in the bottle, invert the bottle and pour off excess water around the collar.

7. Using a dissolved-oxygen test kit, determine the amount of dissolved oxygen and record in the Data Table.

8. Empty the contents of the bottle into the waste container.

PART B. Obtaining Water Samples for Lesson 7

9. Repeat Steps 4 through 6.

10. Completely cover the bottle with aluminum foil so that light cannot enter. Label the bottle with your group name or number.

PART C. In the Laboratory

11. When you return to the classroom, set the bottle in a light-proof, temperature-controlled incubator set at 20°C or in a lightproof laboratory drawer. Record the incubator temperature on the Data Table. The bottles should remain undisturbed in the incubator for five days. You will use this sample for Lesson 7 when you test for biochemical oxygen demand.

© SIU, published by Addison Wesley Longman, Inc.

Observations

Date _____   Location _____

Time _____   Weather Conditions _____

Air Temp (°C) _____

DATA TABLE

Group	Dissolved Oxygen (mg/L)	Water Temperature (°C)

Average =   _____ mg/L   _____ °C

Standard Deviation =   _____   _____

Reported Value =   _____ mg/L ± _____

Percent Saturation =   _____ %

Q-value =   _____ %

Initial Incubator Temperature =   _____ °C

Calculations

12. Obtain and record the water temperature from the other groups.
13. Obtain and record the dissolved oxygen results from the other groups.
14. Using your result and the results from the other groups, calculate and record the average temperature and the average dissolved oxygen (mg/L).
15. Calculate and record the standard deviation for dissolved oxygen.
16. Record the reported value.
17. Using the average temperature and average dissolved oxygen, determine the percent saturation using Figure 6-1 and a straightedge or ruler. Record your result.
18. Convert the percent saturation of dissolved oxygen into its equivalent Q-value using Figure 6-2. Record the Q-value.

Analyses and Conclusions

Q-value for Total Solids	Quality of Water
90–100%	Excellent
70–89%	Good
50–69%	Medium
25–49%	Bad
0–24%	Very bad

© SIU, published by Addison Wesley Longman, Inc.

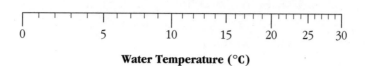

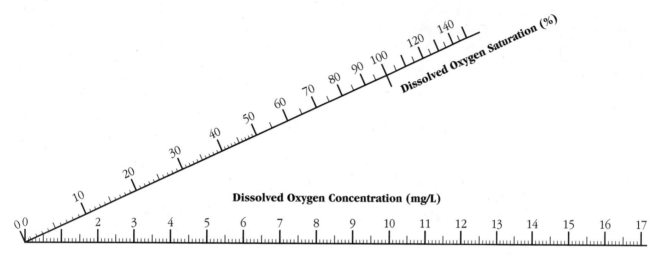

Figure 6-1: Chart for Converting DO Concentration at a Particular Temperature to Percent Saturation

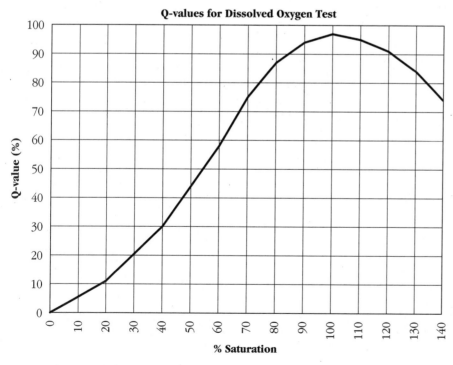

Figure 6-2: Graph for Converting Percent Saturation to Q-value

© SIU, published by Addison Wesley Longman, Inc.

Measuring Dissolved Oxygen in a River or Stream

1. Using your Q-value for dissolved oxygen and the information in the preceding chart, rate your river or stream water from excellent to very bad.
2. Describe your field site. Is the stream or river swift-flowing or sluggish? Do ditches or drains empty matter into your waterway? Are farms, homes, or industries nearby? Are there trees and plants that may drop leaves or other debris into the water? Is the water clear or turbid? What organisms do you see? Are there signs of decomposing matter?
3. What factors do you think add dissolved oxygen to the water at your field site? What factors do you think remove oxygen from the water?
4. What might be done to improve the level of dissolved oxygen in the water at your field site?

Critical Thinking Questions

1. Explain how the amount of dissolved oxygen in the water at your field site might affect the organisms living in the waterway.
2. Predict how the concentration of dissolved oxygen in the water at your field site might vary at different times of the year. Explain your reasoning.
3. Explain how temperature and turbidity might affect the dissolved oxygen level of a river or stream.
4. If you wanted to go trout fishing, what kind of river or stream would be likely to support a population of brook trout?

Keeping Your Journal

1. Write your impressions or feeling about your field site. Do you think it is ugly or pleasing? How might it be improved? What could you do to improve the site?
2. Write a few descriptive phrases about the river or stream that you might later develop into a poem or story about your site. Sketch any unusual or interesting features of the site.

© SIU, published by Addison Wesley Longman, Inc.

LESSON 7 — Biochemical Oxygen Demand in River or Stream Water

Focus	This lesson continues the study of the oxygenation of water, to which students were introduced in Lesson 6. Students will learn what biochemical oxygen demand (BOD) is and how dissolved oxygen is added to and consumed in rivers and streams. They will relate pollution and other human factors to dissolved oxygen levels in waterways. Students will then determine the BOD level in a sample that has been incubated for five days. They will use standard methods to determine the quality of the water.
Learner Outcomes	Students will: 1. Learn what is meant by BOD and the factors that influence it. 2. Learn that BOD is an indirect measure of organic pollution. 3. Learn some of the results of oxygen depletion in river or stream water. 4. Determine the BOD of a river or stream and use their data to determine water quality.
Time	Two to three class periods of 40–50 minutes per period DAY 1: Student Information 7.1: What Is Biochemical Oxygen Demand? DAY 2: Student Activity 7.2: Measuring Biochemical Oxygen Demand in River or Stream Water (Water samples for Student Activity 7.2 are taken in Part A of Student Activity 6.3.)
Safety and Waste Disposal	Follow all laboratory safety procedures presented in Lesson 1. Chemicals used in Student Activity 7.2 are to be placed in a waste container and allowed to evaporate.
Advance Preparation	Prepare to supply students with Student Information 7.1 and Student Activity 7.2. In Student Activity 7.2, three samples of water need to be analyzed. Written material assumes three groups each analyze one water sample. If you do not use three groups, adjust procedures accordingly. Gather all necessary equipment and materials. Make sure the dissolved-oxygen test kit used in Student Activity 6.3 is ready for Student Activity 7.2.

Materials	**Student Activity 7.2: Measuring Biochemical Oxygen Demand in River or Stream Water**

Per student

safety goggles, lab apron, and gloves

Per group

water-filled DO bottle from Student Activity 6.3 that has been incubated for five days

dissolved-oxygen test kit

waste container, 1–2 L

Per class

lightproof incubator set at 20°C, or lab drawer with Celsius thermometer

Vocabulary

bioassay	organic matter
biochemical oxygen demand	

Background for the Teacher

Refer to Lesson 6, Background for the Teacher, for information about the significance of a temperature difference between the water sample collected in Lesson 6 and the incubation temperature. For additional specific teaching activities on BOD, see *Rivers Biology*.

Introducing the Lesson

1. Have students read, answer, and discuss the questions in Student Information 7.1: What Is Biochemical Oxygen Demand? (Answers and solutions for student sheets are in Appendix C.) This sheet gives information about BOD, explores reasons for variations in BOD, and explains the procedure for testing BOD.

Developing the Lesson

1. Have students do Student Activity 7.2: Measuring Biochemical Oxygen Demand in River or Stream Water.
2. Discuss why a river or stream might have a low or high BOD, and relate this to the results of Student Activity 7.2.
3. Have students discuss if they have witnessed an incident of chemical or organic matter being placed in a ditch, sewer, stream, or river. Discuss how this might affect the BOD of a waterway.
4. Have students discuss if they have been exposed to foul-smelling waterways. Discuss possible reasons for the smell.
5. Have students discuss if they have witnessed a waterway that had a large amount of floating dead fish. Discuss possible reasons for the "fish-kill."

Concluding the Lesson

1. Discuss ways to improve the BOD level of a river or stream. What special problems might different environments have? For instance, what natural differences might be expected among waterways flowing through wetlands, woodlands, prairies, and mountains? What industries could have great impact on the BOD of rivers and streams?

2. Plan a field trip to an industrial plant or sewer plant to observe how organic waste is processed. Have an official of an industry or sewer plant visit the class so students can ask questions regarding the issues in this lesson.

Assessing the Lesson

1. Have students add to their water-quality collages.

2. Encourage students to suggest ways BOD could be improved in your river or stream.

Extending the Lesson

1. Have students conduct a survey among other students or families to determine how households in their community dispose of various chemicals such as old paint, insecticide, fertilizer, and used motor oil. Have them contact the local sanitation company (and other resources) to determine recommended procedures for such disposal. For specific teaching activities on interviewing, see *Rivers Language Arts*.

2. Have students debate and decide whether to contact city officials to obtain permission to stencil "DO NOT DUMP" at storm-drain entrances near the school or their homes.

What Is Biochemical Oxygen Demand?

In Lesson 6, you learned that many factors determine the amount of dissolved oxygen in a river or stream. For instance, oxygen gas can become dissolved in water through the natural process of splashing and wave action. Photosynthesis of aquatic plants produces more dissolved oxygen.

Even as such processes are adding oxygen to a waterway, organic matter is removing it. **Organic matter** means anything that is or was alive. The microorganisms in a river or stream feed on the organic matter, and the process by which they break down that organic matter reduces the supply of dissolved oxygen gas in the water.

All rivers and streams naturally contain some organic matter produced by aquatic organisms. Water flowing from swamps and bogs adds organic matter to water, as do falling leaves. Human sources include farms, food-processing plants, paper mills, untreated sewage, and grass clippings. When a river or stream receives excess organic matter, its populations of microorganisms that feed on such matter may increase rapidly, consuming greater amounts of dissolved oxygen.

Chemicals in rivers and streams may also react to deplete dissolved oxygen. Chemical waste from industries and homes often end up in rivers and streams. People dump paint, motor oil, fertilizer, and insecticide into drains and sewers that lead to streams and rivers. Whatever the sources, excess organic and chemical matter can overload a river or stream, so that the stream no longer has a healthy level of dissolved oxygen. **Biochemical oxygen demand** (BOD) is the requirement (demand) for oxygen that matter, organic and chemical, places on water. BOD is a measurement of how much stress is being placed on the dissolved-oxygen system of a waterway. The lower the stress, the more oxygen is available for aquatic organisms such as fish and shellfish.

How Is BOD Measured?

To find the BOD of a river or stream, first measure the amount of dissolved oxygen in the water, as you did in Lesson 6. Then collect another sample of the water and allow it to sit undisturbed in a lightproof compartment at 20°C for five days. At the end of the fifth day, analyze the sample again for dissolved oxygen. If the sample contains organic or chemical matter that has required oxygen, the sample will contain less dissolved oxygen than it did five days earlier. The difference between the initial level and the final level of dissolved oxygen is a measure of BOD. If the difference is zero, then there is

© SIU, published by Addison Wesley Longman, Inc.

no biochemical oxygen demand; the water contains no organic or chemical matter that requires oxygen. If the difference is large, then the water has a large amount of organic or chemical matter, or both.

As with dissolved oxygen, BOD is measured in mg/L. The smaller the BOD number, the better the water quality. A BOD value of 1 mg/L is excellent, and the water is considered "pure." A value of 2 mg/L is good, and a value of 3 or 4 mg/L is fair. Water is considered poor if it has a BOD of 5 mg/L or more.

Example: Assume your water sample contained 22 mg/L of dissolved oxygen when you were at the field site five days ago. At the end of five days, you find that 20 mg/L of dissolved oxygen remains. What created the 2 mg/L difference? (The container was covered.) The water must contain matter that used the 2 mg/L. The BOD is, therefore, 2 mg/L, which is good.

This type of method is a **bioassay.** This means that it does not measure the amount of matter directly; rather, it measures the effect of matter.

If you obtain a difference in dissolved oxygen over the five-day period, you do not know whether the demand comes from organic matter or chemical matter. Some tests can determine which type of source is placing the demand; for most rivers, however, the demand comes primarily from organic matter.

Why Place the Sample in a Lightproof Compartment?

When you collect and store a sample for a BOD analysis, you must protect it from exposure to light. A water sample from a river or stream may contain microscopic plant life. Plants, when exposed to sunlight, produce oxygen gas by photosynthesis. If your sample did have plant life and received exposure to sunlight, then it would produce oxygen by photosynthesis, which would add to the amount of oxygen in the sample. When you did your reading after five days, you would not have a valid measurement of the BOD. To insure that no oxygen gas is added, you will wrap your the stoppered sample and place it in a lightproof compartment.

Why 20°C? Why Five Days?

In order to live, microorganisms need an warm environment. Twenty degrees Celsius is a temperature that provides such an environment. Maintaining the sample temperature close to 20°C helps keep the microorganisms alive throughout the five-day period.

Incubating a water sample for five days as part of BOD testing has become a standard procedure, and here are two interesting tales about why this waiting period developed. One tale states that when BOD measurements were first initiated many years ago, investigators allowed samples to sit for five days simply because that was how long it took for the water from their area to flow to the sea. The second states that scientists' methods were not sensitive enough to

© SIU, published by Addison Wesley Longman, Inc.

obtain a noticeable difference in dissolved oxygen in a shorter waiting period. Whether the tales are true or false, the procedure must allow time for organic matter to use oxygen gas in order that a difference can be obtained. A scientist using an extremely sensitive method can obtain a valid result in less time. Remember, you are finding a difference in the amount of dissolved oxygen. You might be interested in finding BOD for different time periods.

Why Do Rivers and Streams Need a Nice BOD?

If the BOD number is low, a large amount of oxygen remains dissolved in the water. In this case, the small amount of organic matter will decompose into products, such as carbon dioxide, that are not harmful to aquatic life or humans (unless the products are in large amounts). Aquatic life has sufficient dissolved oxygen to flourish.

A high BOD number indicates that a large amount of organic matter is present in the water. In this case, all or nearly all of the dissolved oxygen will soon be depleted, and aquatic life that needs dissolved oxygen, such as fish, will die.

The only remaining organisms will be those that can grow in the absence of dissolved oxygen or at very low levels of dissolved oxygen. The decomposition of these microorganisms produces harmful products such as alcohol and formaldehyde. Some such products are foul smelling and may pollute the air. Even small amounts can give a water supply a very bad taste and odor.

How Can the BOD of a River or Stream Be Improved?

Human actions can improve the BOD of a river or stream by reducing or eliminating the dumping of organic waste into waterways. For instance, in order to keep BOD low, industries and sewage plants often partially decompose their waste before releasing it into waterways. Other plants may artificially aerate the water by bubbling oxygen through it or by increasing the flow rate. Reducing thermal pollution will reduce microorganisms in the waterway, which will, in turn, reduce BOD.

Questions

1. Why is the BOD test considered a bioassay?
2. The dissolved oxygen test in Lesson 6 had to be performed immediately after you collected the water sample. Why must you wait for five days to complete the same test for your BOD analysis?
3. Which is more desirable, a high or low BOD? Explain your answer.
4. What natural and human factors can cause BOD value to be high?
5. Suggest ways to improve the BOD of a river or stream.

© SIU, published by Addison Wesley Longman, Inc.

Measuring Biochemical Oxygen Demand in River or Stream Water

Purpose

To measure the level of biochemical oxygen demand in water samples taken from a river or stream and to use this information to assess water quality.

Background

In this activity you will measure the biochemical oxygen demand in the water sample you collected at the field site as part of Student Activity 6.3. You will use the dissolved oxygen value you obtained in Student Activity 6.3 as your initial value. You will obtain a final dissolved oxygen value by testing the amount of dissolved oxygen in your sample, which has been kept in darkness at 20°C for five days.

To find the BOD level, you will subtract the final dissolved oxygen value from the initial dissolved oxygen value.

Safety and Waste Disposal

Follow all laboratory safety procedures presented in Lesson 1. Be sure to wear safety goggles, gloves, and aprons. Dispose of all liquid waste in the waste container provided by your teacher.

Procedure

1. From Student Activity 6.3, record the sampling date, location, time, air temperature, and weather conditions. Also record the initial dissolved oxygen level that you obtained in Student Activity 6.3.

Record the starting incubator temperature and the final incubator temperature after five days have elapsed.
2. Put on safety goggles, apron, and gloves.
3. Take the DO bottle from the incubator and remove its aluminum-foil wrapping. Unstopper the bottle and determine the amount of dissolved oxygen in the sample by using a dissolved-oxygen test kit. Record the amount of dissolved oxygen (mg/L) in the Data Table.
4. Empty the contents of the DO bottle into the waste container provided by your teacher. Rinse the bottle 2 or 3 times with tap water and dispose of the rinsings in the waste container.

Materials

Per student
- safety goggles, lab apron, and gloves
- calculator with square-root function

Per group
- water-filled DO bottle from Student Activity 6.3 that has been incubated for five days

- dissolved-oxygen test kit
- waste container, 1–2 L

Per class
- lightproof incubator set at 20°C, or lab drawer with Celsius thermometer

© SIU, published by Addison Wesley Longman, Inc.

Observations

Date _____   Location _____

Time _____   Weather Conditions _____

Air Temp (°C) _____

DATA TABLE

Incubator Temperature (Day 1) _____

Incubator Temperature (Day 5) _____

Measurement	Level (mg/L)
Initial DO (Day 1)	_____
Final DO (Day 5)	_____
BOD	

Group	BOD (mg/L)
_____	_____
_____	_____
_____	_____

Average = _____ mg/L

Standard Deviation = _____

Reported Value = _____ mg/L ± ____

Q-value = _____ %

Calculations

5. Calculate the BOD level by subtracting the dissolved oxygen concentration (mg/L) obtained on Day 5 from the dissolved oxygen concentration (mg/L) obtained on Day 1. Record your result in the Data Table.
6. Obtain and record the BOD level from the other groups.
7. Using your result and the results from the other groups, calculate and record the average BOD.
8. Calculate and record the standard deviation.
9. Record the reported value.
10. Convert the average BOD value into its equivalent Q-value using Figure 7-1. Record the Q-value.

© SIU, published by Addison Wesley Longman, Inc.

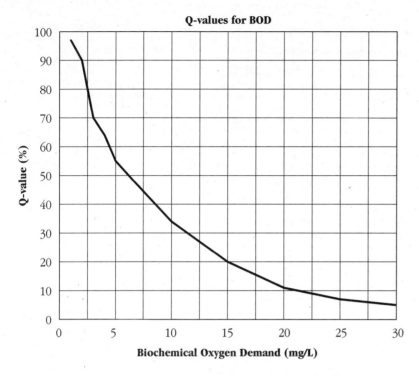

Figure 7-1: Graph for Converting BOD to Q-value

Analyses and Conclusions

Q-value for BOD	Quality of Water
90–100%	Excellent
70–89%	Good
50–69%	Medium
25–49%	Bad
0–24%	Very bad

1. Using your Q-value for biochemical oxygen demand and the preceding table, rate your river or stream water from excellent to very bad.
2. Review the description of your field site from Student Activity 6.3 (Analyses and Conclusions, number 2). What factors do you think contributed to the biochemical oxygen demand of the water at your field site? Explain the possible effect of each factor.
3. What might be done to improve the biochemical oxygen demand level of the water at your field site?

Critical Thinking Questions

1. Explain how the biochemical oxygen demand of the water at your field site might affect organisms living in the river or stream.

© SIU, published by Addison Wesley Longman, Inc.

2. Predict how the biochemical oxygen demand of the water at your field site might vary at different times of the year. Explain your reasoning.
3. Explain how temperature and turbidity might affect the biochemical oxygen demand of a river or stream.

Keeping Your Journal

1. Describe how the biochemical oxygen demand of your river or stream affects your impressions of the site.
2. Describe how this experience has affected your overall feelings about placing matter in a ditch, storm drain, or the river or stream itself.

© SIU, published by Addison Wesley Longman, Inc.

LESSON 8

Phosphates in Rivers and Streams

Focus	Students will learn about the impact of phosphates on rivers and streams. They will learn about eutrophication in waterways. They will measure the concentration of phosphate in a river or stream and use standard methods to determine the quality of the water.
Learner Outcomes	Students will:

1. Learn the causes of high phosphate levels in waterways.
2. Understand the need for monitoring a waterway for phosphates.
3. Learn the effect of excess phosphate.
4. Learn why and how to standardize a phosphate test kit.
5. Determine the phosphate concentration (mg/L) in a river or stream and determine water quality.

Time	Two to three class periods of 40–50 minutes per period and a field trip to a river or stream

DAY 1: Student Information 8.1: Phosphates in Our Waterways

DAY 2: Student Activity 8.2: Standardizing a Phosphate Test Kit
Student Activity 8.3: Measuring Phosphate Levels in a River or Stream, Part A

FIELD TRIP: Student Activity 8.3: Measuring Phosphate Levels in a River or Stream, Part B

DAY 2: Student Activity 8.3: Measuring Phosphate Levels in a River or Stream, Part C

Advanced Preparation	Prepare to supply students with Student Information 8.1 and with Student Activity 8.2 and 8.3. In Student Activity 8.3, three samples of water need to be analyzed. Written material assumed three groups each collect and analyze one water sample. If you do not use three groups, adjust procedures accordingly.

Gather all necessary equipment and materials. Learn the operational procedures for the phosphate test kit your students will be using. If your kits require heating the samples, additional laboratory time and equipment will be needed. Many phosphate kits measure the level of phosphate with a color

wheel or other colorimetric test. Check your kits with a standard solution to determine the accuracy of the color wheel or other colorimetric test. Most phosphate test kits require less than 20 mL of sample per test. Check your test kit to determine the volume of sample required for one test.

Unless your waterway has excess phosphate, it is recommended that students use a standard phosphate solution with a concentration of less than 5 mg/L. Commercial chemical supply houses (listed in Appendix F) have standard solutions available in various concentrations. Instructions for preparing standards are given in Appendix D.

Review Lesson 1 regarding water sampling equipment and technique. Review information in the unit introduction on field trip management.

Safety and Waste Disposal Follow all laboratory and field safety procedures presented in Lesson 1. Used test-kit chemicals from Student Activity 8.2 and 8.3 should be placed in a waste container and allowed to evaporate.

Materials

Student Activity 8.2: Standardizing a Phosphate Test Kit

Per student

safety goggles, lab apron, and gloves

Per group

phosphate test kit

phosphate standard solution

25–30 mL HCl, 6 *M*

waste container, 1–2 L

Student Activity 8.3: Measuring Phosphate Levels in a River or Stream

Per student

safety goggles, lab apron, and gloves

life jacket and tow line (for deeper-water sites)

rubber waders or boots (for shallower-water sites)

calculator with square-root function

Per group

phosphate test kit

sampling bottle, with lid (such as 60–100 mL DO bottle)

25–30 mL HCl, 6 *M*

water-sampling pole, with clamp

label or labeling tape

funnel for filtering

filter paper

funnel support such as ring stand, ring, and porcelain triangle

beaker, 250-mL

sealable plastic bags

waste container, 1–2 L

Vocabulary

algae

cultural eutrophication

eutrophication

phosphate

Background for the Teacher

Though most classrooms use a phosphate test kit with a color wheel or other colorimetric test, an alternate method of measurement is to use a spectrophotometer. This method is described in Appendix E.

Introducing the Lesson

1. Ask students if they know the brand name of the soap or detergent used in their home for cleaning clothes, dishes, floors, and so forth. Have them list factors that are important in choosing a specific product, such as cost, cleaning ability, and package size. Mention that even though a particular detergent has a high degree of cleaning ability, it could contain phosphates.

2. Have students read, discuss, and answer the questions on Student Information 8.1: Phosphates in Our Waterways. (Answers and solutions for student sheets are in Appendix C.) Students may discuss as a group what phosphates are and why they may cause problems in our waterways.

Developing the Lesson

1. Ask students if they have a bathroom scale at home. If they do, ask them how they know it gives correct readings. Ask them how other measuring devices such as a gasoline pump, scale at the meat market, or even the speedometer on their car might be checked for accuracy.
2. Hand out Student Activity 8.2: Standardizing a Phosphate Test Kit. Discuss the activity, and demonstrate how to use a phosphate test kit. Show students how to filter using filter paper and funnel.
3. Have students do Student Activity 8.2.
4. Have students do Part A of Student Activity 8.3: Measuring Phosphate Levels in a River or Stream.

Concluding the Lesson

1. Have students do Part B of Student Activity 8.3 at the field site.
2. Have students complete Student Activity 8.3 in the laboratory.
3. Discuss ways to keep eutrophication from occurring.

Assessing the Lesson

1. Have students do research-oriented Assessment for Lesson 8: Phosphates in Detergent (located in Appendix B).
2. As a simplified version of Assessment for Lesson 8, have students read the label of detergents found in their homes to determine if any contain phosphate and how much.
3. Have students add to their water-quality collages.

Extending the Lesson

1. Invite to class, or have students interview, a lawncare person, farmer, farm supplier, or school agricultural teacher to determine how much phosphate fertilizer is used in the area. Alternatively, do this activity as part of Lesson 9, so students can discuss both nitrates as well as phosphates. For specific teaching activities on interviewing, see *Rivers Language Arts*.

Phosphates in Our Waterways

Phosphates are essential to the growth of all living things. **Phosphate** (FAHS fayt) refers to compounds containing the phosphate ion (PO_4^{-3}). The phosphate ion is found in various minerals, such as calcium phosphate, $Ca_3(PO_4)_2$, as well as in shells, bones, and animal teeth.

Why Test Water for Phosphate?

A plant must receive a sufficient supply of phosphate in order to grow and mature properly. That is why farmers add fertilizers containing phosphate to the soil.

Phosphate is also essential for aquatic plants, such as algae. **Algae** (AL jee) is a general term for chlorophyll-containing plants like seaweed and pond scum. When a waterway has a high level of phosphate (greater than 0.1 mg/L), however, aquatic plants, including algae, mature and reproduce rapidly. Algae may grow so densely across the surface of the water that it prevents the light necessary for photosynthesis from reaching the plants and algae beneath, causing them to die. Then, as you will recall from Lesson 3, that decomposing organic matter reduces the amount of dissolved oxygen in the water. Finally, as discussed in Lesson 6, the decrease in the amount of dissolved oxygen may produce death for aquatic life such as fish.

So, if testing river or stream water reveals a high level of phosphate, it is reasonable to assume that the amount of dissolved oxygen will decrease when the plant population dies, reducing the ability of the waterway to support a variety of aquatic life.

This process of overgrowth of aquatic vegetation followed by death, decay, oxygen depletion, and an imbalance of plants and animals in the water is called **eutrophication** (yoo troh fuh KAY shuhn). Eutrophication that occurs because of human influences is called **cultural eutrophication.**

How Do Excess Phosphates Get into Waterways ?

Excess levels of phosphates in waterways are the result of human activity. Of the several human sources of phosphates in waterways, the main two are fertilizers and detergents. When a phosphate fertilizer is applied to farmlands or lawns, some of the phosphate is absorbed by land plants. The remaining portion may be transported to a river or stream by runoff or groundwater seepage.

© SIU, published by Addison Wesley Longman, Inc.

Industries and homes often use detergents for cleaning dishes, clothes, floors, automobiles, and so forth. Many detergents contain phosphates as builders, compounds that enhance cleaning ability. After detergents are used for cleaning, the waste is released down drains and sewers, or sometimes poured out onto the ground. Once in the water system, that detergent waste, and the phosphate it contains, may end up in a river or stream. In 1990, 475 million pounds of phosphate were used in detergent products in the United States. Much of this ended up in rivers and streams.

How Can Phosphate Levels in Waterways Be Reduced?

One way to reduce phosphate levels in waterways is to remove phosphates from sewage before the sewage is placed into a river or stream. To remove phosphates, the industrial or public treatment plant adds iron (III) chloride ($FeCl_3$) to wastewater that contains phosphate. An insoluble precipitate, iron(III) phosphate ($FePO_4$), is formed. The treatment plant removes this precipitate before releasing the wastewater. This process can reduce the amount of phosphate in wastewater about 90 percent. The only drawback is that removal of the phosphate increases the cost of sewage treatment.

Reduction of the amount of fertilizer used on farms and lawns would decrease phosphate runoff into waterways. A balance must be struck, therefore, between maintaining the productivity of farms and safeguarding rivers and streams. To achieve such a balance requires careful testing and monitoring of phosphate levels in soil and water samples.

The amount of phosphates in detergents has declined in recent years, in response to environmental concerns. Some detergent manufacturers have replaced phosphates with other compounds, such as sodium carbonate (washing soda), silicates, citrates, and zeolites. These compounds are less environmentally harmful, though they may not clean as effectively. As of 1993, 23 states had banned or limited the use of phosphates in detergents. This means that about 40 percent of the population of the United States are using detergents with reduced amounts of phosphate.

DRIFTWOOD

Commercial detergents are available with phosphorus concentrations varying from zero percent to over ten percent by weight. Detergents specially formulated for camping and backpacking contain no phosphorus.

Questions

1. Explain in your own words the difference between eutrophication and cultural eutrophication.
2. Describe two sources of phosphate pollution in rivers and streams.
3. Suggest what can be done in your own community to prevent cultural eutrophication.

© STU, published by Addison Wesley Longman, Inc.

Standardizing a Phosphate Test Kit

Purpose

To make sure your test kit is accurate.

Background

How does a chemist know if a measuring device is accurate? One way is to use the instrument to test a standard solution. As mentioned in Lesson 1, a standard solution is a solution of known concentration, so the chemist knows the ideal result of the test. The closer the actual result is to the ideal result, the more accurate the measuring device.

To standardize your phosphate test kit, you will use your test kit on three samples of standard solution to determine the amount of phosphate (mg/L) in the standard solution. The three results will be averaged, and the percent error will be calculated. (To review

these calculations, see Student Information 1.5: Accuracy and Precision of Data.)

$$\text{Percent error} = \frac{|\text{conc of standard} - \text{average conc}|}{\text{conc of standard}} \times 100\%$$

If your result deviates from the actual concentration of the standard solution by more than 10 to 15 percent, repeat the calibration check.

Safety and Waste Disposal

Follow all laboratory safety procedures presented in Lesson 1, including wearing safety goggles, apron, and gloves. Dispose waste into a waste container as instructed by your teacher.

Procedure

1. Put on safety goggles, apron, and gloves.

2. With soap and water, clean the glass or plastic containers that you will use from your test kit. Rinse thoroughly with tap water, acid wash, and distill wash them, following the procedures from Student Information 1.3, Lab and Field Techniques. Dry them and place the items in sealable plastic bags.

3. Obtain a bottle containing a phosphate standard solution from your teacher. Record the phosphate concentration of the standard solution in the Data Table.

4. Using your test kit, determine the amount of phosphate (mg/L) in the standard solution.

5. Record in the Data Table under Trial 1.

6. Dispose of the contents remaining in your test kit glassware into a waste container as directed by your teacher.

7. Distill wash and standard wash your test kit glassware following the procedures from Student Information 1.3, Lab and Field Techniques

8. Repeat Step 4.

9. Record the result under Trial 2.

10. Repeat Step 7.

11. Repeat Step 4.

12. Record the result under Trial 3.

Materials

Per student
- safety goggles, lab apron, and gloves

Per group
- phosphate test kit
- phosphate standard solution
- 25–30 mL HCl, 6 *M*
- waste container, 1–2 L

© SIU, published by Addison Wesley Longman, Inc.

Observations

Date _____ Time _____

DATA TABLE

Concentration of Standard Solution: _____ mg/L

Trial	Experimental PO_4^{-3} Concentration (mg/L)
1	
2	
3	

Average = _____ mg/L

Percent Error = _____ %

Pass _____

Calculations

1. Calculate the average phosphate concentration (mg/L) for the three trials and record in the Data Table.
2. Calculate percent error and record.
3. Check "pass" if the error is 10 to 15 percent or less. If the error is greater than 10 to 15 percent, repeat the test.

Analyses and Conclusions

1. How accurate is your phosphate test kit?

Critical Thinking Question

1. Why should you not allow waste from this activity be poured down the drain?

Keeping Your Journal

1. Interview a local pharmacist to find how commercial test kits, such as those used by diabetics, are tested for accuracy.

© SIU, published by Addison Wesley Longman, Inc.

Measuring Phosphate Levels in a River or Stream

Purpose

To measure the amount of phosphate in a waterway and assess the impact on water quality.

Background

Try to use a phosphate-free detergent whenever cleaning glassware but particularly in this activity. If the detergent used does contain phosphate, take particular care to rinse the glassware thoroughly with tap water, acid wash, and distill wash it, following the procedures from Student Information 1.3: Lab and Field Techniques. If any phosphate from the detergent remains, the phosphate data obtained on the water sample will be erroneous.

Safety and Waste Disposal

Follow all lab and field safety procedures presented in Lesson 1. Dispose waste into a waste container as instructed by your teacher.

Procedure

PART A. Before Going to the Field Site

1. Clean, acid wash, and distill wash a sampling bottle and stopper, following the procedures from Student Information 1.3: Lab and Field Techniques. Cap the bottle.

2. Label the bottle with your group name or number.

PART B. At the River or Stream

3. Record date, time, location, and weather conditions.
4. Take notes on your site. Do ditches or drains empty into your waterway? Are farms, homes, golf courses, or industries nearby? Check for aquatic plant life such as algae or scum.
5. Put on safety equipment.
6. Using the water-sampling pole, obtain a sample of water. Stopper the sample.

PART C. In the Laboratory

7. Clean with soap and water, thoroughly rinse with tap water, acid wash, distill wash and dry a 250-mL beaker and a funnel.
8. Using the funnel and filter paper, filter the water sample into the beaker.
9. Clean with soap and water, thoroughly rinse with tap water, acid wash, distill wash, and dry all needed containers from your test kit.
10. Using your test kit, determine the amount of phosphate (mg/L) in the water sample.
11. Record the result in the Data Table.
12. Empty the contents into the waste container as directed by your teacher.

Materials

Per student

- safety goggles, lab apron, and gloves
- lifejacket and tow line (for deeper-water sites)
- rubber waders or boots (for shallower-water sites)
- calculator with square-root function

Per group

- phosphate test kit
- sampling bottle, with lid (such as 60–100 mL DO bottle)

- 25–30 mL HCl, 6 *M*
- water-sampling pole, with clamp
- label or labeling tape
- funnel for filtering
- filter paper
- funnel support such as ring stand, ring, and porcelain triangle
- beaker, 250-mL
- sealable plastic bags
- waste container, 1–2 L

© SIU, published by Addison Wesley Longman, Inc.

Observations

Date _____   Location _____

Time _____   Weather Conditions _____

Site Description _____

DATA TABLE

Group	PO$_4^{-3}$ Concentration (mg/L)

Average = _____ mg/L

Standard Deviation = _____

Reported Value = _____ ± mg/L ____

Q-value = _____ %

Calculations

13. Obtain and record the results from the other groups.
14. Using your results and the results from the other group, calculate and record the average phosphate concentration (mg/L).
15. Calculate and record the standard deviation.
16. Record the reported value.
17. Convert the average phosphate concentration (mg/L) into its equivalent Q-value using Figure 8-1. Record the Q-value.

Analyses and Conclusions

Q-value for Phosphates	Quality of Water
90–100%	Excellent
70–89%	Good
50–69%	Medium
25–49%	Bad
0–24%	Very bad

1. Using your Q-value for phosphate and the information in the preceding chart, rate your river or stream water from excellent to very bad.
2. Review your site description. Relate the amount of plant life to your average phosphate concentration.
3. What might be done to reduce the phosphate level at your site?

© SIU, published by Addison Wesley Longman, Inc.

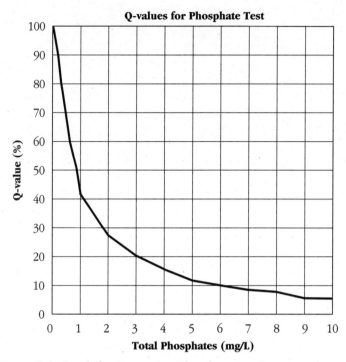

Q-values for Phosphate Test

Figure 8.1: Graph for Converting Phosphate Ion Concentration to Q-value

Critical Thinking Questions

1. What level of phosphate did you expect at your site? On what factors did you base your prediction? Was your test result better or worse than you expected? Why?
2. Explain how the phosphate level at your site might affect the aquatic plant life in or near the water.
3. Predict how phosphate levels might vary at your site at different times of the year. Explain your reasoning.

Keeping Your Journal

1. Imagine you are a phosphorus atom. Describe your travels over a period of time. For example, you might start your journey as an atom in the soil. Then you could be absorbed by a plant, which is eaten by an animal, excreted as waste, washed into a river as runoff, and so on. Alternatively, you could start your journey as part of a detergent molecule.
2. Natural eutrophication is usually a slow process that leads to the gradual filling of a pond or lake. Write a tale of two lakes: one undergoing natural eutrophication and the other experiencing rapid cultural eutrophication.

© SIU, published by Addison Wesley Longman, Inc.

LESSON 9 — *Nitrates in Rivers and Streams*

Focus	Students will learn about the impact of nitrates on rivers and streams and why nitrates are monitored. They will measure the concentration of nitrates in a river or stream and use standard methods to determine the quality of the water.

Learner Outcomes

Students will:

1. Learn the causes of high nitrate levels in waterways.
2. Understand the need for monitoring a waterway for nitrates.
3. Learn the effect of excess nitrate.
4. Determine the nitrate concentration (mg/L) in a river or stream and determine water quality.

Time

Two to three class periods of 40–50 minutes per period and a field trip to a river or stream

DAY 1: Student Information 9.1: Nitrates in Our Waterways

DAY 2: Student Activity 9.2: Standardizing a Nitrate Test Kit
Student Activity 9.3: Measuring Nitrate Levels in a River or Stream, Part A

FIELD TRIP: Student Activity 9.3: Measuring Nitrate Levels in a River or Stream, Part B

DAY 3: Student Activity 9.3: Measuring Nitrate Levels in a River or Stream, Part C

Advanced Preparation

Prepare to supply students with Student Information 9.1 and with Student Activity 9.2 and 9.3. In Student Activity 9.3, at least three samples of water need to be analyzed. Written material assumes three groups each collect and analyze one water sample. If you do not use three groups, adjust procedures accordingly.

Gather all necessary equipment and materials. Learn the operational procedures for the nitrate test kit your students will be using. Many nitrate kits measure the level of nitrate with a color wheel or other colorimetric test. Check your kits with a standard solution to determine the accuracy of the color wheel or other colorimetric test. Most nitrate test kits require less than 20 mL of sample per test. Check your test kit to determine the volume of sample required for one test.

Use a standard nitrate solution with a concentration of 1–10 mg/L. Commercial chemical supply houses (listed in Appendix F) have standard solutions available in various concentrations. Instructions for preparing standard solutions are given in Appendix D.

Review Lesson 1 regarding water sampling equipment and technique. Review information in the unit introduction on field trip management.

Safety and Waste Disposal   Follow all laboratory and field safety procedures presented in Lesson 1. Used test-kit chemicals from Student Activity 9.2 and 9.3 should be placed in a waste container and allowed to evaporate.

Materials

Student Activity 9.2: Standardizing a Nitrate Test Kit
Per student
safety goggles, lab apron, and gloves
Per group
nitrate test kit
25–30 mL HCl, 6 *M*
nitrate standard solution
waste container, 1–2 L

Student Activity 9.3: Measuring Nitrate Levels in a River or Stream
Per student
safety goggles, lab apron, and gloves
life jacket and tow line (for deeper-water sites)
rubber waders or boots (for shallower-water sites)
calculator with square-root function
Per group
nitrate test kit
sampling bottle, with lid (such as 60–100 mL DO bottle)
water-sampling pole, with clamp
label or labeling tape
funnel for filtering
filter paper
funnel support, such as ring stand, ring, and porcelain triangle
beaker, 250-mL
sealable plastic bags
25–30 mL HCl, 6 *M*
waste container, 1–2 L

Vocabulary

infant methemoglobinemia   nitrogen-fixing plant
nitrate

Background for the Teacher

Of all the test kits used thus far, the nitrate kit tends to frustrate students the most. The kit is not more difficult to use than others, but the concentration of nitrates in waterways varies greatly. Though phosphate concentrations in waterways seldom exceed 5 ppm, nitrate concentrations can range from less than 1 ppm to 50 ppm. Reassure students that such variations do not necessarily indicate inaccurate results.

Though most classrooms use a nitrate test kit with a color wheel or other colorimetric test, an alternate method of measurement is to use a spectrophotometer. This method is described in Appendix E.

Introducing the Lesson

1. Ask students if fertilizers are used on their lawns or farms. If they are, ask them how they know what ingredients are in the fertilizers. Mention that many fertilizers contain nitrates.
2. Ask students if they have ever heard of "blue babies." If so, mention what causes "blue babies."
3. Have students read, discuss, and answer the questions in Student Information 9.1: Nitrates in Our Waterways. (Answers and solutions for student sheets are in Appendix C.) Students may discuss as a group why nitrates may cause problems in a waterway.

Developing the Lesson

1. Hand out Student Activity 9.2: Standardizing a Nitrate Test Kit. Demonstrate how to use a nitrate test kit.
2. Have students do Student Activity 9.2.
3. Have students do Part A of Student Activity 9.3: Measuring Nitrate Levels in a River or Stream.

Concluding the Lesson

1. Have students do Part B of Student Activity 9.3 at the field site.
2. Have students complete Student Activity 9.3 in the laboratory.
3. Discuss ways that excess nitrates can be kept from a waterway.

Assessing the Lesson

1. Have students add to their water quality collages.
2. Have students read the label of fertilizers found in their homes to determine if any contain nitrate and how much.

Extending the Lesson

1. Invite to class, or have students interview, a lawncare person, farmer, farm supplier, or school agricultural teacher to determine how much nitrate fertilizer is used in the area. This activity can apply to Lesson 8 also, if students discuss phosphates as well as nitrates.

Nitrates in Our Waterways

Nitrogen is essential for plant and animal life. Most organisms are unable to use the nitrogen that is present as a gas in the air. Instead, nitrogen enters the food chain in the form of ammonia (NH_3) or nitrate (NI trayt) ions that can be absorbed by plants. A **nitrate** ion is composed of a nitrogen atom and three oxygen atoms (NO_3^-).

Nitrate compounds, such as sodium nitrate or potassium nitrate, occur in minerals, plants, and animals. They form the starting material that organisms use to make the many compounds necessary for life. Proteins, enzymes, nucleic acids, hormones, and vitamins all contain nitrogen.

Why Test Water for Nitrates?

You learned in Lesson 8 that plants need phosphates for proper growth and maturity. Proper growth and maturity also require nitrates.

Aquatic plants can obtain the nitrogen they need from dissolved nitrates in a river or stream. As with phosphates, too much nitrate in a waterway can encourage excessive growth of aquatic weeds and algae. This excessive plant growth can degrade the quality of a waterway through eutrophication.

So, one reason waterways are tested for nitrate levels is to monitor and control eutrophication. A second reason directly relates to human health risks, specifically health risks to infants and unborn children. Drinking water that contains high amounts of nitrates may cause "blue babies" or **infant methemoglobinemia** (meht HEE muh Gloh Bih nee mee uh). This is a medical condition of infants in which oxygen does not properly bind to hemoglobin, the oxygen-carrying molecule in the blood. To avoid this condition, pregnant women and infants should not drink water that contains more than 20 mg/L of nitrates.

Human-Based Sources of Nitrates

Nitrogen-containing fertilizers are used on agricultural land and city lawns in larger quantities than any other kind of fertilizer. Farmers supply nitrogen to their crops in various forms. About 80 percent of fertilizer nitrogen is in the form of ammonia, 19 percent is nitrates, and only 1 percent in organic nitrates.

Nitrate fertilizers are usually applied as a water-soluble solid. (In fact, most common nitrates are water-soluble.) Though some of this nitrate is absorbed

© SIU, published by Addison Wesley Longman, Inc.

by plants, some dissolves and washes into rivers and streams via runoff and groundwater.

In the Mississippi River watershed alone, an estimated 4.2 million metric tons (9.2 billion pounds) of nitrogen-based fertilizers are applied to croplands each year. Some of this amount finds its way into rivers and streams. Excess nitrates in rivers and streams also comes from wastewater from treatment plants and home septic systems.

Reducing Nitrate Levels in Rivers and Streams

Limiting the use of nitrate fertilizers would decrease nitrate levels in waterways. An alternative way to supply plants with adequate amounts of nitrogen is by a form of crop rotation. Crop rotation involves varying which crops are planted in a particular field. To increase nitrogen naturally, one season a crop is planted that converts nitrogen from the air into nitrogen in the soil. Such plants are called **nitrogen-fixing plants.** The next season, a crop that requires nitrogen is planted. The most common type of nitrogen-fixing plants are legumes, which includes peas, clover, and soybeans.

Questions

1. Why are nitrates important for plants and other organisms?
2. Give two reasons why waterways should be tested for nitrates.
3. What are two common sources of nitrates in a waterway?
4. What can be done to reduce excess nitrate levels in a river or stream?

© SIU, published by Addison Wesley Longman, Inc.

Standardizing a Nitrate Test Kit

Purpose

To make sure your test kit is accurate.

Background

As in Lesson 8, your test kit needs to be standardized against a standard solution of known nitrate concentration. If your result deviates by more than 10 to 15 percent from the actual concentration of the standard solution, repeat the calibration check.

Safety and Waste Disposal

Follow all laboratory safety procedures presented in Lesson 1, including wearing safety goggles, apron, and gloves. Dispose waste into a waste container as instructed by your teacher.

Procedure

1. Put on safety goggles, apron, and gloves.
2. With soap and water, clean the glass or plastic containers that you will use from your test kit. Rinse thoroughly with tap water, acid wash, and distill wash them, following the procedures from Student Information 1.3, Lab and Field Techniques. Dry them and place the items in sealable plastic bags.
3. Obtain a bottle containing a nitrate standard solution from your teacher. Record the nitrate concentration of the standard solution in the Data Table.
4. Using your test kit, determine the amount of nitrates (mg/L) in the standard solution.
5. Record in the Data Table under Trial 1.
6. Dispose of the contents remaining in your test kit glassware into a waste container as directed by your teacher.
7. Distill wash and standard wash your test kit glassware following the procedures from Student Information 1.3, Lab and Field Techniques
8. Repeat Step 4.
9. Record the result under Trial 2.
10. Repeat Step 7.
11. Repeat Step 4.
12. Record the result under Trial 3.

Materials

Per student
- safety goggles, lab apron, and gloves

Per group
- nitrate test kit
- 25–30 mL HCl, 6 *M*
- nitrate standard solution
- waste container, 1–2 L

© SIU, published by Addison Wesley Longman, Inc.

Observations

Date _____ Time _____

DATA TABLE

Concentration of Standard Solution: _____ mg/L

Trial	Experimental NO_3^{-1} Concentration (mg/L)
1	
2	
3	

Average = _____ mg/L

Percent Error = _____ %

Pass _____

Calculations

1. Calculate the average nitrate concentration (mg/L) for the three trials and record in the Data Table.
2. Calculate percent error and record.
3. Check "pass" if the error is 10 to 15 percent or less. If the error is greater than 10 to 15 percent, repeat the test.

Analyses and Conclusions

1. How accurate is your nitrate test kit?

Critical Thinking Question

1. Why should you not allow waste from this activity to be poured down the drain?

© SIU, published by Addison Wesley Longman, Inc.

Measuring Nitrate Levels in a River or Stream

Purpose

To measure the amount of nitrates in water samples and assess the impact on water quality.

Background

All glassware used in this activity should be cleaned with soap and water, thoroughly rinsed with tap water, acid washed, distilled washed, and dried, following the procedures from Student Information 1.3: Lab and Field Techniques.

Safety and Waste Disposal

Follow all lab and field safety procedures presented in Lesson 1, including wearing safety goggles, apron, and gloves. Dispose waste into a waste container as instructed by your teacher.

Procedure

PART A. Before Going to the Field Site

1. Clean, acid wash, and distill wash a sampling bottle and stopper, following the procedures from Student Information 1.3: Lab and Field Techniques. Cap the bottle.

2. Label the bottle with your group name or number.

PART B. At the Field Site

3. Record date, time, location, and weather conditions.

4. Take notes on your field site. Do ditches or drains empty into your waterway? Are farms, homes, golf courses, or industries nearby? Check your site for aquatic plant life such as algae or pond scum.

5. Put on safety equipment.

6. Obtain a sample of water, stopper the sample, and return to lab.

PART C. In the Laboratory

7. Clean with soap and water, thoroughly rinse with tap water, acid wash, distill wash and dry a 250-mL beaker and a funnel.

8. Using the funnel and filter paper, filter the water sample into the beaker.

9. Clean with soap and water, thoroughly rinse with tap water, acid wash, distill wash, and dry all needed containers from your test kit.

10. Using your test kit, determine the amount of nitrates (mg/L) in the water sample.

11. Record the result in the Data Table.

Materials

Per student

- safety goggles, lab apron, and gloves
- life jacket and tow line (for deeper-water sites)
- rubber waders or boots (for shallower-water sites)
- calculator with square-root function

Per group

- nitrate test kit
- sampling bottle, with lid (such as 60–100 mL DO bottle)

- water-sampling pole, with clamp
- label or labeling tape
- funnel for filtering
- filter paper
- funnel support, such as ring stand, ring, or porcelain triangle
- beaker, 250–mL
- sealable plastic bags
- 25–30 mL HCl, 6 *M*
- waste container, 1–2 L

© SIU, published by Addison Wesley Longman, Inc.

Observations

Date _____   Location _____

Time _____   Weather Conditions _____

Site Description _____

DATA TABLE

Group	Experimental NO_3^{-1} Concentration (mg/L)

Average =   _____ mg/L

Standard Deviation =   _____

Reported Value =   _____ ± mg/L____

Q-value =   _____ %

Calculations

12. Obtain and record the results from the other groups.
13. Using your results and the results from the other groups, calculate and record the average nitrate concentration (mg/L).
14. Calculate and record the standard deviation.
15. Record the reported value.
16. Convert the average nitrate concentration (mg/L) into its equivalent Q-value using Figure 9-1. Record the Q-value.

© SIU, published by Addison Wesley Longman, Inc.

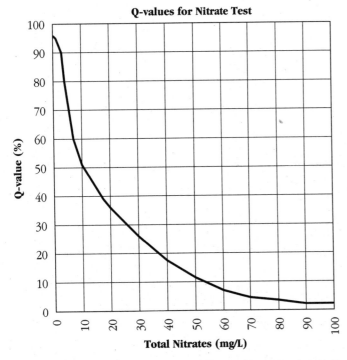

Figure 9-1: Graph for Converting Nitrate Concentration to Q-value

Analyses and Conclusions

Q-value for Nitrates	Quality of Water
90–100%	Excellent
70–89%	Good
50–69%	Medium
25–49%	Bad
0–24%	Very bad

1. Using your Q-value for nitrates and the information in the preceding table, rate your river or stream water from excellent to very bad.

Critical Thinking Questions

1. What level of nitrates did you expect at your site? On what factors did you base your prediction? Was your test result better or worse than you expected? Why?
2. Explain how the nitrate level at your site might affect the aquatic plant life in or near the water.
3. Predict how nitrate levels might vary at your site at different times of the year. Explain your reasoning.

© STU, published by Addison Wesley Longman, Inc.

LESSON 10

Fecal Coliform Bacteria in Rivers and Streams

Focus	Students will learn about fecal coliform bacteria and basic laboratory skills necessary to isolate, culture, and enumerate bacteria. They will learn why fecal coliform bacteria are monitored and how such bacteria enter rivers and streams.

Learner Outcomes	Students will:

1. Learn what fecal coliform bacteria are.
2. Learn why it is important to monitor a waterway for fecal coliform bacteria.
3. Learn how fecal coliform enter a waterway.
4. Learn techniques for isolating, culturing, and enumerating fecal coliform bacteria.
5. Determine the amount of fecal coliform (colonies per 100 mL) in a river or stream and determine water quality.
6. Determine the overall water quality of a river or stream.

Time	Four to five class periods of 40–50 minutes per period and a field trip to a river or stream	
	DAY 1:	Student Information 10.1: What Are Fecal Coliform Bacteria? Student Information 10.2: Sterilization and Sampling Techniques for Fecal Coliform Tests Student Activity 10.3: Measuring Fecal Coliform Levels in a River or Stream, Part A
	FIELD TRIP (DAY 2):	Student Activity 10.3: Measuring Fecal Coliform Levels in a River or Stream, Part B Student Activity 10.3: Measuring Fecal Coliform Levels in a River or Stream, Part C (must be done on the same day as the field trip)
	DAY 3:	Student Activity 10.3: Measuring Fecal Coliform Levels in a River or Stream, Part D (must be done on the day after the field trip)
	DAY 4:	Student Activity 10.4: Calculating the Overall Water-Quality Index for Your River or Stream

Safety and Waste Disposal

Follow all laboratory and field safety procedures presented in Lesson 1. Make sure students understand the importance of the sterilization procedure presented in Student Information 10.1, and are able to perform this procedure before beginning Student Activity 10.3. Also make sure students know how to use a hand pump instead of mouth suction to draw liquids into pipettes.

Ethyl alcohol is used for disinfecting purposes; make sure no alcohol is near an open flame. At the end of Student Activity 10.3, collect all petri dishes and absorbent pads, and have them incinerated.

Advanced Preparation

Prepare to supply students with Student Information 10.1 and 10.2, and with Student Activity 10.3 and 10.4. Gather all necessary equipment and materials. Much of the equipment used in Student Activity 10.3, though not generally found in a physical science lab, is common in a biology lab. Consult a biology teacher regarding the use of the equipment and techniques for bacteria culture. Prepare instructions for students on the use of the microfiltration kit.

If you cannot obtain the equipment required for the fecal coliform test, arrange to have the test performed by an outside agency, and prepare the obtained data for use by your class. If *Rivers Chemistry* is done in tandem with a biology class doing *Rivers Biology,* you may get the data from that class.

Review Lesson 1 regarding water sampling equipment and technique. Review information in the unit introduction on field trip management.

Materials

Student Activity 10.3: Measuring Fecal Coliform Levels in a River or Stream
Per student
safety goggles, lab apron, and gloves
life jacket and tow line (for deeper-water sites)
rubber waders or boots (for shallower-water sites)
calculator with square-root function
Per group
sampling bottle, with lid, 200-mL
water-sampling pole, with clamp
3 petri dishes (each equipped with a sterile pad)
microfiltration (MF) kit, autoclavable or disposable
hand vacuum pump that fits the microfiltration kit
25-mL pipette with bulb or titrator
100-mL pipette
250-mL beaker
500-mL beaker
250-mL volumetric flask
sealable plastic bags

waterproof tape

weights (to submerge cultures in water bath)

distilled water, 2–3 L

refrigerated container, such as ice chest with ice

15–20 mL of fecal coliform culture medium

3 sterile filter pads that fit the microfiltration kit

70% ethyl alcohol, 200 mL

Bunsen burner

forceps

waterproof plastic bags in which to place petri dishes if a water bath is used

labels or waterproof labeling marker

Per class

a method to sterilize equipment such as an autoclave or pressure cooker

constant-temperature environment such as a water bath

Optional

light-source bacteria counter

Student Activity 10.4: Calculating the Overall Water-Quality Index for Your River or Stream

Per student

calculator

completed Observations and Data Tables from Student Activities 2.5, 3.3, 4.5, 5.4, 6.3, 7.2, 8.2, 9.3, and 10.3

Optional

topographic map of field-site area

Lesson 10: Fecal Coliform Bacteria in Rivers and Streams

Vocabulary

colony

culture

dilution

fecal coliforms

medium

pathogenic bacteria

sterile

sterilization

Background for the Teacher

Among the numerous methods for determining the presence of fecal coliforms in water, the microfiltration (MF) method is most applicable for school use. In microfiltration, a water sample is vacuumed through a latex filter, leaving the bacteria on the surface of the filter. The filter is placed in a petri dish containing an absorbent pad saturated with a culture medium. The culture medium contains a blue stain that is specific for fecal coliforms. The culture dishes are incubated for 24 hours at 44.5°C.

Disposable MF kits can be purchased at a reasonable price; autoclavable MF kits are much more expensive. Fecal coliform bacteria culture medium has a limited shelf life. To assure accurate results, use only culture medium that has not expired.

Though having each group have its own hand vacuum pump is convenient, three groups can take turns using a single pump in order to reduce the amount of special equipment needed in order to run this test.

Introducing the Lesson

1. Ask students if they have ever heard of someone becoming ill because of contaminated food. If so, discuss with the students possible reasons for the contamination and ways it could have been avoided.
2. Have students read, discuss, and answer questions on Student Information 10.1: What Are Fecal Coliform Bacteria? (Answers and solutions to student sheets are in Appendix C.)
3. Have students read and discuss Student Information 10.2: Sterilization and Sampling Techniques for Fecal Coliform Tests. If desired, demonstrate the sterilization procedure your students should follow. Provide specific written sterilization procedure if needed.
4. Have students answer the questions for Student Information 10.2.

Developing the Lesson

1. Hand out Student Activity 10.3: Measuring Fecal Coliform Levels in a River or Stream. As appropriate, demonstrate how students should use laboratory equipment for this activity.
2. Have students do Part A of Student Activity 10.3 in lab.
3. At the field site, have student do Part B of Student Activity 10.3.
4. As soon as possible after students return from the field site, have them do Part C of Student Activity 10.3.
5. The next day, have students complete Student Activity 10.3.

Concluding the Lesson

1. As a class, students may discuss the results of Student Activity 10.3 and their responses to its Critical Thinking Questions. For additional specific teaching activities on fecal coliform, see *Rivers Biology*.

Assessing the Lesson

1. Have students do Student Activity 10.4: Calculating the Overall Water-Quality Index for Your River or Stream. For specific teaching activities on topographic maps if students will have access to such maps, see *Rivers Geography*. For specific teaching activities on climate data if students will be adding such information to their field-site description, also see *Rivers Geography*.

2. Have students share the results of Student Activity 10.4 with other Rivers Project classes, either in your school or via the Rivers Project telecommunications system. (For more information on telecommunications options and suggestions, see page xii in unit introduction and pages 190–193 in the Teacher Notes for the Challenge Project for Lesson 10: Telecommunications.)

3. Have students share the results of Student Activity 10.4 with public officials. For specific teaching activities on political action writing, see *Rivers Language Arts*.

4. Have students do computer-oriented Challenge Project for Lesson 10: Telecommunications (located in Appendix B).

5. Have students complete their water quality collages. Students may give oral presentations about their collages. (For suggested scoring rubric, see Appendix A.) Display student collages.

6. Have students complete their portfolios or other unit-long assessment projects. (For suggested scoring rubric for portfolios, see Appendix A.)

Extending the Lesson

1. Invite to class, or have students interview, a home-economics or water-quality professional familiar with fecal coliform bacteria or the testing of fecal coliform, so that students can determine how fecal coliform is assessed.

2. Have a biologist visit the class with prepared slides of fecal coliform and microscope so students can view fecal coliform colonies.

What Are Fecal Coliform Bacteria?

A few years ago, meat shipped to a chain of restaurants in the northwest United States was contaminated with bacteria from the intestines of animals. The meat was not cooked at a high enough temperature to kill the bacteria, and many people who ate the meat became gravely ill; some even died. As a result, the public has become more concerned about bacterial contamination of food and water.

Certain bacteria that propagate in the digestive tracts of humans and animals are known as **fecal coliforms** (FEE kuhl KOH luh forms). Inside the intestines, these bacteria normally do not cause disease. Outside, however, some fecal coliforms may cause disease if they are ingested by humans or if they reach tissues outside the digestive tract.

Why Test Water for Fecal Coliforms?

Although fecal coliforms normally do not cause disease, they often coexist with **pathogenic bacteria** (path uh JEHN ihk bak TIHR ee uh) that are capable of causing human disease such as typhoid fever, cholera, and dysentery.

Usually, waterborne bacteria that cause these types of diseases occur in small numbers and cannot exist outside of living organisms for very long. They are, therefore, difficult to detect and monitor in waterways. Fecal coliforms, however, can exist in greater numbers and for longer periods of time outside the body. This makes them easier to detect and monitor.

Because fecal coliform bacteria coexist with their pathogenic relatives in the same host environment, fecal coliforms are often used as indicators of possible pathogenic bacterial contamination. Thus, if water is tested and found to have a high fecal coliform population, there is a very good possibility that pathogenic bacteria are also present. On the other hand, if water is tested and found to have very few fecal coliforms, then the water probably has very few pathogenic bacteria.

In addition to being a health threat, untreated fecal matter adds excess organic material to a waterway. As the excess organic matter decays, the amount of dissolved oxygen in the water decreases. As you learned in Lesson 6, if large amounts of dissolved oxygen are taken from a waterway, fish kills and loss of other aquatic life could result.

© SIU, published by Addison Wesley Longman, Inc.

How Do Fecal Coliforms Enter a Waterway?

Whenever untreated (raw) animal and human fecal matter enters a waterway, so do fecal coliforms. Fecal waste can come from a number of sources such as untreated sewage, broken sewer lines, overflowing septic tanks, and stockyards.

How Is Fecal Coliform Monitored?

Because bacteria are small and numerous, counting how many individuals are in a water sample is very difficult. To assess the level of fecal coliforms in water samples, scientists **culture** the bacteria, or propagate them in a specially prepared environment that enhances growth. The bacteria are grown on or in a medium. A **medium** is an environment in which microorganisms can live. Each bacterium will divide and grown into a **colony,** or group of bacteria. Bacterial colonies are visible to the naked eye and can be counted relatively easily.

Some colonies have their own distinctive color, which aids the researcher to count the colonies. Fecal coliform colonies have a blue color.

How Much Fecal Coliform Is Too Much?

Drinking water should be free of all fecal coliforms. Before drinking water is released to customers, the water-treatment plant analyzes the water for fecal coliform. If bacteria are found, the water should not be released for human consumption until the bacteria are destroyed. To insure that drinking water is free of bacteria, water-treatment plants add a small quantity of chlorine or other chemical disinfectant to destroy any microorganisms that may be present. The amount of chlorine is carefully measured to be the lowest amount needed to keep the water germ-free.

Water Quality Standards

Category	Maximum Fecal Coliforms per 100 mL of Water
Drinking water	0 colonies
Swimming	200 colonies
Treated sewage	200 colonies
Boating	1000 colonies

Fecal coliform analyses are also performed on treated sewage before it is released into a waterway. If more than 200 colonies per 100 mL are found, the sewage should not be released until the count is reduced by further treatment.

Water that is used for swimming and boating is also periodically tested for fecal coliform levels. If the levels are too high, the area is closed for recreational use.

© SIU, published by Addison Wesley Longman, Inc.

Some people think that if water is clear, it is safe for drinking, swimming, and boating. Clarity is no guarantee that water is bacteria free. Insuring public safety requires regular monitoring of fecal coliform. Usually fecal coliform tests to insure public safety are performed weekly or monthly. In some cities, the drinking water is tested two times a week. At some public boating facilities, analyses are run once a month.

Questions

1. Why is water tested for fecal coliforms rather than for pathogenic bacteria?
2. What are two diseases associated with waterborne pathogenic bacteria?
3. How do fecal coliforms get into waterways?
4. When analyzing water samples for fecal coliforms, why do scientists count bacterial colonies rather than each bacterium?
5. What are the water quality standards for fecal coliforms in drinking water, swimming water, properly treated sewage, and boating water?

© SIU, published by Addison Wesley Longman, Inc.

Sterilization and Sampling Techniques for Fecal Coliform Tests

Bacteria are everywhere—in the air, in the water, on your skin. To get accurate results from a fecal coliform test, you must avoid contaminating the equipment and samples with foreign bacteria. This requires that all equipment be sterilized by heating, boiling, flaming, or treating with a disinfectant. **Sterilization** (sterhr uh luh ZAY shuhn) is a process of creating an environment free from unwanted microorganisms. When equipment or material is **sterile,** it is free of all microorganisms.

In order to avoid contaminating the water samples and the test equipment with bacteria from your skin, you will need to avoid direct contact with them. Wear sterile gloves when doing the fecal coliform tests.

Because some of the bacteria in a water sample may be pathogenic, avoid any direct contact with the sample. Disinfect your lab area and your hands before and after doing the tests.

Sterilization Techniques

Glass and temperature-resistant plastic items can be sterilized by autoclaving at 120°C for 15 to 20 minutes. If an autoclave is not available, a home pressure cooker will work quite well if a pressure of 15 psi (pounds per square inch) is maintained for 20 minutes. If neither an autoclave nor a pressure cooker is available, items can be sterilized by placing them in boiling water for 20 minutes.

During the procedure, work surfaces can be disinfected using 70 percent ethyl alcohol. Hands can be disinfected by thoroughly washing with soap and water. Metallic items, such as forceps, can be disinfected by passing them through the flame of a Bunsen burner. CAUTION: take care no containers of alcohol are near a lit Bunsen burner—alcohol is highly flammable.

Sampling Techniques

Water samples should be collected in sterilized containers using care not to contaminate the containers with foreign bacteria from hands or other sources. Dissolved-oxygen bottles make excellent collecting bottles, but collecting the approximately 200 mL of river or stream water needed will require 3 or 4 60-mL bottles. Once sterilized and stoppered, the bottles remain sterile until the stoppers are removed.

© SIU, published by Addison Wesley Longman, Inc.

To obtain water samples for the fecal coliform test, use the sampling techniques given in Lesson 1. If possible, analyze the water sample immediately. If you cannot conduct the analysis immediately, you must conduct it within five hours of collecting the sample. Until the sample is analyzed, keep it refrigerated. This can be done by packing the sample in ice inside an ice chest. Fecal coliform bacteria has an optimal growth temperature of 44.5°C. The ice will keep the temperature well below 44.5°C. At the temperature of the ice (near 0°C), the reproductive activities of coliforms slow down.

Questions

1. Why is it necessary to collect samples for fecal coliform tests in sterile bottles?
2. How can equipment be sterilized?
3. Why must the water samples be refrigerated if testing for fecal coliforms cannot be done immediately?

© SIU, published by Addison Wesley Longman, Inc.

Measuring Fecal Coliform Levels in a River or Stream

Purpose

To measure the amount of fecal coliform bacteria in water samples and assess the impact on water quality.

Materials

Per student

- safety goggles, lab apron, and gloves
- life jacket and tow line (for deeper-water sites)
- rubber waders or boots (for shallower-water sites)
- calculator with square-root function

Per group

- sampling bottle, with stopper, 200-mL
- water-sampling pole, with clamp
- 3 petri dishes (each equipped with a sterile pad)
- microfiltration (MF) kit, autoclavable or disposable
- hand vacuum pump that fits the microfiltration kit
- 25-mL pipette with bulb or titrator
- 100-mL pipette
- 250-mL beaker
- 500-mL beaker
- 250-mL volumetric flask
- sealable plastic bags

- waterproof tape
- weights (to submerge cultures in water bath)
- distilled water, 2–3 L
- refrigerated container, such as ice chest with ice
- 15–20 mL of fecal coliform culture medium
- 3 sterile filter pads that fit the microfiltration kit
- 70% ethyl alcohol, 200 mL
- Bunsen burner
- forceps
- waterproof plastic bags in which to place petri dishes if a water bath is used
- labels or waterproof labeling marker

Per class

- a method to sterilize equipment such as an autoclave or pressure cooker
- constant-temperature environment such as a water bath

Optional

- light-source bacteria counter

Background

In this activity, you will collect a sample from a waterway and determine how many fecal coliform bacteria are in the sample. To determine the bacteria count, you will culture a control and three prepared samples at 44.5°C for 24 hours. Following the incubation period, you will count the number of colonies.

Government standards require that microfiltration for fecal coliform testing be conducted with 100 mL of water. In highly contaminated water, 100 mL of undiluted water produces so many colonies that they are difficult to count. In such cases, testing involves diluting the sample before incubating it. **Dilution** (di LOO shuhn) is a process that reduces the concentration of matter per unit volume. In this activity, you will do a 1:10 dilution and a 1:100 dilution of the water sample. Also included are instructions for converting colony counts of those diluted samples into the corresponding number of fecal coliform colonies per 100 mL of river or stream water. If you analyze a particular waterway several times, you will find a particular dilution that works best for

© SIU, published by Addison Wesley Longman, Inc.

your river or stream. (Aim for a dilution that gives a count of between 20 to 80 fecal coliform colonies per culture.)

Safety and Waste Disposal

Follow all lab and field safety procedures presented in Lesson 1. Because some of the bacteria in a water sample may be pathogenic, avoid any direct contact with the sample. Use a hand pump rather than a mouth pipette to transfer liquids. Disinfect your lab area and your hands before and after doing the tests.

At no time during the activity should you open the sealed petri dishes. At the end of the activity, give the unopened petri dishes to your teacher for disposal.

Procedure

PART A. Before Going to the Field Site

1. Put on safety goggles, lab apron, and gloves.
2. Sterilize sampling bottle and stopper using the procedure presented in Student Information 10.2. Stopper the bottle and place it in a sealable plastic bag labeled with your group name or number.
3. Sterilize a microfiltration (MF) kit, 25-mL pipette, 250-mL beaker, 500-mL beaker, 100-mL pipette, and 250-mL volumetric flask. Place each item in a sealable plastic bag labeled with your group name or number.

PART B. At the Field Site

4. Record date, time, location, and weather conditions.
5. Describe your field site. Do ditches or drains empty into your waterway? Are farms or stockyards nearby?
6. Put on safety goggles, gloves, and other safety equipment.
7. Remove your sampling bottle from its bag, unstopper the bottle, and obtain a water sample, using procedures for water sampling presented in Lesson 1. Restopper the bottle and place in a refrigerated container. Return to the lab.

PART C. In the Laboratory (Must Be Same Day as Field Trip)

8. Put on safety goggles, apron, and gloves.
9. From your teacher, obtain 15–20 mL of fecal coliform culture medium, three petri dishes (each equipped with a sterile absorbent pad), and three sterile filter pads.

Steps 10 through 21 will yield an incubating sample of sterile distilled water.

10. Place 400–450 mL of distilled water in the 500-mL beaker.
11. Heat the water until it just begins to boil. Allow it to cool.
12. Disinfect your work area by wiping it with 70% ethyl alcohol. Allow the alcohol fumes to dissipate before continuing.
13. Light a Bunsen burner. Place the end of your open forceps into the flame for 2–3 seconds. Rotate the forceps and flame again.

14. With the sterile forceps, place a sterile filter pad in your MF kit.
15. Using the 100-mL pipette, measure 100 mL of sterile distilled water and transfer it to the MF kit.
16. Vacuum the water through the filter pad, following instructions supplied with your kit or by your teacher.
17. Open a petri dish equipped with a sterile absorbent pad. Saturate the pad with 2–4 mL of fecal coliform culture medium.
18. With sterile forceps, remove the filter pad from the MF kit and place it directly on top of the saturated pad inside the petri dish.
19. Close the dish and label the bottom "Sterile Distilled Water."
20. If a water bath will be used to provide the constant-temperature environment, seal the dish with waterproof tape. Place the dish in a sterile, waterproof plastic bag. Seal the bag and label it "Sterile Distilled Water."
21. Place the dish in a constant-temperature environment set at 44.5°C. If using a water bath, place the bagged dish in the water bath upside down and submerge it with a weight. (When placed upside down, only a small amount of condensation will form on the top of the dish during incubation. This facilitates counting bacterial colonies after the incubation period.)

© SIU, published by Addison Wesley Longman, Inc.

Steps 22 through 26 will yield an incubating sample of undiluted river water, labeled "Sample One."

22. Repeat Steps 13 and 14.
23. Remove the water sample from the ice chest and swirl until it is thoroughly mixed.
24. Using the 100-mL pipette, measure 100 mL of water sample. Transfer the contents to the MF kit. Vacuum the sample through the filter pad.
25. Thoroughly rinse the 100-mL pipette with sterile distilled water.
26. Repeat Steps 16–21, using a label of "Sample One."

Steps 27 through 30 will yield a solution of river or stream water with a dilution factor of 10, labeled "Solution Two."

27. Swirl the water sample to thoroughly mix it.
28. Using the sterile 25-mL pipette, transfer 25 mL of the water sample into a sterile 250-mL volumetric flask.
29. Add sterile distilled water to the flask until a volume of 250 mL is obtained. Label the solution "Solution Two."
30. Thoroughly rinse the 25-mL pipette with sterile distilled water.

Steps 31 through 35 will yield an incubating sample of 1:10 diluted river or stream water labeled "Sample Two."

31. Repeat Steps 13 and 14.
32. Swirl Solution Two until it is thoroughly mixed.
33. Using the 100-mL pipette, measure 100 mL of Solution Two. Transfer the volume to the MF kit. Vacuum the sample through the filter pad.
34. Thoroughly rinse the 100-mL pipette with sterile distilled water.
35. Repeat Steps 16–21, using a label of "Sample Two."

Steps 36 through 39 will yield a solution of river or stream water with a dilution factor of 100, labeled "Solution Three."

36. Transfer the remaining amount of Solution Two from the 250-mL volumetric flask into a sterile 250-mL beaker.
37. Thoroughly rinse the 250-mL volumetric flask with sterile distilled water.
38. Using the 25-mL pipette, transfer 25 mL of Solution Two to the 250-mL volumetric flask.
39. Add sterile distilled water to the flask until a volume of 250 mL is obtained. Label the solution "Solution Three."

Steps 40 through 43 will yield an incubating sample of 1:100 diluted river or stream water, labeled "Sample Three."

40. Repeat Steps 13 and 14.
41. Swirl Solution Three until it is thoroughly mixed.
42. Using the 100-mL pipette, measure 100 mL of Solution Three. Thoroughly mix the solution and transfer the volume to the MF kit. Vacuum the sample through the filter pad.
43. Repeat Steps 16–21, using a label of "Sample Three."

44. Flush any remaining samples into the sink. Thoroughly rinse all used glassware with distilled water. Flame metal equipment. Put away your equipment. Disinfect your lab area with 70 percent ethyl alcohol. Wash your hands thoroughly with soap and water.
45. Allow the samples to incubate at 44.5°C for 24 hours.

PART D. In the Laboratory (Next Day)

46. Put on safety goggles, apron, and gloves.
47. Remove the petri dishes from the constant-temperature environment and place right-side up on the lab surface. (If a water bath was used, remove the sealed dishes from the plastic bags.) CAUTION: do not remove the waterproof tape or open the dishes. Some of the bacteria inside may be hazardous.
48. Check the dish labeled "Sterile Distilled Water." If it contains any blue circular fecal coliform colonies, count the number of colonies and record the result on Line A of the Data Table. (Ignore any colonies that are not blue; these are not fecal coliforms.) If any fecal coliform colonies are present, a fresh supply of sterile distilled water will have to be obtained and the entire analysis will have to be repeated. If the dish contains no fecal coliform colonies, continue to the next step.

© SIU, published by Addison Wesley Longman, Inc.

49. Count the number of blue circular fecal coliform colonies in the dish labeled "Sample One" and record the result on Line B of the Data Table.

50. Count the number of fecal coliform colonies in dish labeled "Sample Two" and record the result on Line C of the Data Table. To account for the dilution that was performed to obtain Solution Two, multiply Line C by ten and record the result on Line D.

51. Count the number of fecal coliform colonies in dish labeled "Sample Three" and record the result on Line E of the Data Table. To account for the dilution that was performed to obtain Solution Three, multiply Line E by 100 and record the result on Line F.

52. Give the unopened dishes to your teacher for disposal.

© SIU, published by Addison Wesley Longman, Inc.

Observations

Date _____   Location _____

Time _____   Weather Conditions _____

Site Description _____

DATA TABLE

	Actual Fecal Coliform Count (colonies/100 mL)	Fecal Coliform Count Equivalent to Undiluted Sample (colonies/100 mL)
(A) Sterile distilled water		////////////
(B) Sample One (undiluted)		
(C) Sample Two (1:10 dilution)		////////////
(D) Line (C) × 10	////////////	
(E) Sample Three (1:100 dilution)		////////////
(F) Line (E) × 100	////////////	

Average for B, D, and F= _____ colonies/100 mL

Standard Deviation = _____ colonies/100 mL

Reported Value = _____ colonies/100 mL ± ____

Q-Value = _____ %

Calculations

53. Using the result from Lines B, D, and F, calculate the average colonies of fecal coliform per 100 mL and record.
54. Compute the standard deviation and record.
55. Record the reported value.
56. Convert the average number of fecal coliform colonies per 100 mL into its equivalent Q-value percent by using Figure 10-1 on the following page. Record the result in the Data Table.

Analyses and Conclusions

Q-value for Fecal Coliforms	Quality of Water
90–100%	Excellent
70–89%	Good
50–69%	Medium
25–49%	Bad
0–24%	Very bad

© SIU, published by Addison Wesley Longman, Inc.

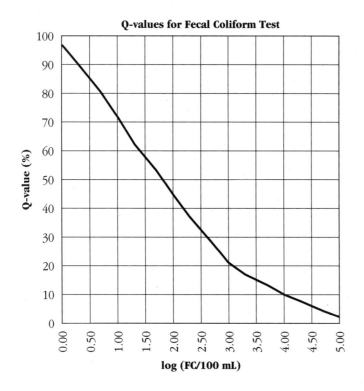

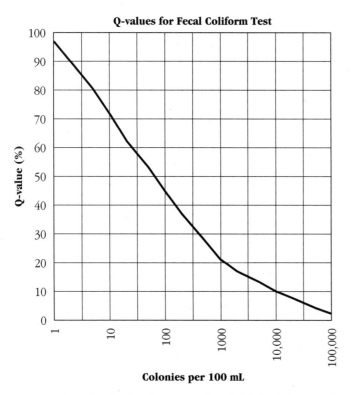

Figure 10-1: Graphs for Converting Fecal Coliform Data to Q-value

Measuring Fecal Coliform Levels in a River or Stream

© SIU, published by Addison Wesley Longman, Inc.

1. Using your Q-value for fecal coliforms and the preceding chart, rate your waterway from excellent to very bad.
2. Referring to the water quality standards given in Student Information 10.1, is the water in your river or stream safe to drink? Is it safe for swimming? Is it safe for boating?
3. Describe the major natural and human-made features of your site. Begin by describing its predominant type, such as wooded, clear-cut, industrial, farmland, park, residential, or wetland. What features may be sources of fecal coliforms at your site?
4. What must be done to improve the fecal coliform levels and water quality at your site?

Critical Thinking Questions

1. What level of fecal coliforms did you expect at your site? On what factors did you base your predictions? Was your test result better or worse than you expected? Why?
2. Explain how the fecal coliform level at your site might affect the organisms living in or near the waterway.
3. Predict how fecal coliform levels might vary at your site at different times of the year. Explain your reasoning.

Keeping Your Journal

1. Write your impressions or feelings about your field site. Do you think it is ugly or pleasing? How might it be improved? What could you do to improve the site?
2. Write a few descriptive phrases about the river or stream that you might later develop into a poem or story about your site. Sketch any unusual or interesting features of the site.

© SIU, published by Addison Wesley Longman, Inc.

Measuring Fecal Coliform Levels in a River or Stream

Calculating the Overall Water-Quality Index for Your River or Stream

Purpose

To use the results of the water-quality tests you have performed in *Rivers Chemistry* and determine the overall water-quality index for your river or stream at your field site.

Background

As you recall from Lesson 1, when the results of all nine water-quality tests are weighted according to their importance and added together, they comprise the overall water-quality index for a waterway. Ideally, before computing the overall water-quality index for your river or stream, you will have conducted all nine water-quality tests. This activity includes steps on how to calculate water quality if you do not have results from all nine tests; in such cases, refer to the result as water-quality index, not overall water-quality index.

For most accurate results, all tests should be run on samples taken at the same site and at nearly the same time. If your testing took place at multiple times or locations, annotate your results to show what happened.

As you consider the significance of your results, remember that the use of the waterway determines which tests are most important in assessing quality and safety. For example, if the river or stream is used for swimming, a high fecal coliform count would indicate that no swimming should be permitted, even though the other eight tests may show excellent quality. On the other hand, a low fecal coliform count with poor results in other categories may indicate water that is acceptable for swimming but threatening to many aquatic species.

The water-quality index was developed as a guide for judging water. It is a very general index that gives an overview of the quality of a water system. The index includes measurements of many common pollutants, the importance of which have been ranked by experts. Excluded from the index and the rankings are some dangerous materials, such as heavy metals, pesticides, and herbicides. The weighting scheme that is part of the index allows analysts to condense complex test results into a common water-quality measurement that can be readily communicated to the public.

Procedure

1. Enter the field-site description in the accompanying Water-Quality Index (WQI) sheet. Adapt as necessary to reflect multiple field sites. Give specific information so others using your data can locate your field site. If available, use a topographic map for your area.
2. Using the Observations and Data Tables from earlier Student Activities, fill in information about test results on the WQI sheet.

Materials

Per student
- calculator
- completed Observations and Data Tables from Student Activities 2.5, 3.3, 4.5, 5.4, 6.3, 7.2, 8.2, 9.3, and 10.3

Optional
- topographic map of field-site area

© SIU, published by Addison Wesley Longman, Inc.

Calculations

3. Multiply each Q-value by the corresponding weighting factor on the WQI sheet and record your weighted value in the "Total" column on the WQI sheet.
4. Sum the totals to obtain your overall water-quality index.
5. If you do not have data for all tests, sum the weights of all the tests for which data are available. Then divide the water-quality index obtained in Step 4 by the sum of the weight of the tests, obtained in Step 5. For example, if all tests were completed except fecal coliform, and the calculated water quality without this test was 65%, and the total of all the weighting factors except the one for fecal coliform is 0.84, then the water-quality index is 65% divided by .84 = 77%.

Analyses and Conclusions

1. Using the overall water-quality index value you obtained and the chart at the bottom on the WQI sheet, determine the overall quality of your water.
2. Reviewing your observations throughout *Rivers Chemistry,* what natural factors do you think have significantly impacted the water quality of your river or stream positively? Which have had significant negative impact? Explain your answers.
3. Reviewing your observations throughout *Rivers Chemistry,* what human factors do you think have significantly impacted the water quality of your river or stream positively? Which have had significant negative impact? Explain your answers.

Critical Thinking Questions

1. If you made a prediction in Lesson 1 about the water quality of your river or stream, how does your finding compare with your prediction? Explain why your prediction and result are the same or different.
2. Do you think students such as yourself can do something to improve quality of the waterway? If so, describe your suggestions.
3. What are the most important steps public agencies and private industries and businesses can do to improve the quality of your river or stream?

Keeping Your Journal

1. What do you feel about the overall quality of your waterway now? Do you feel different having a quantitative value for that water quality? Explain your thoughts.
2. Do you have a different relationship with your river or stream now compared with when you began *Rivers Chemistry?* Explain your thoughts.

© SIU, published by Addison Wesley Longman, Inc.

Water-Quality Index (WQI)

River/Stream _____   River Mile Marker _____

School _____   Location   Latitude: _____ ° _____ ' _____ "

Date _____ Time _____   Longitude: _____ ° _____ ' _____ "

Water Conditions _____   County _____ Quadrangle _____

Weather Conditions _____   Legal Description: _____ 1/4 of the_____ 1/4 of the _____ 1/4

_____   Section_____ of Township _____ Range _____

Air temperature _____ °C   Nearest Town _____ _____

Flow rate_____ m/s   Site Location or Address_____

Test	Test Results (mean values)	Standard Deviation	Q-Value	Weighting Factor	Total (%)
Dissolved Oxygen	_____ mg/L ($DO_{day\ 1}$) _____ % Sat			0.17	
Fecal Coliform	_____ colonies/100 mL			0.16	
pH	_____ units			0.11	
BOD	DO_{day1} _____ mg/L – DO_{day5} _____ mg/L BOD = _____ mg/L			0.11	
Temperature Change	$Temp_{site\ 1}$ _____ °C $Temp_{site\ 2}$ _____ °C ΔT = _____ °C			0.10	
Phosphate	_____ mg/L			0.10	
Nitrate	_____ mg/L			0.10	
Turbidity	_____ meters or JTU/NTU			0.08	
Total Solids	_____ mg/L			0.07	

OVERALL WATER-QUALITY INDEX _____ %

Overall Water-Quality Index	Quality of Water
90–100%	Excellent
70–89%	Good
50–69%	Medium
25–49%	Bad
0–24%	Very Bad

© SIU, published by Addison Wesley Longman, Inc.

Assessment Tools

This appendix covers assessment tools on which students may work throughout *Rivers Chemistry,* specifically a science notebook, collage, and portfolio. The Teacher Notes (with scoring rubrics) appear first, followed by student sheets for each assessment tool. If you prefer, substitute your own evaluating tool or student handout.

Teacher Notes for Keeping a Science Notebook (pages 168–169)

Focus

Students learn and practice the skills of keeping a science notebook. In their notebooks, students demonstrate their understanding of the ideas presented in *Rivers Chemistry* and offer insights into the interrelationship of these ideas.

Does a Science Notebook Replace or Complement a Journal?

The Rivers Project curriculum promotes the writing of journals in which students enter impressions, feelings, data, poems, and all other project tracking. Students are encouraged to write their private thoughts and feelings, with the understanding that their journals will not be collected by the teacher. The journals also serve as sources of ideas, data, and impressions for writing formal assignments to be turned in for evaluation.

If you want to review entries but still give students privacy, you may choose to have students keep a science notebook as well as a journal. In the journal, students can make private responses and informal entries. In the notebook, students enter data, calculations, and all other scientific predictions, observations, analysis, and conclusions; the teacher collects the science notebooks periodically for review. If desired, you may instruct students to use their science notebook to record their answers to the Student Information and Student Activity sheets in *Rivers Chemistry.* The keeping of the notebook can also give students experience with the more formal notebook methods practiced in many scientific fields. Students are instructed to use only the front of each page, so that if water is spilled on the notebook, the writing will be more legible than if both sides are used.

Student Information: Keeping a Journal (in Lesson 1) has been included in the basic *Rivers Chemistry* curriculum because its use successfully integrates writing into scientific inquiry. If you wish to evaluate student recordkeeping, also use Student Assessment: Keeping a Science Notebook.

Materials

Per student

bound notebook, so pages cannot be removed or inserted

pen or pencil

markers

scissors

glue

Per class

magazines for cutting up

Advanced Preparation

Prepare to supply students with Student Assessment: Keeping a Science Notebook (located on pages 168–169). Gather all necessary materials, or give students a copy of the handout ahead of time, so they can gather what they will need.

Prepare several sample pages to show students the required format for entries. Prepare samples of different writings, such as observations and results.

Developing the Lesson

1. Have students read Student Assessment: Keeping a Science Notebook. Discuss the procedures for making entries. Show sample pages to the class. Read to the students several types of notebook entries.
2. Explain to them that they will use this notebook throughout the *Rivers Chemistry* unit, and that they should include all relevant observations in it. Clarify the differences between the journal and the science notebook. Discuss how frequently you will review the contents of the science notebook.
3. You may have them decorate this notebook at home or during class, working in small groups to share ideas and materials.
4. If students should use science notebooks to record data during lab and field activities, remind them at the beginning of such activities to copy data tables from their student activity sheets into their notebooks.
5. Collect and review science notebooks periodically, to evaluate student work. Depending on your preference, you may do this at the conclusion of each student sheet or at the conclusion of each *Rivers Chemistry* lesson.

Performance Criteria

The successful science notebook features:

- Organized and focused entries, with ample explanation to identify the data, calculations, and conclusions.

- Complete and correct calculations and data analyses.

- Results and conclusions based on the experimental data collected, showing an understanding of the procedures and expectations for the activities.

- Results of prior activities integrated into current work.

- Demonstrated improvement over the project, both in mechanics of keeping the notebook and in clarity and completeness of the writings.

- Use of correct, standard written English.

Scoring Rubric

Score	Expectations
0	No response is attempted. A notebook has not been used.
1	A notebook is kept, but entries have little organization. Work shows little understanding of chemistry concepts.
2	The notebook is organized and mostly complete. A limited understanding of the chemistry concepts is shown. Writings are logical but often incomplete.
3	The notebook is organized and complete. A satisfactory understanding of concepts and applications is shown. Writings are logical, often including additional observations and readings.
4	The notebook is organized and complete. Chemistry concepts are understood and readily applied to analyze data and draw conclusions. Additional observations, readings, and resources are frequently cited.

Teacher Notes for River Collage (pages 170–171)

Focus

Each student constructs a collage that represents his or her feelings, gives a message, or shows concern for a river or stream. The collage is developed throughout the project and should include material that represents each of the lessons covered.

You may display the collages during the project or at an open house for parents and the community. The partially finished posters may be displayed during the unit so students may share ideas on making collages. Students may present their poster to the class with short (five-minute) presentations.

Materials
Per student
poster board
large envelope for holding collected materials
scissors
markers
glue stick
Per class
magazines from which pictures and text can be cut
colored paper

Advanced Preparation

Prepare to supply students with Student Assessment: River Collage (located on pages 170–171). Decide whether students will have class time for this assignment or should do it at home. Collect all equipment and materials necessary for the collage work students will do in class.

Make arrangements to display the completed posters, such as in the classroom, in hallways, in school display cases, or at special events. Decide whether to have students deliver oral presentations in conjunction with their completed posters.

You may wish to invite your school art teacher or local artists to talk to your students about designing a collage. Ask for guidelines they would use to evaluate artistic merit. Invite them to view the finished projects.

Developing the Lesson

1. Have students read Student Assessment: River Collage, for ideas and suggestions about making a collage. Explain that they will work on their collages during each lesson segment of the *Rivers Chemistry* unit. Suggest that, in the early lessons, students make sketches of their collage, starting to glue materials onto their posters only after covering two or three lessons. Make sure they understand that they will have to allow for additions during later lessons. Indicate what materials are available for their collages. Give minimum and maximum sizes for posters.

2. Making a collage is an unusual type of assessment for most science classes. Emphasize to your students that you will evaluate the collages like all assignments, so they require careful planning and execution.

3. Tell students whether the posters will be displayed throughout the project in the classroom. Explain where the completed posters will be displayed.

4. If students will do oral presentations, indicate how long each presentation should be. As the presentation date approaches, provide students with any other appropriate guidance on the presentations.

5. As the completion date approaches, arrange for publicity for the posters and presentations as appropriate, such as contacting school and local newspapers, sending notes home to parents, and so forth. You may have students participate in these activities.

Performance Criteria

Students should be given artistic freedom in their use of printed materials and pictures for their display. The successful collage:

- Features a single message or theme throughout the collage. The message is evident through pictures and organization and may also be stated in print.

- Contains materials representing each *Rivers Chemistry* lesson studied.

- Clearly demonstrates organization and planning. The collage is neatly constructed.

- Reflects artistic considerations, such as use of color, space, balance, and line.

- Has an accompanying sheet containing complete answers to the assessment questions listed on the student handout. Answers show insights into the use of a collage to present a message.

- Is complemented by an oral presentation (if assigned) that emphasizes the message and the relationship of the different parts of the collage to the message.

Scoring Rubric

Score	Expectations
0	No collage is completed.
1	A collage was started, but is incomplete or shows no theme or message.
2	A collage is completed and a theme or message is used. Only a few of the lessons are represented by the collage. Questions are completed.
3	A collage is completed and a theme or message is evident. Materials from most lessons were included and mostly supported the theme. Questions are completed and some understanding of the strengths and limitations of collages is shown.
4	A collage is completed that conveys a theme or message using ideas from all the lessons. The display is neatly constructed and shows good use of space. Responses to questions show an understanding of the use of collages to convey a message.

Teacher Notes for Portfolio (pages 172–173)

Focus

Each student selects and arranges multiple assessment items that demonstrate the student's learning of scientific content, attitude, and skills.

Materials

Per student

Manila folder

Plastic report cover or three-ring notebook

Advanced Preparation

Look through one or more of the lessons in *Rivers Chemistry*. In each lesson, a Teacher Notes section gives suggestions on using the Student Information sheets, Student Activity sheets, and additional projects for assessing and extending the lesson. As you select which assignments you will give, make sure students will have a variety of opportunities to express their abilities and interests during this study of *Rivers Chemistry*.

Based on your assignment plans, decide what kinds of items students may (or must) include in their portfolios. Modify the accompanying handout,

Student Assessment: Portfolio (located on pages 172–173), as appropriate to reflect your approach.

If you have used portfolio assessments for special projects, collect good examples to share with your students. If not, select some ideas from different lessons to make a sample portfolio.

As the *Rivers Chemistry* unit progresses, students should collect their choices of what they plan to include in their portfolios. Ideally, they should keep their selections in manila folders in the classroom. To conserve space, you may limit the total items per folder to five at any time.

Developing the Lesson

1. Have students read the handout, Student Assessment: Portfolio (pages 172–173). Illustrate the diversity of work students may select for their portfolio by showing a sample portfolio that includes a variety of items such as special reports, laboratory work, writings, and group reports.
2. Show students where in the classroom they should keep their portfolio selections during the *Rivers Chemistry* project.
3. Show how students should prepare the portfolio for final submission, such as in a bound notebook, folder, or a three-ring notebook.

Performance Criteria

The portfolio may take a number of forms, but any successful portfolio assessment program has certain considerations:

- focuses on students taking responsibility for identifying the extent of their learning and demonstrating that it is part of their personal knowledge system.

- shows growth over time; is a cumulative document.

- features students' best work; illustrates capabilities, not weaknesses.

- expresses student competencies in multiple forms, because learning is multidimensional.

- emphasizes not only solutions to problems but descriptions of the problem-solving process as well.

Scoring Rubric

Score	Expectations
0	The portfolio has not been collected and documented. Only random papers are included, and no summary statement is written.
1	A portfolio has been collected, but work has not been selected to reflect student performance; work is incomplete; portfolio does not have introduction, afterword, or other reflective analysis.

2   The notebook is organized and mostly complete. A limited understanding of chemistry concepts is shown. Writings are logical but often incomplete.

3   The notebook is organized and complete. A satisfactory understanding of concepts and applications is shown. Writings are logical, often including additional observations and readings.

4   The notebook is organized and complete. Chemistry concepts are understood and readily applied to analyze data and draw conclusions. Additional observations, readings, and resources are frequently cited.

Keeping a Science Notebook

Introduction

During the Rivers Project, having a record of your laboratory work to refer to as you do the various water tests will be important. You may simply need to check what day you started some activity, or you may need to make a more complicated inquiry, such as comparing actual test readings with results. Keep your science notebook with you whenever you are working in the laboratory or in the field. Use this notebook as the first place you record data. Add observations, ideas, and explanatory notes as they occur to you. By using a science notebook for *Rivers Chemistry,* you will become more familiar and comfortable with the ways scientists handle record-keeping during investigations.

Procedure

1. Write your name in the front, along with your class and "Rivers Chemistry Science Notebook."
2. Number all pages consecutively, using only the front of each page. Label pages 1 and 2 as "Contents." On these pages, the left column should read, "Title," and the right column should read, "Pages."
3. Beginning with page 3, place the following information at the top of each page:
   Date:
   Time:
   Location:
   Purpose:
   Each time you use your notebook, fill in this information so each entry is clearly distinguished from prior entries.

4. Bring your notebook to every class meeting to record instructions, class notes, and ideas. Also take it into the field, to interviews, field trips, and other presentations. Make notes at every class meeting or other *Rivers Chemistry* event.

- Before you start a lab or field activity, copy data tables from your activity sheets into your notebook. This will help you record all the information you need.

- Make detailed observations of your work. Record these as they occur. Note if the observations were what you expected. If working in the field, include weather conditions, the appearance of the site, plants and animals you see, and other observations that you make.

- Take notes of any outside research done as part of any *Rivers Chemistry* assignments.

- Complete all calculations in your notebook.

- When you have completed the activity, write a summary of the activity, an analysis of your results, and your conclusions.

Materials

Per student
- bound notebook, so pages cannot be removed or inserted
- pen or pencil
- markers

- scissors
- glue

Per class
- magazines for cutting up

© SIU, published by Addison Wesley Longman, Inc.

5. You may use your notebook to record answers to questions, to write about the project or your feelings about the "Rivers Project," and for other writings. Note each assignment or other activity in the Contents pages of your notebook, indicating the pages used.

6. Write all entries legibly, preferably in ink. If you make a mistake, one line through an entry is sufficient. Do not erase or completely obliterate any entries. If you make a correction or revise an entry, add the date and your initials to show that you are the person making the change.

Performance Criteria

Your science notebook will be graded regularly along with your other assignments. Your grade will be based on whether you have followed the procedures described in this sheet. Important points include the following:

- Have you completed all your assignments?

- Are your entries organized and focused, with ample explanations that identify the data, calculations, and conclusions?

- Are your data entered completely? Have you completed calculations?

- Have you analyzed your data correctly?

- Do your conclusions follow from your experimental results? Do you demonstrate that you understand the activity?

- As appropriate, do you integrate the results of prior *Rivers Chemistry* activities into current work?

- Have you given detailed observations?

- Have you followed the procedures and written legibly?

© SIU, published by Addison Wesley Longman, Inc.

River Collage

Introduction

When you try to explain a situation or feeling to others, often a picture works better than words. A collection of pictures may be even more effective. A collage is a collection of pictures and other materials, selected and arranged to present a message to the viewer.

Over the course of the *Rivers Chemistry* unit, you will construct a collage whose message relates to water quality and the uses of rivers and streams. As you will learn in greater detail, this unit concentrates on testing and determining water quality in your river or stream.

Before starting your collage, you will need to decide what message you want to convey. Your message should involve each of the lessons you will study in the *Rivers Chemistry* unit, but it should not just be a summary of the unit, nor an unfocused jumble of pictures about water and rivers. As you reflect on the quality of your river or stream, think about what specific message you want to communicate to others.

Here are some questions to guide you in discovering the message you want to communicate. How is the river important to you and your community? How does its water quality affect you, and how does your community affect the river? Do you use it for boating or fishing? Do you hike or picnic along its shore? Is it used for your drinking water? Does treated sewage water end up there? What industries rely on the river? Decide what you want others to be more aware of. You may want to consider the beauty of the river or stream; its value as habitat; its value to humans as a water supply, a source of transportation, or a recreational resource; its power and destructiveness in a flood; or the effects of the such human actions as removal of vegetation from stream banks, construction of dams, drainage of wetlands, dredging, pollution, or overuse by industries or municipalities.

Procedure

1. Decide on a general topic or theme. Write out the message you want to convey. List kinds of pictures you could use to convey that message. Decide if you will need to include other materials or verbal messages. Make sketches of possible arrangements.

2. Select and gather materials. Each time you consider materials for your collage, ask yourself, "How will this express my message?" If you have no answer, look for different materials instead. Do not attach materials to your board until you have covered several lessons.

3. Collect your collage materials in a large envelope labeled with your name and class. Keep the

Materials

Per student
- poster board
- large envelope for holding collected materials
- scissors
- markers
- glue stick

Per class
- magazines from which pictures and text can be cut
- colored paper

© SIU, published by Addison Wesley Longman, Inc.

envelope in the classroom (as directed by your teacher) until you attach them to your poster.

4. Experiment with the sizes, shapes, and colors you have collected. Anticipate what you might want to add after upcoming lessons. The arrangement should be visually pleasing, with thought given to color, form, shape, and line. Balance of pictures, print, and white space contribute to the effectiveness of a collage.

5. When you are satisfied with your arrangements, glue the materials to the poster board.

6. After completing each lesson, add to your collage. Does your message weave through the different lessons? Do all the materials connect to your theme?

7. When your collage is completed, make sure that it is labeled on the back with your name, class, and date. Include a title.

8. When you have finished your collage, answer the following questions and turn in your responses with your collage.

Questions

1. What is your theme or topic?
2. What message do you wish to convey?
3. Did all the materials on your display contribute in projecting this message? Explain why or why not.
4. What features were helpful in conveying your message?
5. When you showed your collage to others, was the message clear? Were other messages conveyed?
6. What changes could improve your collage?
7. What can a collage convey better than other forms of communication? What is difficult to convey with a collage?

Performance Criteria

You have artistic freedom in your use of pictures, printed materials and other items for your collage. Your grade will be based on whether you have followed the procedures described in this sheet. The successful collage will:

- Feature a single message or theme throughout the collage. The message is evident through pictures and organization and may also be stated in print.

- Contain materials representing each *Rivers Chemistry* lesson studied.

- Clearly demonstrate organization and planning. The collage is neatly constructed.

- Reflect artistic considerations, such as use of color, space, balance, and line.

- Have an accompanying sheet containing complete answers to the assessment questions listed on the student handout. Answers show insights into the use of a collage to present a message.

- Be complemented by an oral presentation (if assigned) that emphasizes the message and the relationship of the different parts of the collage to the message.

© SIU, published by Addison Wesley Longman, Inc.

Portfolio

Introduction

A portfolio is a collection of work that you deem to be your best and most representative. In preparing your portfolio, you should include material that you would be proud to show others and that you may keep. The purpose of a portfolio is to enable you to see your own progress and to share what you have learned with others. A well thought-out portfolio will allow you, your classmates, and your teachers to assess what you have learned and done.

Procedure

1. During this study of *Rivers Chemistry,* you will keep some of your best papers in a manila folder in the classroom. You may update the contents of this folder regularly, so that the folder contents represents your best work. These items may include a compilation of entries

from your journal, laboratory reports, poems or stories, artwork, articles you have written for a newspaper or published journal, or any other evidence of the effectiveness or benefits of this project.

2. You may also include articles you have found in newspapers, books or magazines regarding environmental issues (such as water quality and industrial spills), national or international water issues, or comments and happenings related to the local river or stream. For maximum impact, include your own observations about the significance of the content or impact on the community of each article you include.

3. Complete your portfolio by writing an overview of the *Rivers Chemistry* project. This overview should include a brief introduction, a reflection on what you have learned and done, and an afterword or concluding statement. Address your writing to an adult who has no knowledge of this project, but whom you want to impress positively.

    In *Introduction,* include information about the project and state the source or assignments for the works you included in your portfolio.

In *Reflections,* answer the following questions:

- What did you expect to learn or discover during this project? What skills did you expect to gain?

- What part of the project was most important? What was most fun? What part was most useful?

- In what ways have you become more aware of your environment during this project? Have your attitudes changed?

    In *Conclusion,* reflect on where you have been and where you might go because of your interest in the environment in general, in rivers and stream specifically.

4. Complete your portfolio by assembling all materials into a binder, such as a plastic report holder or a three-ring notebook. Place your materials in the following order:

- Title page, including your name, class, and date

- Project overview

- Your collection of works, ordered by date of completion of the work

Materials

Per student

- Manila folder
- Plastic report cover or three-ring notebook

© SIU, published by Addison Wesley Longman, Inc.

Performance Criteria

Your portfolio will be graded at the end of the *Rivers Chemistry* unit. Your grade will be based on whether you have followed the procedures described in this sheet. The material in your portfolio should reflect the following:

- Acquisition of new knowledge and skills
- Ability to express ideas clearly and to think critically
- Ability to analyze data and draw conclusions
- Ability to revise and expand your understanding
- Not only solutions to problems but description of the problem-solving process as well
- Connection of information from several disciplines
- Self-reflection and evaluation

© SIU, published by Addison Wesley Longman, Inc.

Assessment Activities for Specific Lessons

Each of the following assessments serves as a performance-based assessment tool for a specific lesson in *Rivers Chemistry*. Some are lab-based, but others feature role-playing, research, written analysis, and telecommunications activities. These assessments are optional, but many teachers find that these help both students and instructors discover what a student really understands about the relevant lesson.

Teacher Notes Assessment for Lesson 2: Dilution of an Acid (pages 194–196)

Focus

In the laboratory, students investigate the effect of dilution of an acid on its pH. Students explore the relationship between the concentration of a strong monoprotic acid (hydrochloric acid) and the pH of the solution.

Time

One class period of 40–50 minutes, plus additional time in class or as homework

Advanced Preparation

Prepare to supply students with Assessment for Lesson 2: Dilution of an Acid (located on pages 194–196). Obtain all necessary equipment and materials.

Prepare 0.01 M HCl. To make 1 L of 0.01 M HCl from concentrated (12 M) acid, first make a 0.1 M solution using 8.33 mL of HCl and dilute to one liter. 100 mL of 0.1 M dilution, diluted to 1 liter, will give the 0.01 M solution.

Because of possible contamination from carbon dioxide in the air and small errors in measurement, the pH of this solution will probably not be exactly 2.0. You may wish to adjust the pH by adding more HCl or more water to give a pH of 2.0.

Safety

Follow all laboratory safety guidelines presented in Lesson 1. Students should be reminded to wear goggles. The solutions are very dilute and may be discarded by pouring into the sink with additional water.

Materials

Per student
safety goggles, apron, and gloves
graph paper

Per group
wax marking pencil
5 medicine cups
11 mL of 10^{-2} *M* HCl acid
graduated cylinder, 10-mL
50 mL distilled water
pH wide-range indicator solution, paper, or meter

Developing the Lesson

1. Have students read and do Assessment for Lesson 2: Dilution of an Acid.
2. Have students complete graph and writing assignment in class or as homework.

Notes

You may wish to have students record the pH of the distilled water that is used to make the dilutions. Even if the distilled water has a pH of 7.0, each dilution rarely changes the pH by exactly one pH unit. A typical set of results is shown in the following table and in the graph on the next page. (Form of pH reading depends on method used.)

ASSESSMENT TABLE 2-1

Typical Data Table Results for Dilution of an Acid

Concentration [*M*]	$-\log[M]$	Color (pH paper)	Color (indicator solution)	pH (pH meter)
10^{-2}	2	red-orange		
	2.0	1.9		
10^{-3}	3	orange-red	2.8	3.0
10^{-4}	4	orange	4.0	4.2
10^{-5}	5	yellow (no green)		
	5.8	5.7		

In order to graph pH versus concentration using linear graph paper, students should record the concentrations as $-\log[M]$, the same units used for pH. If pH and logarithms have not been covered, you may need to help students fill in the data table.

A similar dilution activity could be done using a basic solution such as sodium hydroxide. Tenfold dilutions should decrease the pH about 1.0 pH unit. Discuss with the class that the change for either the acidic or the basic solution is true only to pH of 7 and only approximately true from 6 to 7 for acids and 8 to 7 for bases.

Performance Criteria

- The student works safely in lab, following the given procedure.
- If students work in groups, tasks are shared and all members of the group participate.

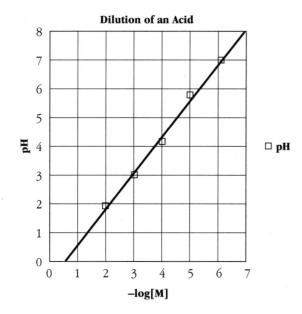

Dilution of an Acid

y=1.260x − 0.710

Assessment Figure 2-1: Typical Graph Results for Dilution of an Acid

- Data are collected and reported on a data table.

- A graph is constructed and used to predict a dilution not made in the lab.

- A report is written, showing an understanding of the problem and variables investigated. An appropriate conclusion is made. The report uses correct grammar and spelling and is written in paragraph form.

Scoring Rubric

Laboratory Work and Data Collection

Score	Expectations
0	The student has not completed the activity, or/and the data collected are not useful.
1	The activity is completed, and minimal, but useful, data are recorded. This score might be given for students in groups who contributed minimally to the task.
2	The activity is completed, and useful data are recorded in a data table. Students working in groups shared tasks in completing the activity.
3	The activity is completed, and useful data are recorded in a data table. Students working in groups share equally in completing the task. Reserve a three for students who follow all prescribed laboratory rules and work together in groups.

Graph and Prediction

Score	Expectations
0	No information is shown, or minimal information is recorded but information is not useful in understanding what the student did.
1	Minimal information is recorded, and basic rules for graphing data are followed.
2	At least one axis has been correctly identified and labeled, with some data points plotted.
3	Both axes are correctly identified and labeled, data points are plotted, and a title is given.
4	The criteria for a three are met, and students have also drawn a best-fit line which, when extrapolated, is used to predict the fourth dilution.

Writing Sample

Read the student's entire writing sample. Then reread, using the following criteria as guidelines. If students do not use complete sentences, paragraph form, or have a large number of misspelled words, decrease the score by one mark.

Score	Expectations
0	Nothing is written.
1	Narrative is minimal, or the narrative does not describe the activity correctly.
2	The student poses the problem and identifies at least one of the variables correctly.
3	The student fulfills all the expectations for a two and also identifies both the independent and dependent variables and describes a logical procedure.
4	In addition to the requirements for a score of three, the student relates a conclusion to the problem and justifies it.

Teacher Notes for Assessment for Lesson 3: More Than One Answer—Evaluating Change (pages 197–199)

Focus

Students are divided into special-interest groups to role-play a scenario in which an industry wishes to build a plant on a river and use river water as coolant in the plant. You may wish to change or expand this assessment to include local issues or concerns.

Students work with others in their interest group to discuss issues and come to consensus about the pros and cons of the plant construction from their point of view. Conclude this activity with a general discussion where groups share their concerns and different points of view.

Time

Two class periods of 40–50 minutes. Allow extra time if doing calorimetric calculations in class.

DAY ONE: Students work in small groups

DAY TWO: Town meeting

Advanced Preparation

Prepare to supply students with Assessment for Lesson 3: More Than One Answer—Evaluating Change (located on pages 197–199). Decide whether students will perform the calorimetric calculations that quantify the effect on river temperature of using the river water as coolant. Alternatively, you may demonstrate the calculations, have a few more-skilled students demonstrate the process, or simply provide your students with the results.

Developing the Lesson

1. Distribute Assessment for Lesson 3: More Than One Answer—Evaluating Change. As a class or in small groups have students read and discuss this handout. Assign students to specific special-interest groups. Although you may ask students to select which interest group they wish to join, some adjustment of roles may be needed in order to have balanced groups.

2. If students will do calorimetric calculations, discuss this process in class and have students complete the calculations in small groups or as individuals. Otherwise, you may demonstrate the process or provide the results.

3. In their special-interest groups, have students prepare responses to the questions on the student handout. Decide if additional questions should be raised, and assign individual members of their group to speak to each issue. Students should write their responses in the journals (or notebooks) for reference during the town meeting.

4. The next day, hold a "town meeting" to debate the pros and cons of the plant and its cooling process. Select one student (or yourself) to run the town meeting, which everyone is invited to attend. Remind students to support the opinions of their interest group throughout the discussion. At the meeting, the facilitator should encourage everyone to speak, but individuals must raise their hands in order to be recognized and should begin by giving the name of the group they represent.

5. You may wish to organize the town meeting so that the "plant officials" go first, presenting their plans. Then request questions or comments from the audience. Alternately, each group may be assigned to present their group's viewpoint before opening the meeting to questions and comments.

6. At the end of the town meeting, you may wish to have a paper ballot to determine if the citizens would support having the plant in their community. As an out-of-class or extra assignment, students might investigate the procedure a company would follow if they did wish to locate facilities in

your community. Do individuals or special-interest groups have the opportunity to ask questions and voice opinions in their community?

Notes

Students may want to know more precisely how much the proposed use of river water as coolant for the plant would affect the river temperature downstream. They may also want to be able to evaluate the significance of the increase in plant cooling needs proposed for the future. If students have studied specific heat and calorimetry, you may have them analyze the data given by the engineers. (Otherwise, you may simply provide them with the results of the calculations, as given here.) The specific heat of water is defined by

$$C_p = 1.00 \text{ cal}/(g \bullet C) \text{ or } C_p = 4.18 \text{ J}/(g \bullet °C)$$

The heat gained by water is then

$$\text{heat gained (q)} = C_p \text{ (water)} \bullet \text{ mass of water} \bullet \text{ change in temperature}$$

$$= \frac{4.18 \text{ J}}{g \bullet °C} \bullet \text{ mass} \bullet (T_{final} - T_{initial})$$

$$\text{Heat gained} = \text{Heat lost}$$

$$C_p \bullet \text{mass}_{river\ water} \bullet (T_f - T_{i\text{-}river}) = -C_p \bullet \text{mass}_{plant\ water} \bullet (T_f - T_{i\text{-}plant})$$

To calculate the temperature of the river after the plant has discharged the warmer water into it, use the data from this problem. The specific heat (C_p) of water is the same on both sides of the equation, and the initial temperature of the water discharged by the plant $(T_{i\text{-}plant})$ is equal to the initial temperature of the river water plus 10°C $(T_{i\text{-}river} + 10°C)$. One milliliter of water has a mass of one gram; therefore, 1 L of water would have a mass of 1000 g.

$$\text{mass}_{river\ water} \bullet (T_f - T_{i\text{-}river}) = -\text{mass}_{plant\ water} \bullet (T_f - T_{i\text{-}river} + 10°C)$$

$$43.2 \bullet 10^9 \text{ g } (T_f - T_{i\text{-}river}) = -5 \bullet 10^6 \text{ g } (T_f - T_{i\text{-}river} + 10°C)$$

$$T_f = T_i + 0.0012°C$$

As long as the amount of water used by the plant is small compared with the volume or mass of river flow, the change in river temperature as a result of the use of water as coolant will be insignificant. In this example, the ratio of volume of heated water to volume of river water is about 1:8000.

Larger amounts of cooling water, a greater temperature difference, or a smaller stream volume or flow rate would result in a greater temperature change. You may, therefore, want to calculate the temperature change using a different set of conditions. For example, if on a hot summer day the water discharged by the plant is 25°C higher than the temperature of the river water and the flow rate is only 0.10 m/s because the water level has dropped to an average of 7.0 m in width and 2.0 m in depth, then a similar calculation gives a final temperature, $T_f = T_i + 0.25°C$. (These calculations assume even mixing of the discharge water with the river and do not consider local variations in temperature where the two meet.)

Performance Criteria

■ Students work cooperatively in their group, sharing ideas and strategies.

■ Responsibility for speaking at the town meeting is divided among everyone in the group.

■ Questions and responses express the interests of the group rather than a single individual.

■ Students listen to the views of the other groups, respect different points of view, and make rational responses.

Scoring Rubric

Base scoring on quality of ideas and strategies, ability to work within a group, and questions and debate at the town meeting. Discussions can become heated, and questions pointed to individuals rather than to a group. Any group that dominates the discussion or whose members do not work with their group should receive a score lowered by one point.

Score	Expectations
0	The group does not participate in the town meeting.
1	At least one member of the group speaks to ask or answer questions or state an opinion consistent with the interests of the group.
2	Two or more members speak and statements are consistent with the interests of the group.
3	All expectations for a two, and participation shows evidence of pre-planning by the group.
4	All members of the group speak (if time allows) and respond within the interests of the group, with evidence of planned questions and strategy. Students share ideas (paper and pencil note-passing to reduce noise) for others to include in their response.

Teacher Notes for Assessment for Lesson 4: The Turbidity of Milk (pages 200–202)

Focus

Students investigate the measurement of turbidity using homogenized milk in water to give a cloudy liquid. They model a simple turbidimeter in which the height of liquid that masks a black and white mark is compared with the amount of milk added to water.

Time

One class period of 40–50 minutes, plus additional time in class or as homework

---

Advanced Preparation

Prepare to supply students with Assessment for Lesson 4: The Turbidity of Milk (located on pages 200–202). Obtain all necessary equipment and materials. Provide graph paper or remind students to bring their own.

Safety and Waste Disposal

Have students follow all laboratory safety guidelines presented in Lesson 1. All waste can be discarded in the sink with lukewarm (not hot) water.

Materials

Per student
safety goggles, lab apron, and gloves
graph paper
Per group
white card (3" × 5")
permanent marker
graduated cylinder, 25-mL
7 pipettes or droppers (3, if rinsed between uses)
glass cylinder, 2.5-cm diameter × 9.5-cm tall
metric ruler
beaker
125 mL water
20 mL milk, homogenized

Developing the Lesson

1. Have students read the handout, Student Assessment: The Turbidity of Milk. Discuss the importance of using a clean pipette or dropper for each sample.
2. Have students do Procedure for Turbidity of Milk. Students may work individually or in groups. Results will vary with the fat content of milk used. If time permits, students may repeat the procedures and average two or three sets of data.
3. Have students complete their graph and writing assignment in class or as homework. The graph of turbidity versus concentration of milk is not linear but curved. Show students various examples of this type of graph.
4. If desired, have students discuss their results as a group.

Notes

Sample data, using 2 percent fat-content milk, are shown in the following table and graph. Two trials gave similar heights and a reasonably smooth curve. For this experiment, the height predicted for 50 drops of milk, interpolated from the graph, is 1.9 cm.

ASSESSMENT TABLE 4-1

Sample Data Table for Turbidity of Milk

Trial	Drops of Milk	Series 1 Height (cm)	Series 2 Height (cm)	Average Height (cm)
1	20	4.1	4.2	4.2
2	40	2.2	2.2	2.2
3	60	1.7	1.5	1.6
4	80	1.2	1.4	1.3
5	100	1.2	1.2	1.2

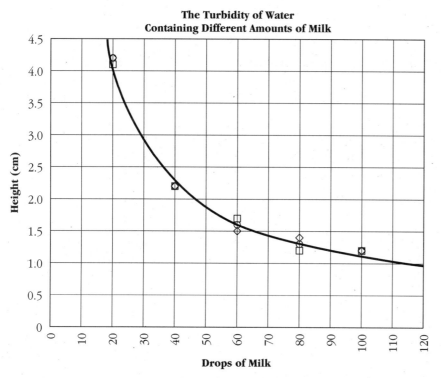

Assessment Figure 4-1: Sample Graph for Turbidity of Water Containing Different Amounts of Milk

Performance Criteria

- The student works safely in lab, following the given procedure.

- If students work in groups, tasks are shared and all members of the group participate.

- Data are collected and reported on a data table.

- A graph is constructed and used to predict the height of a different concentration of milk.

- A report is written, showing an understanding of the problem and variables investigated. An appropriate conclusion is made. The report uses correct grammar and spelling and is written in paragraph form.

Scoring Rubric

Laboratory Work and Data Collection

Score	Expectations
0	The student did not complete the activity, or/and the data collected are not useful.
1	The activity was completed and minimal, but useful data are recorded. This score might be given for students in groups who contributed minimally to the task.
2	The activity was completed, and useful data are recorded in a data table. Students working in groups shared tasks in completing the activity.
3	The activity was completed, and useful data are recorded in a data table. Students working in groups shared equally in completing the task. Reserve a three for students who followed all prescribed laboratory rules and worked together in groups.

Graph and Prediction

Score	Expectations
0	No information is shown, or information is minimal and not useful in understanding what the student did.
1	Minimal information is recorded, and basic rules for graphing data are followed.
2	At least one axis has been correctly identified and labeled, with some data points plotted.
3	Both axes are correctly identified and labeled, data points are plotted, and a title is given.
4	The criteria for a three are met, and students also have drawn a smooth curve which is used to predict a different concentration.

Writing Sample

Read the student's entire writing sample. Then reread using the following criteria as guidelines. If students do not use complete sentences, paragraph form, or have a large number of misspelled words, decrease the score by one mark.

Score	Expectations
0	Score a zero if nothing is written.
1	Narrative is minimal or does not correctly describe the activity.
2	The student poses the problem and identifies at least one of the variables correctly.
3	The student fulfills all the expectations for a two and identifies both the independent and dependent variables and describes a logical procedure.

4   In addition to the requirements for a score of three, the student relates a conclusion to the problem and justifies it.

Teacher Notes for Assessment for Lesson 6: How Much Oxygen in the Fish Tanks? (pages 203–204)

Focus

Students will predict the amount of oxygen in water under different conditions of temperature and aeration and compare their predictions with measured levels. The activity is designed as a demonstration, in which some students set up the water tanks, then others perform the dissolved oxygen tests, while the rest of the class observes. Students write about the activity using three basic components of scientific inquiry—prediction, analysis, and application.

Time

Two class periods of 40–50 minutes

Day One: Assessment for Lesson 6: How Much Oxygen in the Fish Tanks, Part A (requires only a partial period)

Day Two: (At least two days after Day One) Assessment for Lesson 6: How Much Oxygen in the Fish Tanks, Part B

Advanced Preparation

Prepare to supply students with Assessment for Lesson 6: How Much Oxygen in the Fish Tanks? (located on pages 203–204). Gather all necessary equipment and materials.

Safety

Have students performing the dissolved oxygen tests follow all laboratory safety guidelines presented in Lesson 1.

Materials

Per student doing dissolved oxygen test
safety goggles, lab apron, and gloves
Per class
4 aquariums or large bowls
2 aquarium aerators
aquarium heater
Celsius thermometer
1–4 dissolved oxygen (DO) bottles with stoppers
dissolved oxygen test kit
waste container

Developing the Lesson

1. Have students read Assessment for Lesson 6: How Much Oxygen in the Fish Tanks? Have selected students do Part A, setting up the fish tanks. Encourage all students to observe the tanks carefully each day and base their predictions on their observations and their readings.

2. At least two days after having students set up the fish tanks, have selected students do Part B of the assessment, running the dissolved oxygen tests on the tanks.

3. Have students complete the writing assignments in class or as homework.

Notes

Students' initial predictions (or guesses) of the dissolved oxygen rankings of the tanks are likely to be wrong because students will not have sufficient information to make an informed choice. Base evaluation of their predictions not on accuracy but on how they justify their rankings.

Students should be able to compare Tank 3 and Tank 4 correctly, because the only difference is the temperature of the water; Tank 3 would be expected to have more dissolved oxygen than Tank 4. They should also be able to interpret the relationship between Tanks 1 and 2 correctly, because the aerator on a water faucet will cause the freshly drawn water to be supersaturated in oxygen. As the water stands, air bubbles will form on the sides of the tank, decreasing the dissolved gases in the water. Comparison of Tanks 1 and 2 with Tanks 3 and 4 is more complicated, because the aerator in Tank 3 will agitate the water, causing a rapid loss of excess dissolved gases, but it will also add dissolved gases to the tank. In fact, the ordering of the tanks may vary with how the experiment is prepared.

Performance Criteria and Scoring Rubric

The three one-paragraph writing assignments in this assessment provide the performance basis for assessing students' skills at three components of scientific inquiry—prediction, analysis, and application.

Paragraph One: Prediction

The knowledge base and observations on which the students base their prediction include:

- The higher the temperature, the lower the level of dissolved oxygen.

- The observation of gas bubbles on the sides of Tank 2.

- Bubbling air through water increases the gas-to-liquid surface and the level of dissolved gas.

Score	Expectations
0	No explanation is given for ordering the tanks, or explanation is not based on observations and scientific reasoning.
1	One reasonable explanation for ordering any two of the tanks is given. Reasons for the other orders are not given or are not based on observations and scientific reasoning.
2	Two reasonable explanations for ordering any three of the tanks are given.
3	Three reasonable explanations for ordering the four tanks are given.

Paragraph Two: Analysis

The knowledge base and observations on which the students base their analysis include:

- Results of the DO analysis

- Prior knowledge base and observations listed under Prediction

Score	Expectations
0	No explanation is given for correct or incorrect predictions. Explanation is not based on observations and scientific reasoning.
1	One reasonable explanation for ordering any two of the tanks is given. Reasons for the other orders are not given or are not based on observations and scientific reasoning.
2	Two reasonable explanations for ordering any three of the tanks are given.
3	Three reasonable explanations for ordering the four tanks are given.

Paragraph Three: Application

The knowledge base and observations on which the students base their application include:

- The level of dissolved oxygen is greater in cooler water than in warmer water; therefore, a stream would be expected to have a higher DO level when the water is cold than when it is hot.

- As it stands, water will lose excess dissolved gases; therefore, a quiet section of a stream would have a lower DO level than a quickly moving section, because excess dissolved gases are slowly lost on standing.

- Bubbling air through water will increase the contact between the two surfaces, increasing the dissolving process; therefore, streams agitated by rapids and waterfalls will have a high level of DO.

- Disturbing water that contains an excess of dissolved gases will cause these gases to be given off; therefore, still ponds supersaturated with dissolved gases would lose the excess gases more rapidly if agitated (by natural or man-made actions).

Score	Expectations
0	No application is given, or applications listed are not based on scientific reasoning.
1	One reasonable application is given.
2	Two reasonable applications are given.
3	Three reasonable applications are given.
4	Four reasonable applications are given.

Assessment Activities for Specific Lessons

Teacher Notes for Assessment for Lesson 8:
Phosphates in Detergents (pages 205–206)

Focus

Students explore the phosphate levels of different types of detergents or cleaners available in local stores. They research a specific aspect of detergents and prepare a written or oral report.

Time

This assessment is primarily a research-based assignment, requiring little class time.

Advanced Preparation

Prepare to supply students with Assessment for Lesson 8: Phosphates in Detergents (located on pages 205–206). Gather materials that student may use for their reports. If students have limited access to references, collect reference materials on phosphates and detergents into folders for their use. After doing *Rivers Chemistry* several times, you may have a wide range of materials and topic ideas for students. Sources for information are listed in the appendix. Collect a variety of detergent labels and boxes.

Decide whether students should do their research individually or in groups. If students must use a specific reference citation format, prepare a handout giving examples of how to cite various types of articles, books, pamphlets, and other resources. Prepare a handout of written or oral report guidelines, including requirements of structure, format, elements, length, references, and deadlines.

Materials

Per class (if available)

detergent labels and boxes

pamphlets from detergent manufacturers

articles on phosphates and phosphate detergents from consumer magazines and other sources

articles and pamphlets from federal, state, and local environmental protection agencies

Developing the Lesson

1. Distribute and discuss Assessment for Lesson 8: Phosphates in Detergents. Discuss how the three steps of this assessment fit together.

2. Distribute and discuss handouts on references and on report guidelines. Discuss available research sources, such as in-class materials, school library, public library, and manufacturers. You may want to discuss potential research topics.

3. Have students discuss the results of Step 1, looking at the phosphate content of specific products. Compare manufacturers of different brands of detergents, and note that competitive products are often made by the same company. You may wish to collect written student responses to Step 1 at

this point, and perhaps to some portion of Step 2, and discuss research topics individually or in groups before students finalize their topics.

4. Have students finalize their research topics, do their research, and prepare their reports.

Notes

In states and other areas in which phosphate is not allowed in most cleaning products, the percent weight for phosphate in all laundry and dish detergents used in the home is likely to be zero. The exception is dishwasher detergents. Challenge students to find other cleansers that still contain phosphates: Do restaurants and hospitals use phosphate-containing detergents? Do garages and auto-repair centers have special detergents that may contain phosphates? Do window cleaners or household cleaning supplies contain detergents that may contain phosphates?

Performance Criteria

■ The student examines the phosphate contents of at least three commercially available detergents or cleansers and includes at least one product containing phosphate.

■ The student lists two or more references, with good content and presentation.

■ The student's written (or oral) research report has a topic relevant to phosphates in detergent and follows prescribed guidelines for structure, format, elements, length, references, and timeliness.

Scoring Rubric

Percent Phosphate in Detergents or Cleansers

Score	Expectations
0	Answer is not given or is incomplete.
1	Three products are given, and all have 0 percent phosphate.
2	Three products are given, and at least one contains phosphate.

Written or Oral Report

Score	Expectations
0	Report has no references; very limited content and presentation.
1	At least one reference or source of information is cited; limited or disorganized content. The presentation, written or oral, is generally poor.
2	At least one reference or source of information is cited; content is adequate, and presentation is good.
3	Two or more references or sources of information are cited; content and presentation are good.
4	Two or more references or sources of information are cited; content and presentation are excellent.

Teacher Notes for Challenge Project for Lesson 10: Telecommunications (pages 207–208)

Focus

In this culminating activity, students use data from other schools to expand their knowledge of water quality in river and streams. This activity emphasizes the importance of analyzing collected data, looking at results over time and distance. Once students have retrieved additional river data electronically, they will interpret and report those data.

Time

Three or four class periods of 40–50 minutes, with additional homework time for preparing presentation

Materials

Per group
computer
telecommunications system
data from a Rivers bulletin board
maps of rivers, streams, and watersheds being studied
graph paper
Optional
spreadsheet program for sorting and managing data

Advanced Preparation

Prepare to supply students with Challenge Project for Lesson 10: Telecommunications (located on pages 207–208). Gather all necessary equipment and materials. If your class must share computer capabilities with others in the school, make arrangements for your class to have appropriate access.

Before having students try to connect electronically with the Rivers Project, make these connections yourself, to make sure you can give clear, accurate, and up-to-date instructions on this process. As necessary, create and distribute a handout on making these connections. As necessary work with your school's computer resource person or other skilled individual to give students proper preparation and guidance for the telecommunications portion of this activity.

Decide how students will present their investigations, such as written reports, oral presentations, poster presentations, and so forth. Prepare a handout of presentation guidelines if different from what is included on the student sheet. If students will make group presentations, decide how the group and the individuals will be evaluated.

Developing the Lesson

1. Have students read and discuss Challenge Project for Lesson 10: Telecommunications.
2. Explain that the rivers bulletin board that the students will be accessing includes the results of water-quality tests from thousands of students in many geographic areas. Explain the school or classroom computer capabil-

ities and your class access to such facilities. Ascertain which students have experience communicating via e-mail and the World Wide Web.

3. Describe the form in which students will present the results of their research, such as written, oral, poster, and so forth. Distribute handout of presentation guidelines as appropriate, including deadlines.

4. Divide the class into three or more groups to work on the telecommunications portion of this activity. Try to distribute students with computer networking skills evenly among the groups working on this project. Each group should choose a specific river, watershed, or geographic area to investigate. As a group, have them explore the database to see what sites within that watershed or geographic area have data available, and the dates and water-quality tests for which such data are available.

5. Working with the rest of his or her group, have each student select an area for individual research that fits within the group's general area.

6. Working in groups, have students retrieve from the rivers bulletin board observations and tests required for each student's individual research endeavor. Peer coaching in using telecommunications should help students with little background in this technology.

7. While some students are working with the computers, have others investigate their test sites(s) using maps, geography books, and other library resources. For specific teaching activities on map reading and on land use, see *Rivers Geography*.

8. Have students graph their data. For specific teaching activities on graphing, see *Rivers Mathematics*.

9. Have students complete their written reports, poster, or other presentation.

Notes

Accessing information via telecommunications may be a new venture for many students. The technology for supporting a database for information changes too quickly to adequately explain in detail all the steps that are needed to access the information.

As was mentioned in the introduction to the Rivers Project curriculum, the Rivers Project includes two telecommunications systems designed for students to use in exchanging data with students at other schools. Information on how to access the Rivers Project via e-mail and on the World Wide Web is included on page xii. *Southern Illinois University at Edwardsville (SIUE)*, the *Office of Science and Mathematics Education (OSME)*, and *Rivers Project* are key words to finding the Rivers Project home page for information on using the database, for asking questions about the project, and for connecting with other schools testing their local river or stream.

You may decide to have all students in the class select rivers and streams within the same watershed as the field site you investigated. If enough data are available, students could even choose sites upstream and downstream from the field site. As students work in groups to select their individual topics, you may require that they coordinate their selection of topics, so they investigate related issues. For instance, projects within each group, when taken as a whole, may involve:

- investigation of all nine tests

- investigation of test results under particular conditions, such as: a specific test under different weather conditions or seasons; a specific test at different sites along one river or stream; a series of tests upstream and downstream from a specific area of interest (such as a city or industrial complex)

- inclusion of local site and class test results in each report

- inclusion of certain common elements, such as historical background, geology, or weather conditions

You might want students to research their topic or area as background for their findings. This might include historical background on uses of the river and land along the river, a study of the geology along the river, or the typical (or special) weather conditions of the area. Maps of the area with the location of the different sites shown may be required. Data should be displayed in tables and graphs. References should be cited when appropriate.

Performance Criteria

Because this challenge project can take many forms, assessment criteria should fit the specific tasks and activities involved. In most cases, the assessment criteria can be the same already presented for other assessments, such as those for written analysis and for group participation. Criteria for the telecommunications portion of the assessment will depend on student access to and experience with telecommunications systems.

Scoring Rubric

For certain activities, you may want specific scoring rubrics. Here are some possibilities.

Written Analysis of Telecommunications Data

Do students convey their knowledge through their writings? Are their written presentations logical, persuasive, and informative? Read the student's entire writing sample. Then reread, using the following criteria as guidelines. If students do not use complete sentences and paragraph form, or if they have a large number of misspelled words, decrease the score by one mark. As appropriate, consider whether the student has included charts and graphs to make explanations easier to understand. Did the student cite references as appropriate?

Score	Expectations
0	Nothing is written.
1	Narrative is minimal, has little relevance to water-quality tests or standards, or does not describe the work correctly. The group relied on others outside their group to retrieve information from the Rivers Project database.

2   Students adequately describe the test results and make some connections between the test results and site conditions. Cause-and-effect relationships are usually missing. At least one student in the group was able to manipulate the telecommunications system.

3   Students make meaningful connections between test results and site conditions. They describe variables, detail the procedure, and relate the conclusion to the problem. Topics are discussed in a logical sequence and information is summarized. All students in the group have accessed the telecommunications system with minimal help.

4   The group fulfills the requirements for a three and has reasonable explanations or correlations among test data, researched water testing beyond requirements for the course to include in their discussion, or otherwise shows interest and scholarship in environmental concerns.

Group Poster Presentations

If poster presentations are made during parent night, for an environmental program, or other school function, students may present their results several times to different audiences. An evaluation form may be used for general comments from others about the presentations. If the oral report is for the class, peer review may be included along with your review.

If the poster presentation is a group project, it should reflect the different areas investigated by each of the students in the group.

Score	Expectations
0	No poster/presentation is made.
1	The poster/presentation shows little preparation or has incorrect or meaningless information.
2	Students have followed the criteria for preparing the poster and have some correct and meaningful information. If a group project, the presentation is the result of efforts of most, if not all, of the group. This score may be given for groups in which one element (either poster or presentation) is good but the other is poor.
3	Both the poster and presentation meet most of the criteria. All members of the group participate.
4	Reserve a four for groups that meet all criteria. Exceptional efforts should be shown in either the poster or the presentation. All members of the groups participate in preparing the poster and in the presentation.

Dilution of an Acid

Introduction

What happens to the pH of an acid when you mix it with water? In this activity, you will dilute a strong acid, hydrochloric acid, several times and measure the pH of each dilution. You will be assessed on your ability to: carry out the experiment safely and properly, record and graph the change in pH with concentration of an acid, and prepare a written summary of your experiment, data, and conclusions.

Safety

Follow all lab safety guidelines presented in Lesson 1. If any acid should spill, wash the area with

lots of cold water. Dispose of excess acid by diluting with water and washing down the drain.

Procedure

1. Put on your safety goggles, lab apron, and gloves.
2. Label the cups: "10^{-2} M," "10^{-3} M," "10^{-4} M," "10^{-5} M," and "water."
3. Pour 11 mL of 10^{-2} M acid into the medicine cup labeled "10^{-2} M" and 12 mL of distilled water into the cup labeled "water."

4. Place 1 mL of the 10^{-2} M acid into the graduated cylinder as shown in the figure following.

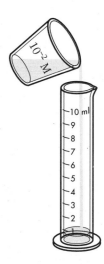

5. Fill the graduated cylinder to the 10-mL line with distilled water as shown in the figure following.

Materials

Per student
- safety goggles, lab apron, and gloves
- graph paper

Per group
- wax marking pencil
- 5 medicine cups
- 11 mL of 10^{-2} M HCl acid
- graduated cylinder, 10-mL
- 50 mL distilled water
- pH wide-range indicator solution, paper, or meter

© SIU, published by Addison Wesley Longman, Inc.

6. Pour the contents of the graduated cylinder into the cup labeled "$10^{-3}\ M$" as shown in the figure following.

Pour the $10^{-3}\ M$ solution back and forth several times to mix it thoroughly.

7. Refill the water cup with distilled water. Place 1 mL of the $10^{-3}\ M$ acid into the graduated cylinder and fill to the 10-mL line with distilled water.

8. Pour the contents of the graduated cylinder into the cup labeled "$10^{-4}\ M$." Pour the solution back and forth several times to mix it thoroughly.

9. Refill the water cup with distilled water. Place 1 mL of the $10{-}4\ M$ acid into the graduated cylinder and fill to the 10-mL line with distilled water.

10. Pour the contents of the graduated cylinder into the cup labeled "$10^{-5}\ M$." Pour the solution back and forth several times to mix it thoroughly.

11. Measure the pH of each of the four acid solutions using a wide-range pH indicator solution, pH paper, or a pH meter. *Record your results in a data table.* If using color indicator (solution or paper), record the color, estimate the pH to one-tenth of a pH unit, and record your estimate. If using a pH meter, record the pH to one-tenth of a pH unit.

12. Clean up your lab area. Dilute all your solutions with extra water and wash down the drain.

© SIU, published by Addison Wesley Longman, Inc.

DATA TABLE

Concentration [M]	$-\log[M]$	Color (ph paper or indicator solution)	pH (ph meter)

13. *Graph your results on graph paper,* recording each concentration as $-\log[M]$. For example, 10^{-2} M would equal 2.

14. *Prediction*: Based on your graph, if you made one more dilution (10^{-6} M), what would you predict the pH of the solution to be?

Writing Assignment

15. Think about the experiment you have just completed. Prepare a lab report describing your investigation to the members of your class. Be sure your report contains a description of your investigation and summarizes the results of your investigation. Write your paper using the following guidelines:

- State the problem that you investigated.

- Describe all the variables in the experiment.

- Identify the independent and dependent variables.

- Indicate the result of your experiment.

- Tell what happened during your experiment that led to this result.

- Include your data table, graph, and predictions.

- Explain how you made your prediction.

Also keep the following points in mind as you do this writing assignment:

- Take time to plan your paper before you actually write it.

- Organize your ideas carefully.

- Use language and information appropriate for the students in your class.

- Write in complete paragraphs and check your sentences, punctuation, and spelling for correctness.

© SIU, published by Addison Wesley Longman, Inc.

More Than One Answer: Evaluating Change

Introduction

In this assessment activity, you will be given a real-life scenario involving river usage and thermal pollution. You will read the scenario and determine what further information you need to know. Then your class will divide up into different special-interest groups to develop arguments for and against the proposed change. Special-interest groups will then meet all together in a town meeting to debate this proposal.

Proposed Change

A company proposes to build a manufacturing plant in your community. The proposed plant will generate a great deal of heat that must be quickly and continuously removed. The company officials want to use water from your local river as a coolant to remove the excess heat. In winter, they will use the heated water to provide hot water and heating in the plant. They will then discharge used coolant water—which is no more than 10°C above the initial water temperature of the river—back into the river.

The company engineers have calculated that the plant will need 5000 liters (1320 gallons) of river water every hour for 24 hours a day. The river near the plant site has an average flow rate of 0.50 meters per second (m/s) and averages 8.0 m in width and 3.0 m in depth. About 12 cubic meters (12 m³) of water flows past the site each second. Because 1 m³ equals 1000 L and one hour contains 3600 seconds, the river carries 43×10^6 L of water each hour. For each hour of plant operation, the heat lost by each 5000 L of hot water would be transferred to 43×10^6 L of river water. Based on these figures, the overall temperature change in the river will be very small.

The manufacturing plant will hire 50 employees to work in the plant. Company officials are anxious to minimize any environmental problems, because they would like to expand the plant within the next three years. Once the plant is expanded, the company will hire 100 additional employees. Company engineers estimate that the larger facility would require five to ten times more river water for cooling.

© SIU, published by Addison Wesley Longman, Inc.

Questions

1. What additional information would you want to know before deciding whether or not to recommend that the plant be built in your community?
2. Have environmental concerns been adequately researched to determine if problems will occur once the plant is in operation?
3. What special-interest groups would you expect to favor construction of the new plant?
4. What groups might oppose having the plant located in the community?
5. What positive and negative arguments might different groups offer?

Role-Play

Your class will role-play the parts of the following special-interest groups:

City Officials: The city has lost some industry over the past five years, but the opening of a few new businesses and the expansion of existing companies have kept employment at an even level. The city encourages new development, so city officials favor building the plant.

Plant Officials: Company engineers have studied the environmental impact of the plant on the river water and surrounding areas. When the plant is expanded in the next three years, they promise to study the impact of the expansion to ensure that the environment is not harmed. New jobs provided by the company should have a positive impact on the local economy.

Labor Representatives: Labor groups favor the proposed plant because it will increase employment opportunities in the community.

Parks and Recreation Representatives: The river is a source of recreation in the community, and parks have been built along the river in many parts of the city. Questions have been raised about changes in water levels during different seasons and whether low water levels will make the river less usable for recreation. Most recreational use occurs during the summer when the water level of the river is likely to be low.

Environmental Activists: There are concerns about whether the river should be used for cooling in the summer when rainfall is small and the river level is only about half its average depth. The flow rate is also less in the summer. The company proposes to expand the plant. Will the river suffer from thermal pollution if the plant is enlarged?

Working as a Special-Interest Group

Working together with your special-interest group, prepare for the town meeting. Determine whether your group needs additional information before deciding whether or not to support the proposed plant. Discuss what information you would like to get from other groups.

What points of view should you express to the other town members? Decide among yourselves who will ask certain questions of other groups,

© SIU, published by Addison Wesley Longman, Inc.

who will raise specific issues, and who will give particular responses to questions your group is likely to be asked. Involve each member of your group in planning and discussion.

During the town meeting, listen to other groups and share your interest group's perspective with the rest of the town. Compare your responses with those of the other groups. Do all the groups have nearly the same questions or different ones? With the information given, would you vote for or against building the plant?

Performance Criteria

Your grade for this activity will be based on your participation within your special-interest group and on your group's questions and responses at the town meeting. You are expected to:

- work cooperatively in your group, share answers, and develop questions and strategies for the town meeting.

- have everyone in your group have a role in the town meeting. Questions that are asked, issues to be raised, and responses should be divided among the members of the group.

- maintain the interests of the group you represent, even if you personally disagree with them.

- listen to the views of the other groups, respect different points of view, and make rational responses.

© SIU, published by Addison Wesley Longman, Inc.

The Turbidity of Milk

Introduction

In this assessment activity, you will model how a Jackson Candle Turbidimeter works, using a black "X" instead of a candle. You will be assessed on your ability to carry out the experiment safely and properly, to record and graph data, and to prepare a written summary of your experiment, data, and conclusions.

Safety

Follow all laboratory safety guidelines presented in Lesson 1. The glass cylinder used in this activity may be somewhat unstable, so take care pouring liquids into it. If the cylinder accidentally breaks, do not pick up the broken pieces with your bare hands. Place the broken glass in a special container provided by your teacher.

All the samples can be discarded in a sink with lukewarm water. Rinse the containers and pipettes with lukewarm to cold water (rather than hot water) so that the milk does not congeal and adhere to surfaces.

Procedure

1. Put on your safety goggles, lab apron, and gloves.
2. Make an "X" on the white card with the permanent marker. Make the "X" less than 2.5 cm on a side so that it can be covered by the glass cylinder or viewing tube. Place the card beneath the viewing tube so that the "X" is centered within the walls of the cylinder as shown in the accompanying figure.

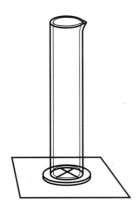

3. Using the dropping pipette, transfer 20 drops of milk to the graduated cylinder, as shown in the figure following.

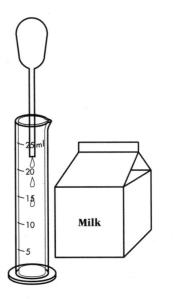

Materials

Per student
- safety goggles, lab apron, and gloves
- graph paper

Per group
- white card (3" × 5")
- permanent marker
- graduated cylinder, 25-mL

- 7 pipettes or droppers (3 if rinsed between uses)
- glass cylinder, 2.5-cm diameter × 9.5-cm tall
- metric ruler
- beaker
- 125 mL water
- 20 mL milk, homogenized

© SIU, published by Addison Wesley Longman, Inc.

4. Fill the graduated cylinder with water to the 25-mL level, using a second pipette to add water until the meniscus falls exactly on the 25-mL line, as shown in the figure following.

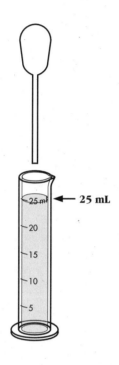

5. With a third pipette, stir the solution in the graduated cylinder. Add solution to the viewing tube just to the height at

which you can no longer see the "X" when you look through the top of the tube, as shown in the figure following. Measure the height of the solution in the tube and record your result in your data table.

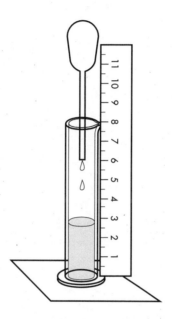

6. Repeat Steps 4 through 6 four more times, starting with 40 drops of milk for Trial 2, 60 drops for Trial 3, 80 drops for Trial 4, and 100 drops for

Trial 5. Record each result in your data table. Use a clean pipette for each trial, or rinse and drain your pipettes after each trial.

7. If instructed by your teacher, repeat Steps 4–7 again, entering your data in the table under "Series 2." Average the results for Series 1 and Series 2.

8. Pour all the solutions down the sink and rinse all the equipment with lukewarm water. Air-dry the pipettes, graduated cylinder, and viewing tube.

© SIU, published by Addison Wesley Longman, Inc.

The Turbidity of Milk

DATA TABLE

Trial	Drops of Milk	Series 1 Height (cm)	Series 2 Height (cm)	Average Height (cm)
1				
2				
3				
4				
5				

9. Graph your results on graph paper.

10. Prediction: Based on your graph, if you started with 50 drops of milk, at what height do you think the "X" would disappear from view?

Writing Assignment

11. Think about the experiment that you have just completed. Prepare a lab report describing your investigation to the members of your class. Be sure your report contains a description of your investigation and summarizes the results of your investigation. Write your paper using the following guidelines:

   - State the problem that you investigated.

   - Describe all the variables in the experiment.

   - Identify the independent and dependent variables.

   - Indicate the result of your experiment.

   - Tell what happened during your experiment that led to this result.

   - Include your data table, graph, and prediction.

   - Explain how you made your prediction.

   Also keep the following points in mind as you do this writing assignment:

   - Take time to plan your paper before you actually write it.

   - Organize your ideas carefully.

   - Use language and information appropriate for the students in your class.

   - Write in complete paragraphs and check your sentences, punctuation, and spelling for correctness.

© SIU, published by Addison Wesley Longman, Inc.

How Much Oxygen in the Fish Tanks?

Introduction

In this assessment activity, you will set up four different aquariums. Then you will predict their dissolved oxygen rankings—from the highest level of dissolved oxygen to the lowest level. You will compare your predicted rankings with the actual dissolved oxygen levels in each aquarium. Finally, you will apply to a local river or stream what you learned during the aquarium activity.

Safety

Students should follow all laboratory safety guidelines presented in Lesson 1, including wearing safety goggles and gloves when performing the dissolved oxygen tests. All liquid wastes from the dissolved oxygen tests should be poured into a waste container for evaporation and proper disposal.

Procedure

Part A. Setting Up the Fish Tanks (Two Days Before Testing for Dissolved Oxygen)

1. Label the aquariums or bowls "Tank 1," "Tank 2," "Tank 3," and "Tank 4." Leave Tank 1 empty until the day of testing.
2. Fill Tank 2 with water from the faucet and leave undisturbed for two days.
3. Fill Tank 3 with water from the faucet and fit it with an aquarium aerator. Aerate Tank 3 for two days before testing.
4. Fill Tank 4 with water from the faucet and fit it with an aquarium aerator, heater, and thermometer. Heat the water to 24°C (75°F). Maintain at a constant temperature of 24°C and aerate for two days. If your lab is near 24°C, increase the temperature for Tank 4 to at least 3°C above room temperature.

5. Predict what the dissolved oxygen rankings of the tanks will be in two days. Rank them from highest level (mg/L) of dissolved oxygen to lowest level, using a table such as the following:

Highest   _____
Second   _____
Third   _____
Lowest   _____

6. *Paragraph one: Prediction*
   In a short paragraph, explain the criteria you used to rank the tanks and why you expect the tanks to be in the predicted order.

Part B. Testing the DO of the Water in the Tanks (At Least Two Days After Part A)

7. After Tanks 2, 3, and 4 have been allowed to sit undisturbed for at least two days, fill the empty tank (Tank 1) with water freshly drawn from the faucet.
8. If your teacher assigns you or your team to test the DO of the tanks, put on your safety goggles and gloves. Take a water sample from each tank and use the dissolved oxygen test kit to determine the oxygen level (mg/L). Record your data in the Data Table.
9. Clean up your lab area, placing all liquid wastes from the oxygen test kit into the waste container.

Materials

Per student doing dissolved oxygen test
- safety goggles, lab apron, and gloves

Per class
- 4 aquariums or large bowls
- 2 aquarium aerators

- aquarium heater
- Celsius thermometer
- 1–4 dissolved oxygen (DO) bottles with stoppers
- dissolved oxygen test kit
- waste container

© SIU, published by Addison Wesley Longman, Inc.

Observations

DATA TABLE

Tank Number	Dissolved Oxygen (mg/L)
1	
2	
3	
4	

Analyses and Conclusions

1. Rank the tanks from highest to lowest in dissolved oxygen.

   Highest   Second   Third   Lowest

   _____   _____   _____   _____

2. *Paragraph two: Analysis* Compare your predicted rankings with the actual rankings. Write a paragraph explaining which rankings agreed with your predictions and which did not agree and why.

3. *Paragraph three: Application* Write a paragraph applying the results of this assessment activity to the levels of dissolved oxygen that you might expect to find in a local stream or river under various conditions.

Performance Criteria

Your grade for this activity will be based on the three paragraphs you write expressing your predictions, analysis, and application of your measurement of dissolved oxygen in the fish tanks. You are expected to:

- Base your predictions on observations and readings.

- Offer reasonable explanations for your predictions.

- Give explanations for comparisons of predictions with measured results, explaining both predictions that were correct and those that were not.

- Relate the significance of the conditions you observed in the fish tanks to a stream or river at various points in its path and under various weather conditions.

© SIU, published by Addison Wesley Longman, Inc.

Phosphates in Detergents

Introduction

In this assessment activity, you will select a topic relating to the phosphate content of detergents. Then you will research the topic and present your findings in a written or an oral report. In doing this task, you should demonstrate an understanding of phosphates and their impact on the environment. You also will demonstrate your library research and communication skills.

Procedure

1. Identify at least three commercially available detergents or cleansers and determine the phosphorus content by percent weight from the package label or by contacting the manufacturer. Try to identify at least one product that does contain phosphates. For each product, list brand name, manufacturer, and percent phosphorus.
2. Select a topic related to phosphates, detergents, and water quality. Thoroughly research this topic by looking in the library, contacting the manufacturer(s), contacting your local or state Environmental Protection Agency, and using other resources suggested by your teacher. Prepare a bibliographic listing of these resources and references.
3. Based on your research and on your work in *Rivers Chemistry*, prepare a written or an oral report on your topic. Follow report criteria provided by your teacher. Be sure to include visual aids (graphs and diagrams) and a list of your sources of information.

Possible Topics for Study

The following list of possible research topics for this assessment is not comprehensive, but it may help you identify and focus your topic.

- Alternatives to Phosphates in Detergents and How They Work
  (Hint: You can begin to answer this question by trying to find information about biodegradable cleaners, such as borax or washing soda—also called sodium carbonate. Key words include: *surfactants, brighteners, zeolites, oxylicates,* and *bleaches.*)

© SIU, published by Addison Wesley Longman, Inc.

- A Comparison of the Cleaning Ability of Phosphate and Phosphate-Free Detergents

- Variations in Phosphate Levels Among Laundry Detergents, Liquid Dishwashing Detergents, Automatic Dishwashing Detergents, and Industrial Detergents (You could rank these products from environmentally friendly to environmentally unfriendly.)

- The Effects of State Legislation Limiting Phosphates in Detergents (You could research which states have passed such legislation and the impact of this legislation on cultural eutrophication.)

- The Pros and Cons of Phosphate Bans

- Why Detergent Manufacturers Oppose Phosphate Bans

- Assessing the Role of Phosphate Detergents in Eutrophication

Performance Criteria

- Check a variety of cleaning agents, and list different kinds. Your list should include at least one phosphate-containing product.

- In research for your report, use more than one reference and resource. Your reference and resource listings are complete and accurate.

- Follow report criteria provided by your teacher, including good content, organization, and visual aids.

© SIU, published by Addison Wesley Longman, Inc.

Telecommunications

Introduction

In this project, you will use the information acquired during your study of water quality to analyze and evaluate a waterway. You will utilize a telecommunications system to collect data about water-quality tests conducted by other students along rivers and streams. You will select a particular topic relating to such data. You will prepare tables and graphs of your data and collect maps and additional information from the library. Finally, you will interpret all this information and organize and write a paper about your findings. You may also work in groups to develop a poster presentation to share the data and information you collect.

Materials

Per group
- computer
- telecommunications system
- data from a Rivers bulletin board
- maps of rivers, streams, and watersheds being studied
- graph paper

Optional
- spreadsheet program for sorting and managing data

Procedure

1. Based on your knowledge of the variables that determine water quality, select as a group a river, stream, or other geographic area as the focus of your study. Access the database to make sure the water system chosen has a minimum of five test sites with data.
2. Based on your knowledge of available data, select one of the water-quality tests to investigate on this river or stream.
3. Choose the conditions to consider in your analysis, such as season of the year, weather conditions, or temperature. Specify your individual research topic.
4. Retrieve test results for the water system from the Rivers bulletin board. Check the amount of data available. If too little or too much information is available, modify the amount by changing the size of the system you are studying or limiting the time period for which you are collecting data. Average the data from one site that falls within your specified time periods and conditions.
5. Locate the test sites on maps and find out how the land is being used near each site. Note what communities, industrial areas, farming areas, or other land uses are nearby. To find this information, you may need to do research at a local library or refer to a geography textbook.
6. Devise a scheme for graphing your test data, comparing test results to site location and land use. Consider whether your data should be represented by a line, point, bar, or pie graph.
7. Analyze your results, and prepare a presentation of your findings. In your presentation, answer the following questions:

   - Using the Q-value for your test, what is the water quality for the water system you have chosen?

   - What natural factors affect this water quality?

   - What human factors affect this water quality?

   - How does land use affect this water quality?

   - What might be done to improve or maintain water quality for your water system?

© SIU, published by Addison Wesley Longman, Inc.

Performance Criteria

A written report should:

- demonstrate that you can access data electronically

- show that you understand the water-quality parameter reviewed

- show that you have researched and performed critical thinking in evaluating the relationship between land use and water quality

- include suggestions for improving or maintaining the water quality

- reference resources used in preparing the report

A group poster presentation should:

- represent the efforts of everyone in the group

- have a poster with a title large enough to be easily read; a map of the geographic area; data tables, charts, and graphs showing different tests; and narrative discussing the purpose, method, and results of the analysis

- include an oral presentation in which everyone in the group participates. The presentation should be well-organized and the poster used as a visual aid.

- include an opportunity for the audience to ask questions; all members of the group should respond to questions, especially those about their individual areas.

© SIU, published by Addison Wesley Longman, Inc.

Answers and Solutions for Student Information and Student Activity Sheets

Lesson 1: Answer to Questions

Student Information 1.1
Questions

1. Answers will vary: "Old Man River," "The Blue Danube," and so forth.
2. Answers will vary: *The Old Man and the Sea, On Walden Pond,* and so forth.

Student Information 1.2
Questions

1. Answers will vary but may include: She took off her glasses before the other students had finished (Rule 4); she picked up a chemical with her hand (Rule 5); she placed a chemical in acid (Rule 1); she wore sandals (Rule 6); she poured acid contents down drain (Rule 14); she spilled acid on the floor (Rule 13); she placed excess into original bottle (Rule 15); she did not clean her lab area (Rule 16).

2. Answers will vary but may include: An accident nearby (acid spill, broken glass, etc.) could have struck her eyes; the chemical could have harmed her; an explosion could have resulted or toxic fumes could have formed; her feet could have been harmed; the acid contents could be harmful to drains and other sewage facilities; the spilled acid could have damaged the floor, or another student could have stepped in it; she could have contaminated the bottle contents; a student using the lab area after she left could have been harmed by chemicals she might have left; she might be affected later by chemicals with which she had come in contact.

3. Answers will vary but may include: Jack did not stay with the group (Rule 2); he did not stay within the designated area (Rule 1); he climbed a fence (Rule 1).

4. Answers will vary but may include: He could have been hurt and no one known where he was; the glittering metal object might not have been a silver dollar and he could have been injured when he picked it up.

Student Information 1.3
Questions

1. An acid wash solution is prepared by adding concentrated HCl acid (12 M) to an equal volume of distilled water.
2. a. Glassware is acid washed to remove any matter that might have been left behind by soap and water. b. The distill wash removes any remaining acid wash solution.

3. If the bottom is disturbed, silt and mud may get inside the sampling bottle and, if so, the sample would not be representative of the water at the site.

4. The first sample is released so that the inside of the bottle will be thoroughly wet with river or stream water. This will help insure more accurate results.

5. The bottle is lowered upside down so that a minimum amount of surface water will be obtained.

6. Gloves should be worn to protect hands from possible hazards in the water and to prevent contamination of the sample by the individual's hands.

Student Information 1.4
Questions

1. Weighting factor is the decimal equivalent of the percent of the WQI for a particular test.

2. The Q-value is used to convert the units of each of the nine tests into a common unit (percent) so the results of the test can be added together.

3. The WQI is obtained by adding the total percent of the nine tests.

4.

Test	Units	Q-value (%)	Weighting Factor	Total (%)
1. Dissolved oxygen	46% Sat	38	0.17	**6.5**
2. Fecal coliform	16,000 colonies/100 mL	8.0	0.16	**1.3**
3. pH	7.7 units	91	0.11	**10.0**
4. BOD	4.39 mg/L	63	0.11	**6.9**
5. Temperature change	0.1°C	93	0.10	**9.3**
6. Phosphate	0.63 mg/L	51	0.10	**5.1**
7. Nitrate	10.37 mg/L	48	0.10	**4.8**
8. Turbidity	0.30 meters	5.0	0.08	**0.4**
9. Total solids	475 mg/L	36	0.07	**2.5**

WQI = **46.8%**

Quality of Water = **bad**

5. Q-value = approximately 79%
   Total % = 5.5

Student Information 1.5
Problems (for Percent Error)

1. Mean = $\dfrac{0.8 \text{ mg/L} + 0.8 \text{ mg/L} + 1.0 \text{ mg/L} + 1.0 \text{ mg/L}}{4} = \dfrac{3.6 \text{ mg/L}}{4} = 0.9 \text{ mg/L}$

Percent Error = $\dfrac{|1.0\ \text{mg/L} - 0.9\ \text{mg/L}|}{1.0\ \text{mg/L}} \times 100\% =$ **10%**

2. Mean = $\dfrac{4.8\ \text{mg/L} + 5.1\ \text{mg/L} + 5.4\text{mg/L}}{3} = \dfrac{15.3\ \text{mg/L}}{3} = 5.1\ \text{mg/L}$

Percent error = $\dfrac{|5.0\ \text{mg/L} - 5.1\ \text{mg/L}|}{5.0\ \text{mg/L}} \times 100\% =$ **2.0%**

Problems (for Standard Deviation)

1. a. Mean = $\dfrac{(950 + 760 + 1213 + 894 + 1116)\ \text{colonies/100 mL}}{5} =$ **987 colonies/100 mL**

b. $d_1 = |950 - 987| = 37$
$d_2 = |760 - 987| = 227$
$d_3 = |1213 - 987| = 226$
$d_4 = |894 - 987| = 93$
$d_5 = |1116 - 987| = 129$

$(37)^2 = 1{,}369$
$(227)^2 = 51{,}529$
$(226)^2 = 51{,}076$
$(93)^2 = 8{,}649$
$(129)^2 = 16{,}641$
$\text{sum}\quad 129{,}264$

$\dfrac{\sqrt{129{,}264}}{(5-1)} =$ **± 180 colonies/100 mL**

c. Reported value = **987 ± 180 colonies/100 mL**

2. a. Mean = $\dfrac{(18.6 + 17.5 + 19.2)\ \text{mg/L}}{3} =$ **18.4 mg/L**

b. $d_1 = |18.6 - 18.4| = 0.2$
$d_2 = |17.5 - 18.4| = 0.9$
$d_3 = |19.2 - 18.4| = 0.8$

$(0.2)^2 = 0.04$
$(0.9)^2 = 0.81$
$(0.8)^2 = 0.64$
$\text{sum} = 1.49$

$\dfrac{\sqrt{1.49}}{(3-1)} =$ **± 0.9 mg/L**

c. Reported value = **18.4 ± 0.9 mg/L**

Student Information 1.6
Problems

1. Range = 214 − 203 = 11 mg/L

(214 − 207) mg/L = 7 mg/L

Calculated quotient = $\frac{7 \text{ mg/L}}{11 \text{ mg/L}}$ = 0.64

Tabulated quotient from Figure 1 = 0.76

0.64 < 0.76; therefore, **214 mg/L should not be rejected.**

2. a. Range = 2520 − 810 = 1710

    2520 − 900 = 1620

    Calculated quotient = $\frac{1620}{1710}$ = 0.95

    0.95 > 0.94; therefore, **2520 mg/L should be rejected.**

    b. 900 − 810 = 90

    Calculated quotient = $\frac{90}{1710}$ = 0.05

    0.05 < 0.94; therefore, **810 mg/L should not be rejected.**

3. 26°C 27°C 28°C 28°C 29°C 31°C

    a. Range = 31°C − 26°C = 5°C

    31°C − 29°C = 2°C

    Calculated quotient = $\frac{2°C}{5°C}$ = 0.4

    0.4 < 0.56; therefore, **31°C should not be rejected.**

    b. 27°C − 26°C = 1°C

    Calculated quotient = $\frac{1°C}{5°C}$ = 0.2

    0.2 < 0.56; therefore, **26°C should not be rejected.**

Lesson 2: Answers to Questions

Student Information 2.1
Questions

1. Two definitions are (1) an acid is a substance that releases hydronium ions in water solution; and (2) an acid is a substance that reacts with a base to produce a salt and water.

2. Most acids have a sour taste.

3. Two definitions of a base are (1) a base is a substance that yields hydroxide ions in water solution; and (2) a base is a substance that accepts hydronium ions.

4. Most bases feel slippery to the touch and taste bitter.

5. A neutralization reaction is the process of an acid reacting with a base to produce a salt and water.

6. Answers will vary but may include: Hydrochloric acid reacts with sodium hydroxide to produce sodium chloride and water; sulfuric acid reacts with sodium hydroxide to produce sodium sulfate and water.

Student Information 2.2
Questions

1. Answers will vary somewhat but may include: Higher pH numbers indicate a substance is more basic, while lower number means it is more acidic. Another answer might be: Numbers on the pH scale are divided into three categories—numbers less than 7 indicate an acid; numbers greater than

7 indicate a base; the number 7 indicates a neutral substance, such as pure water.

2. Any substance that has a pH less than 7 is an acid.

3. Any substance that has a pH greater than 7 is a base.

4. A neutral liquid has a pH of 7.

5. One "drawback" of litmus paper is that litmus paper can indicate only if a substance is an acid, a base, or neutral. It doesn't yield pH values.

6. A buffer is a substance capable of maintaining a constant pH even when small amounts of acid or base are added.

7. a. Liquid B has more hydronium ions.

   b. Liquid B is more acidic.

8. Liquid B is more basic.

Student Activity 2.3
Analyses and Conclusions

1. Answers will vary, but acidic materials should include vinegar, noncola drinks, apple juice, and grapefruit juice. Most of the acidic materials are food products and some have a sour taste.

2. Answers will vary, but basic materials should include ammonia cleaner, dish detergent, liquid antacid, and tap water. Some of the materials are cleaning agents and have a slippery feeling. Dish detergents vary and may test acidic, basic, or neutral.

3. Of all the materials tested, distilled water should measure nearest neutral.

4. Answers will vary.

5. Answers will vary. Either method should correctly identify acids and bases.

6. Results of different groups should be the same. Most discrepancies should occur for liquids having a pH close to 7.

7. Answers will vary. Variations in the method of wetting the pH paper, the amount of red cabbage juice added, and contamination of glassware, samples, or indicator solutions could cause discrepancies.

Critical Thinking Questions

1. Baking soda is a base.

2. The pH would increase.

3. Window cleaner is a base, because the cleaning items were bases. Orange juice is an acid, because apple juice was an acid. Dill pickles are acidic, because vinegar was an acid. Shampoo is a base because the cleaning items were bases.

Student Information 2.4
Questions

1. It could be expected that the pH of rivers and streams flowing through the area would be 7. Even though acid rain would be produced due to the large amount of rainfall and the oxides of sulfur and nitrogen, the limestone cliffs would neutralize the acid.

2. A waterway could have a low pH if large amounts of acids were dumped into the waterway. It could also have a low pH if it receives a large amount of acid rain that is not neutralized by bases in or around the waterway.

Lesson 3: Answers to Questions

Student Information 3.1
Questions

1. Answers will vary. Typical answer: Four natural processes that may cause temperature change in a river or stream are: (1) a shift in the temperature of water flowing into a river or stream; (2) the amount of sunlight a river or stream receives; (3) the flow rate of a river or stream; and (4) a shift in the amount of water in the waterway.

2. If a power plant or industry places high-temperature water into a waterway, thermal pollution can occur.

3. Benefits of dams and other structures such as dikes and agricultural diversions include providing needed water for river traffic, irrigation, and hydroelectric power production. Holding areas can be used to provide water during dry seasons. Negative aspects include reducing flow rate (which increases temperature) and disrupting natural wetlands and fish migration.

4. Some negative ecological effects of thermal pollution are a decrease in dissolved oxygen and possible overpopulation of microorganisms.

5. Excess thermal energy can help warm water and enhance commercial farming such as catfish and oyster.

Student Information 3.2
Questions

1. To determine temperature change, measure the temperature at two different sites 1.6 kilometers apart and then subtract one measurement from the other.

2. Mercury-filled thermometers are not recommended because, if this kind of thermometer breaks, the exposed mercury it contains can escape into the water, with toxic effects on humans and animals.

3. In order to determine flow rate, measure the time a floating object requires in order to travel a known distance between two locations. To compute the flow rate, divide the distance by the time.

Student Activity 3.3
Analyses and Conclusions

1. Answers will vary.

2. Answers will vary.

3. Answers will vary. If downstream temperature is higher than upstream temperature, then students may suggest possible sources of thermal pollution. If downstream temperature is lower than upstream temperature, then perhaps an underground spring or a colder tributary is between the two locations.

4. Answers will vary. Flow rate is usually greater in the middle of a waterway than near the shore if the channel is straight, especially if dikes, rock piles, or a shallow shore are present.

Critical Thinking Questions

1. a. $\Delta T = 22.3°C - 25.8°C = -3.5°C$; Q-value is approximately 69%
   b. 69% = medium. c. Two possible explanations are (1) the two smaller streams might lower the temperature and (2) as the river flows downstream, it will lose some of its heat to its surroundings. (Note: The farms would not be expected to lower the water temperature.)

Lesson 4: Answers to Questions

Student Information 4.1
Questions

1. Turbidity refers to how clear or cloudy water appears.
2. Answers will vary.
3. High turbidity may affect the amount of sunlight reaching aquatic plants. This would decrease the amount of dissolvable oxygen that plants produce. Also, silt in waterways with high turbidity may settle to the bottom and cover bottom-dwelling species such as clams.
4. One natural cause of increased turbidity is forest fires. One human-related cause of increased turbidity is poor farming techniques.

Student Information 4.2
Questions

1. Solid matter reduces the amount of light transmitted through water; all devices that measure turbidity actually measure light transmission.

Student Information 4.3
Questions

1. Floc is a gelatinous or fluffy solid that sinks to the bottom of a holding area. It captures suspended matter.
2. Sedimentation refers to the natural process of suspended matter in water settling to the bottom, whereas flocculation refers to the addition of chemicals that help suspended matter in water settle to the bottom.

Student Activity 4.4
Analyses and Conclusions

1. Answers will vary. Usually iron (II) chloride treatment produces the clearest water.
2. Allowing the samples to sit longer usually results in more solids settling to the bottom, with the water becoming less turbid.

Critical Thinking Questions

1. Answers will depend upon the results of the experiment. Students should consider both the time for the sample to settle and the final clarity of the sample in their answer. If available, provide students with the costs of the chemicals used, so that students can make a cost comparison.
2. Dangerous dissolved materials or microscopic organisms may be present, but not detectable visually in the water.
3. Flocculating agents would not be used in an aquatic environment because the gelatinous and fluffy solids would sink to the bottom and increase the

amount of matter covering bottom dwellers. Also, the flocculating agents may be harmful to aquatic species.

Student Activity 4.5
Analyses and Conclusions

1. Answers will vary.
2. Answers will vary.
3. Answers will vary. Generally, students should describe ways to solve any problems cited in their responses to Question 2.

Critical Thinking Questions

1. If the site is very turbid, plants may not grow very well, because they will have reduced light. The turbid water also may be unsuitable for animal life, because of the reduced supply of plants for food. Silt, settling to the bottom of the river or stream, may cover the natural habitat for organisms living on the bottom or may cover the eggs of aquatic organisms, disrupting the life cycle.
2. Answers will vary but usually would include: When rainfall is great, erosion increases and so would turbidity. When rainfall is low or absent, erosion decreases, and so would turbidity.

Lesson 5: Answers to Questions

Student Information 5.1
Questions

1. Turbidity refers just to matter that is suspended in water, whereas total solids refers both to matter suspended in water and to matter dissolved in water.
2. A container of known mass is filled with a known volume of river or stream water. The water is allowed to evaporate, leaving the total solids in the container. The mass of the container with the total solids is found. The mass of the container is subtracted from the second measurement of mass, yielding the mass of total solids per original known volume of the river water.
3. Total solids are measured in milligrams per liter (mg/L).
4. Drinking water should have no more than 0.5 mg/L of total solids.

Problems

1. 0.75 grams/L = 750 mg/L = 750 ppm
2. Total solids = 0.65 g = 650 mg; volume of H_2O = 0.80 L
   Total solids = $\frac{650 \text{ mg}}{0.80 \text{ L}}$ = 812.5 mg/L rounds to 810 mg/L
   810 mg/L = 810 ppm

Student Information 5.2
Questions

1. Hard water contains magnesium, calcium, and iron. Soft water has little or no magnesium, calcium, or iron.
2. Over a long period of time, limestone ($CaCO_3$) dissolved in water, forming tunnels in the rock, which became the caves. As the water receded, some limestone remained, as stalactites and stalagmites.

3. Three practical problems that may be caused by hard water are: (1) Hard water leaves deposits in appliances such as steam irons; (2) Hard water requires more soap for cleaning; and (3) Hard water leaves a "scum" on clothes and bathtubs.

4. a. The solvent is tea; the solute is sugar.

   b. Add a small amount of solute; if it dissolves, the solution was unsaturated. If it does not dissolve, the solution is saturated.

   c. Obtain a known volume of tea. While maintaining constant temperature, add small amounts of sugar until a saturated solution is produced. Add a small amount of sugar; it will sink to the bottom and not dissolve. Slowly allow the temperature to increase, and observe whether the undissolved sugar dissolves. If it does, then the increased temperature caused the original undissolved sugar to dissolve.

5. Limestone and marble contain $CaCO_3$. $CaCO_3$ will dissolve in acid rain, thereby causing the structures to disintegrate. The acid in the acid rain reacts with the limestone or marble, which are basic, to form water and a salt. This removes limestone or marble from the structure, eroding it over time.

Student Activity 5.3
Analyses and Conclusions

1. Answers will vary.

2. Answers will vary. If the water is hard, then it may have an undesirable taste, leave deposits in water pipes, damage steam irons, and make cleaning clothes more expensive. Soft water causes few or no problems.

Critical Thinking Questions

1. Answers will vary. One reason a person would want to know if tap water is soft or hard is to be better prepared for doing laundry and other cleaning activities.

2. This activity analyzed water for calcium only. Water may contain other metal ions, such as magnesium and iron, as well. Therefore, the results of this test may not reflect the total amount of ions.

Student Activity 5.4
Analyses and Conclusions

1. Answers will vary.

2. Answers will vary.

3. Answers will vary, but students should mention factors such as rock formations; ditches or drains that empty into the waterway; bare, eroded soil; farms, homes or industries; trees and plants; decomposing matter.

4. If the level of total solids is unsatisfactory, efforts should be made to reduce the amount of inorganic and organic matter that enters the water, such as reducing erosion and runoff.

Critical Thinking Questions

1. Answers will vary, but if the level of total solids is too high, it can be an indicator of pollution. In this case, the diversity of species will probably be less than normal and there may be signs of death of aquatic species that cannot tolerate high levels of total solids.

2. Answers will vary, but during periods of heavy rainfall or melting snow, erosion and runoff may greatly increase the level of total solids in the water. In the fall, in places where waterways are heavily shaded by deciduous trees, the water will contain large amounts of leafy matter.

3. Where turbidity is high, totals solids are usually high. A river may have a low turbidity level, however, and still contain significant amounts of dissolved solids.

4. Higher temperatures would increase the rate of decay of organic matter and increase the solubilities of certain inorganic chemicals, raising the amount of total solids in the water. Water with a low pH would dissolve more chemicals, increasing the amount of dissolved matter. At the same time, a low pH would kill off many life-forms, ultimately reducing the amount of organic matter in the water.

Lesson 6: Answers to Questions

Student Information 6.1
Questions

1. Dissolved oxygen refers to the amount of oxygen gas (measured in mg) that is dissolved in river water (measured in L).

2. The amount of gas soluble in a liquid decreases as the temperature increases, and the amount of gas soluble in a liquid increases as the temperature decreases (inverse proportion).

3. The amount of gas soluble in a liquid increases as the air pressure increases, and the amount of gas soluble in a liquid decreases as the air pressure decreases (direct proportion).

4. The amount of dissolved oxygen can be decreased when aquatic plants die and decay.

5. Daily variations in dissolved oxygen are common because the amount of sunlight received by the water varies. In bright sunlight, the water temperature increases, which decreases the dissolved oxygen. At night, the water temperature decreases, so dissolved oxygen increases. If plants are present, oxygen is produced during the day, increasing the available oxygen, and used at night, decreasing the dissolved oxygen. Seasonal variations in dissolved oxygen are common because of changes in temperature.

6. Answers will vary but may include: To insure that water has a sufficient amount of dissolved oxygen, people should not dump decayable matter such as leaves and grass clippings into the waterway; waste-disposable plants should treat sewage before it is placed in the river; and thermal pollution should be minimized.

Student Activity 6.2
Analyses and Conclusions

1. The can weighed less because the carbon dioxide gas that was originally dissolved escaped out of the liquid as the pressure decreased to atmospheric pressure over the 15-minute time period.

2. If the can sat overnight, carbon dioxide gas would escape until the pressure became constant at atmospheric pressure. At that point, any carbon dioxide that was still dissolved would remain dissolved; the weight of the can would stabilize.

3. As the temperature increased, the mass of the can decreased because more dissolved carbon dioxide was converted to a gas and escaped.

Critical Thinking Questions

1. As the temperature in the car trunk increased, carbon dioxide that was dissolved inside the cans came out of the liquid. Because the can was sealed, the carbon dioxide could not escape out of the can; pressure inside the can increased until it became so great that it ruptured the can.

2. On a hot summer day, water near the surface has less dissolved oxygen than water several meters below. In order to have a more comfortable oxygen supply, most of the fish went to the deeper water. Because Marita was fishing in deeper water, she had better chances of catching fish than did Joe.

Student Activity 6.3
Analyses and Conclusions

1. Answers will vary.

2. Answers will vary.

3. Answers will vary. Dissolved oxygen would be added by aquatic green plants and by physical aeration processes, such as wave action and the rippling of the water over boulders and rocks. Oxygen would be removed if there is heat pollution from a power plant or if the water is very shallow and sluggish and air temperatures are high.

4. Answers will vary. Increasing the depth and current by clearing away debris might improve the level of dissolved oxygen. Controlling the temperature of any water that enters the river or stream could also improve oxygen levels.

Critical Thinking Questions

1. If the water has a sufficient amount of dissolved oxygen, then it should be able to sustain a diversity of aquatic life. If life in the river is diverse and abundant, it will provide an abundant food supply for shore animals, such as birds, that feed on aquatic animals and plants. Thus, a healthy river will support a greater variety of life near the river.

2. During hot summer months, the amount of dissolved oxygen will be less because of the higher water temperatures. During the colder winter months, the amount of dissolved oxygen will be greater because of the lower water temperatures.

3. Temperature: As the temperature of the river increases, the amount of dissolved oxygen decreases. Turbidity: High turbidity will prevent sunlight from reaching green aquatic plants, preventing photosynthesis and the release of oxygen.

4. A river or stream likely to support a population of brook trout would have a relatively high level of dissolved oxygen; therefore, it would probably be cool, with some deep pools.

Lesson 7: Answers to Questions

Student Information 7.1
Questions

1. Biochemical oxygen demand is a bioassay because it does not directly measure the amount of matter in water; it measures the effect of that matter on organisms living in the water.

2. In order to determine how much dissolved oxygen is consumed by the microorganisms in the sample, the organisms must have sufficient time to consume a large enough quantity of dissolved oxygen to be measurable with the equipment used.

3. A low biochemical oxygen demand is more desirable because if the biochemical oxygen demand is low, then the amount of organic matter in the water is low.

4. Natural factors that cause biochemical oxygen demand to be high include: a large amount of organic matter, such as decaying plants; or naturally stagnant water, such as a bog or pond. Human factors that cause biochemical oxygen demand value to be high include large amounts of organic matter, such as untreated sewage or organic industrial waste dumped in the waterway.

5. The biochemical oxygen demand of a river or stream could be improved by: properly treating sewage before placing it in the waterway; reducing agricultural waste; and by individuals refraining from dumping organic matter, such as raked leaves or grass clippings, in the water.

Student Activity 7.2
Analyses and Conclusions

1. Answers will vary.
2. Answers will vary.
3. Answers will vary.

Critical Thinking Questions

1. A high BOD indicates a large amount of organic matter and a large population of microorganisms. As the microorganisms feed on the organic matter, the level of dissolved oxygen in the water will decrease, making it difficult for many species of fish to survive. Other species that live near the river or stream also may be adversely affected by a high BOD if they drink the water and ingest disease-causing microorganisms.

2. During the fall, the river may have more organic matter due to falling leaves. During the summer, water temperatures are higher. Both of these factors will produce a larger population of microorganisms, causing the BOD level to be higher than it would be in the winter.

3. If the temperature is high, then anaerobic organisms increase in population. This increase in population would decrease the amount of dissolved oxygen, thus producing a high biochemical oxygen demand. High turbidity could indicate the presence of a large amount of organic matter. As the organic matter decays, the amount of dissolved oxygen is reduced, thus producing a high biochemical oxygen demand.

Answers and Solutions

Lesson 8: Answer to Questions

Student Information 8.1
Questions

1. Eutrophication refers to an imbalance between plants and animals due to the overgrowth of plant life. Cultural eutrophication refers to eutrophication in which the overgrowth of plant life is due to human influences such as large amounts of introduced phosphates.

2. Phosphate pollution can occur (1) when people use phosphate-containing detergents and allow the detergents to enter a waterway and (2) when phosphate-containing fertilizers are used in a way that allows the fertilizer not used by plants to enter a waterway.

3. To prevent cultural eutrophication (1) use nonphosphate detergents and (2) use conservative amounts of phosphate-containing fertilizers.

Student Activity 8.2
Analyses and Conclusions

1. Answers will vary.

Critical Thinking Question

1. Because the activity uses a phosphate standard solution, the waste should not be poured down the drain, because if it ended up in a waterway, it would be adding to contamination of the waterway with phosphates.

Student Activity 8.3
Analyses and Conclusions

1. Answers will vary.

2. Answers will vary. Detergents and fertilizers used in residential areas may add excess phosphates to waterways. Homes connected with septic tanks rather than city sewers may also be sources of phosphates. Farms, recreational facilities, businesses, and industries can release phosphates into the environment. The general landscape (hills versus flatland, evidence of erosion, floodplains, and types of vegetation) also may affect the amount of phosphates that enter waterways due to runoff.

3. Answers will vary. Phosphate levels may be low, indicating that no change is necessary. If there are high levels of phosphates, students should focus on possible sources and ways to reduce the amounts of phosphate that are released into the environment.

Critical Thinking Questions

1. Answers will vary.

2. If phosphate levels are high, they may induce rapid eutrophication.
   If phosphate levels are low, they may inhibit the growth of aquatic vegetation.

3. Answers will vary. Phosphate levels will vary with the season and with weather conditions. Heavy rainfalls may wash fertilizers into streams and rivers rather than allowing them to be absorbed by land plants. In places with seasonal tourists, phosphate levels may rise when the tourist population is high due to heavy loads on sewage systems and increased discharge of pollutants.

Lesson 9: Answers to Questions

Student Information 9.1
Questions

1. Nitrates are necessary for proper growth of plants and animals because they help produce proteins, enzymes, hormones, nucleic acids, and vitamins.
2. Water should be tested for nitrates in order (1) to better prevent human health problems such as "blue-babies" and (2) to better prevent rapid growth of aquatic plants, resulting in eutrophication.
3. Two common sources of nitrates are nitrate-containing fertilizers and untreated animal waste.
4. To reduce nitrates in water, use conservative amounts of nitrate-containing fertilizers and treat animal waste before allowing runoff from the animal waste to enter a waterway.

Student Activity 9.2
Analyses and Conclusions

1. Answers will vary.

Critical Thinking Questions

1. Because the activity uses a nitrate standard solution, the waste should not be poured down the drain because, if it ended up in a waterway, it would add to the contamination of the waterway with nitrates.

Student Activity 9.3
Analyses and Conclusions

1. Answers will vary.

Critical Thinking Questions

1. Answers will vary.
2. High nitrate levels would increase plant growth, possibly causing eutrophication. At low levels, few plants could grow, limiting the presence of aquatic life.
3. Nitrates from agricultural sources vary with the season, as do home use of fertilizers. Nitrates are more likely to wash into streams and rivers during the rainy season.

Lesson 10: Answers to Questions

Student Information 10.1
Questions

1. Water is tested for fecal coliforms rather than pathogenic bacteria because fecal coliforms can exist outside of the body for longer periods of time, thus allowing for easier monitoring.
2. Answers should mention at least two of the following diseases: typhoid fever, cholera, and dysentery.
3. Answers will vary. Fecal coliform enter waterways via untreated sewage, broken sewer lines, faulty or overflowing septic tanks, and stockyards.

4. Scientists count bacterial colonies because individual bacteria are small and difficult to monitor; colonies are easier to see.

5. Drinking water = 0 colonies/100 mL; swimming water = 200 colonies/100 mL; treated sewage = 200 colonies/100 mL; boating water = 1000 colonies/100 mL.

Student Information 10.2
Questions

1. It is necessary to use sterile bottles because if the bottles had bacteria in them before the water sample was taken, then erroneous data would be obtained. In such circumstances, the sample water might be free of bacteria, yet the test data would indicate the presence of bacteria.

2. Here are three methods of sterilizing equipment: (1) autoclaving at 120°C for 15–20 minutes; (2) pressure cooking at 15 psi for 15–20 minutes; and (3) placing in boiling water for 20 minutes.

3. After the sample is collected, it must be kept well below 44–45°C in order to keep any bacteria from multiplying. If the bacteria multiply between the time of sample and the time of counting, then the test data will indicate a higher colony count than actually exists in the waterway.

Student Activity 10.3
Analyses and Conclusions

1. Answers will vary.
2. Answers will vary.
3. Answers will vary. Sewage effluents, barnyard runoff, and faulty septic tanks can be sources of fecal coliforms.
4. Answers will vary. Depending on the use, untreated sewage entering the waterway should be totally eliminated or restricted.

Critical Thinking Questions

1. Answers will vary. Accept all reasonable responses.
2. If a high fecal coliform count is obtained, then there is a high probability that animals living in or near the river will be diseased. A low count probably would have little or no negative impact on the health of organisms.
3. The growth of fecal coliform bacteria is highly enhanced at 44.5°C. At higher or lower temperatures, the bacteria will be destroyed or their rate of growth will decrease. Therefore, in cold winter and hot summer conditions, fecal coliform levels usually will be lower.

Student Activity 10.4
Analyses and Conclusions

1. Answers will vary.
2. Positive natural factors might include a rapid flow of water to increase dissolved oxygen, little evidence of decaying vegetation, and plants along banks that control erosion and offer shade. Negative natural factors might include extreme weather conditions, such as rains, flooding, drought, or temperatures high or low enough to disrupt the balance of aquatic life.
3. Human factors that have positive influences might be improved farming practices to minimize erosion, optimal use of fertilizers, updated sewage

---

Answers and Solutions   **223** treatment facilities, and the planting of trees along banks. Negative factors might include the reverse of the postive factors, such as no control of erosion at new building sites, or uncorrected sewage treatment problems.

Critical Thinking Questions

1. Answers will vary.

2. Answers will vary. (*Rivers Language Arts* includes suggestions for student action projects. Students may list personal actions such as picking up litter and taking care not to pollute.)

3. Answers will vary. Suggestions may include making, monitoring, and enforcement of tougher standards for water quality and for treatment of materials that may wind up in the water supply.

Preparing Standard Solutions

How do you know whether a test or procedure gives the "right" answer or whether it really measures what it is supposed to measure? One way to check the accuracy of a test is to run it using a standard solution, a sample of known concentration.

Checking the accuracy of analytical tests, whenever possible, is important. Because standards are readily available for measuring pH, nitrates, and phosphates, these standards should be used on a regular basis to check the accuracy of the tests. Some tests, however—such as those for dissolved oxygen, biochemical oxygen demand, and fecal coliform—have no standards that can be readily purchased or prepared. Other tests—such as those for turbidity, total solids, and temperature—have standards that are difficult to prepare or use. The accuracy of these tests is determined by using more than one method or type of equipment, then comparing the results.

Purchasing Standard Solutions

Standard solutions may be purchased for some of the water-quality tests, specifically the tests for pH, nitrates, and phosphates. For pH testing, buffer solutions with pH values of 4.0, 7.0, and 10.0 are commonly used, and buffers for many other values are also available. In order to test the accuracy of colorimetric tests, such as acid-base color indicator solutions, standards must be colorless.

Concentrations of standard solutions for nitrate and phosphate tests are given either in parts per million of nitrate or phosphate or in parts per million of nitrogen or phosphorus. Checking the accuracy of a test over a range of concentrations requires preparation of more dilute concentrations from these solutions.

Preparing Standard Solutions from a Salt

Instead of purchasing such standard solutions, you can also prepare them from salts containing nitrate or phosphate ions. You need to prepare only one concentrated standard from the salt and use it to prepare dilute solutions. Dry the salt in an oven for several hours to remove moisture, then cool in a desiccator until used.

A concentrated nitrate standard solution may be made from either sodium nitrate ($NaNO_3$) or potassium nitrate (KNO_3). To prepare a 1000 ppm nitrate (NO_3^-) solution, 1.371 g of $NaNO_3$ is needed to make 1 L of solution:

$$\frac{1.00 \text{ g } (NO_3^-)}{L} \times \frac{1 \text{ mol } (NO_3^-)}{62.00 \text{ g } (NO_3^-)} \times \frac{1 \text{ mol } (NaNO_3)}{1 \text{ mol } (NO_3^-)} \times \frac{84.98 \text{ g } (NaNO_3)}{1 \text{ mol } (NaNO_3)} = 1.371 \text{ g } (NaNO_3)$$

For KNO_3, preparing 1 L of a 1000 ppm nitrate solution requires 1.631 g of KNO_3.

Phosphate standard solutions may be prepared using other sodium or potassium salts. To prepare 1 L of a 1000 ppm phosphate (PO_4^{3-}) solution, the following salts and masses would be used: 1.263 g NaH_2PO_4, 1.495 g Na_2HPO_4, 1.433 g KH_2PO_4, or 1.834 g K_2HPO_4.

Nitrate and phosphate standards should have at least one year of shelf life remaining when used.

Preparing Dilute Solutions From More Concentrated Solutions

Measuring the accuracy of a kit should involve using solutions of several different concentrations in the range expected for river samples. To make dilutions, the following formula is used.

Concentration (1) × Volume (1) = Concentration (2) × Volume (2), or

$$C_1 \times V_1 = C_2 \times V_2$$

Making accurate dilutions involves using pipettes and volumetric flasks, so tailor your procedure to the sizes of available equipment. For example, to make a 10.0 ppm solution from the 1000 ppm standard using a 1-L volumetric flask,

$$1000 \text{ ppm} \times V_1 = 10 \text{ ppm} \times 1000 \text{ mL},$$
$$V_1 = 10 \text{ mL}$$

use a 10-mL pipette to accurately transfer 10.00 mL of the concentrated solution into the flask and fill to the 1-L mark with distilled or deionized water. Similarly, 5-mL, 2-mL, and 1-mL pipettes would be used to make 1 L of 5.00, 2.00, and 1.00 ppm solutions.

Because the concentration of phosphate ions found in rivers and streams is frequently less than 1 ppm, accurate testing may require the preparation of two dilutions; first make a standard in the range of 1 to 5 ppm and then, using this standard, make a standard lower than 1 ppm.

Using a Spectrophotometer
(Optional Color Analyzer)

Overview

The measurement of some pollutants, most typically nitrates and phosphates, is usually based on a colorimetric method. The intensity of color serves as a quantitative measure of the amount of nitrate or phosphate in the solution. Test kits use some kind of color comparator, such as a printed color wheel or a series of colored vials, to match with the unknown sample. In place of the color comparator system included in such kits, a spectrophotometer may be used. A spectrophotometer measures light intensity at a single wavelength or color, giving more accurate and sensitive results, especially on river samples that are discolored.

Visible light is the part of the total energy spectrum we know as light, the part our eyes interpret as objects and colors. The spectrophotometer functions similarly to our eyes, measuring colors and the lightness or darkness of colors. We measure colors using words such as "red" or "yellow;" the spectrophotometer uses the wavelengths of light. We describe colors as "light" or "dark," while the spectrophotometer uses a numbering system.

Many different brands of test kits and spectrophotometers are available. The general instructions provided here may need to be modified to match the procedures for the specific kit and instrument used. You may have students compare results from using the kit color comparator and the spectrophotometer to determine any differences between the two methods.

Determination of Wavelength

What wavelength of light is being absorbed in a colorimetric test? You know that the wavelength that is absorbed is not the color seen but the color missing from white light. This is not enough information, however, to allow you to set the dial on a spectrophotometer to an exact wavelength.

The manufacturer of any colorimetric test kit should be able to supply the wavelength used in developing that kit. If the wavelength is not included in kit instructions, obtain this information by calling or writing the company. Different brands of kits may be based on the same chemical reactions and, therefore, use the same wavelength for determining concentration. Similarly,

© STU, published by Addison Wesley Longman, Inc.

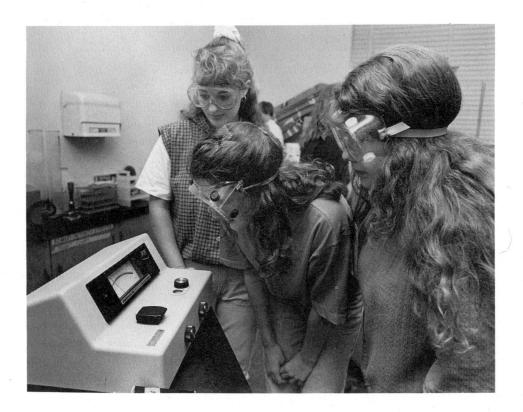

kits that use different chemical changes would not use the same wavelength, even if they are testing for the same pollutant. For example, the wavelength (in nanometers) for the HACH nitrate NitraVer 3/6 kit is 540 nm, while for the NitraVer 5 kit, the wavelength is 400 nm. The wavelength used for the HACH phosphate PhosVer 3 kit is 650 nm.

If you find no information on what wavelength to use, determine the wavelength by measuring the absorbance curve of the colored sample over the full range of the spectrophotometer. At each wavelength, zero the instrument with no sample cell in place, insert a blank to set the 100-percent transmittance, and then insert the colored sample to measure the absorbance. A plot of absorbance versus wavelength will show where the sample absorbs energy.

Determination of Transmittance

A spectrophotometer uses two systems to measure the lightness or darkness of a solution. The first measures the amount of light that passes through the sample and compares this with the light that passes through a blank. When standards are run, the blank is a test tube filled with distilled or deionized water. When river samples are run, the blank is filtered river water. Assuming that 100 percent of the light passes through the blank, the instrument should be set at 100 with the blank. The comparison of standard and sample is called percent transmittance,

$$I/I_o \times 100\% = \%T,$$

© SIU, published by Addison Wesley Longman, Inc.

where I is the intensity of light through the sample, I_o is the intensity of light through the blank, and $\%T$ is percent transmittance.

Beer's Law

The relationship between transmittance and the concentration of a solution is called Beer's Law and is expressed as

$$\log I/I_o = -\alpha\, l\, c,$$

where α is the absorption coefficient, a constant that depends on the substance and wavelength used; l is the thickness of the sample the light passes through; and c is the concentration (ppm) of the solution. A new term, absorbance, A, is used to simplify the expression:

$$A = -\log I/I_o = -\alpha\, l\, c$$

Absorbance is directly related to concentration as long as Beer's Law is applicable.

When measurements are made over a wide range of concentrations, some deviation from Beer's Law should be expected. A calibration curve should be made covering the range of concentrations expected for all samples tested. If more than one spectrophotometer is used, a calibration curve must be run for each instrument.

Preparation of a Calibration Curve

1. Prepare calibration standard solutions as discussed in Appendix D. The standard solutions should have concentration ranges that cover the expected levels of pollutant in your river or stream samples. As a starting point, phosphate standards should cover the range from 0 to 10 ppm and nitrate standards from 0 to 30 ppm. These ranges should be adjusted to match your river or stream results.
2. Follow the instructions for your test kit to develop the color for each of the standard solutions.
3. Run each of the samples in the spectrophotometer, following the instructions for the instrument.
4. Graph the concentration (ppm) versus the absorbance. This graph can now be used to analyze the results on the river or stream samples. Sample graph is shown in Appendix Figure E-1.
5. A different calibration curve must be made for each different spectrophotometer and should be repeated frequently, because instruments may drift slightly from day to day.

© SIU, published by Addison Wesley Longman, Inc.

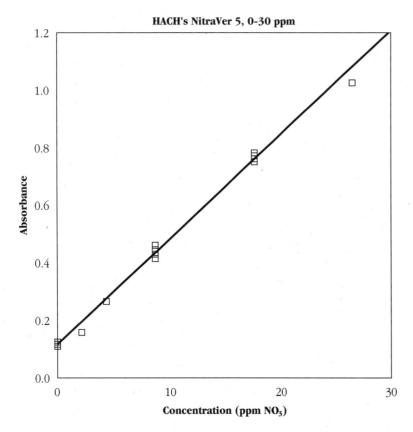

Figure E-1: Sample Graph of Concentration and Absorbance Data Using Spectrophotometer

Sample Spectrophotometer Procedure

These instructions apply specifically to a popular model, the Bausch & Lomb Spectronic 20 spectrophotometer. This material gives information pertinent to almost every spectrophotometer.

1. Turn on the spectrophotometer for at least 20 minutes to warm up the instrument. (See Figure E-2 for generalized diagram of spectrophotometer control panel.)
2. Set wavelength to the specified wavelength for your particular test.
3. With nothing inserted and with the door closed, set transmittance to 0, using the dial on the left.
4. If running a standard solution, prepare a blank sample by filling a test tube about ⅔ full of 4 mL distilled or deionized water. If running tests on river or stream water, use 4 mL of filtered river or stream water as the blank. Wipe the test tube with a tissue (or laboratory wipe) to dry the outside and remove fingerprints before inserting it in the sample compartment. Place the test tube into the sample chamber and line up the label of the tube with the marker on the spectrophotometer chamber. Close the door.
5. Using the dial on the right, set percent transmittance ($\%T$) to 100.

© SIU, published by Addison Wesley Longman, Inc.

6. Remove the blank and empty its contents into a waste container. Rinse the test tube with the sample to be analyzed (for a small amount, rinse three times). Fill about ⅔ full, wipe the outside with a tissue, place in the sample compartment with the marks aligned, and close the door. If a series of standards is being analyzed, start with the lowest concentration and work up to the highest concentration, in order to minimize effects of contamination from sample to sample.

7. If your spectrophotometer has a dial display, read the %T and record in a data table. Absorbance (A) may be recorded also, but this value is difficult to read accurately. Convert the %T results to absorbance (A) using the following equations:

$$T = \%T/100 \quad \text{and then} \quad A = \log [1/T].$$

If your instrument has a digital display, read and record %T and A.

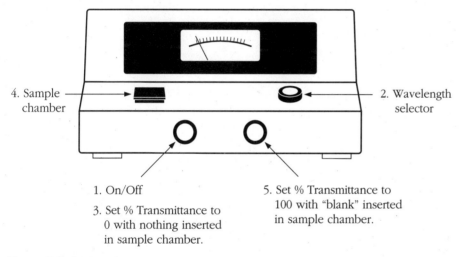

4. Sample chamber   2. Wavelength selector

1. On/Off

3. Set % Transmittance to 0 with nothing inserted in sample chamber.

5. Set % Transmittance to 100 with "blank" inserted in sample chamber.

Figure E-2: Spectrophotometer

© SIU, published by Addison Wesley Longman, Inc.

Using a Spectrophotometer

Resources

Suppliers—Chemistry Unit

CHEMetrics, Inc.
Route 28
Calverton, VA 22106
800-356-3072 • Fax 703-788-4856
in VA: 703-788-9026

Cole-Palmer
7425 North Oak Park Avenue
Niles, IL 60714
800-323-4340
within area codes 312 and 708: 708-647-7600
Fax 708-647-9660

HACH Company
P.O. Box 389
Loveland, CO 80539-0389
800-227-4224 • Fax 303-669-2932
303-669-3050
(for test kits, instrumentation, and standard solutions)

LaMotte Chemical Products Company
P.O. Box 329
Chestertown, MD 21620
800-344-3100 • Fax 301-778-6394
in MD: 301-778-3100
(for test kits)

Millipore Corporation

East	*West*
Bedford, MA 01730	448 Grandview Drive
	South San Francisco, CA 94080
800-645-5476	800-632-2708
Fax 617-275-8200	Fax 415-952-1740
in MA: 617-275-9200	

(for fecal coliform equipment)

Hydrolab Corporation
P.O. Box 50116
Austin, TX 78763
800-949-3766
Outside U.S. and Canada: 512-255-8841
Fax 512-255-3106
(for water-monitoring instrumentation)

General Scientific Suppliers

Carolina Biological Supply Company
2700 York Road
Burlington, NC 27215
800-334-5551
Fax 800-222-7112

Connecticut Valley Biological
82 Valley Road
P.O. Box 326
Southampton, MA 01073
800-628-7748 • Fax 413-527-8286

Fisher-EMD
4901 W. LeMoyne Street
Chicago, IL 60651
800-955-1177 • Fax 312-378-7174
312-378-7770

Flinn Chemical Catalog
P.O. Box 219
131 Flinn Street
Batavia, IL 60510-0219
800-452-1261 • Fax 708-879-6962

Forestry Suppliers, Inc.
P.O. Box 8397
Jackson, MS 39284-8397
800-647-5368 • Fax 800-543-4203

Sargent-Welch Scientific Company
911 Commerce Court
Buffalo Grove, IL 60089-2362
800-727-4368 • Fax 708-677-0624

Ward's

East

5100 West Henrietta Road

P.O. Box 92912

Rochester, NY 14692-9012

800-962-2660 • Fax 800-635-8439

West

815 Fiero Lane

P.O. Box 5010

San Luis Obispo, CA 93403-5010

800-872-7289 • Fax 805-781-2704

Organizations

In addition to your state, local, and regional offices of environmental protection, energy, natural resources, soil and water conservation, and geological survey, the following organizations and federal government agencies can provide useful information for use in the classroom:

Academy of Natural Sciences, 1900 Benjamin Franklin Parkway, Philadelphia, PA 19103-1195.

Adopt-A-Stream, P.O. Box 435, Pittsford, NY 14534-0435. Water-quality monitoring, cleanup programs.

American Rivers, 801 Pennsylvania Avenue SE, Suite 400G, Washington, DC 20003-2167. Preservation and restoration of rivers.

American Water Resources Association, 5410 Grosvenor Lane, Suite 220, Bethesda, MD 20814-2192. Posters and booklets.

American Water Works Association, 6666 West Quincy Avenue, Denver, CO 80235-3098. Campaign to preserve water resources.

America's Clean Water Foundation, 750 First Street NE, Suite 911, Washington, DC 20002-4241. Educational materials.

Center for Environmental Information, 46 Prince Street, Rochester, NY 14607. Phone: 716-271-3550. Great Lakes information.

Earth Science Information Center, U.S. Geological Survey, 507 National Center, Reston, VA 22092. Phone: 703-648-6892 or 800-USA-MAPS. Request list of publications. New classroom map lesson packets include *Exploring Maps* and *What Do Maps Show?*

EPA Wetlands Information Hotline: 800-832-7828. Mon.–Fri. 9:00 A.M.–5:30 P.M. EST.

Greenpeace USA, 1436 U Street NW, Washington, DC 20009. Phone: 202-462-1177.

Izaak Walton League of America, 1401 Wilson Boulevard, Level B, Arlington, VA 22209-2318. "Save Our Streams" program, publications.

National Arbor Day Foundation, The, 100 Arbor Avenue, Nebraska City, NE 68410. Phone: 402-474-5655.

National Audubon Society, National Education Office, Route 4, Box 171, Sharon, CT 06069.

National Geographic Society, 1145 17th Street NW, Washington, DC 20036. Publishes *National Geographic, National Geographic World,* and *National Geographic Traveler.*

National Geographic Society, Educational Services, P.O. Box 98019, Washington, DC 20090-8019. Phone: 800-368-2728. Classroom materials: printed materials, maps, atlases, films, filmstrips, telecommunications, videodisks.

National Geographic Society, Geography Education Program: Geographic Alliances, P.O. Box 37138, Washington, DC 20013-7138. Summer programs for teachers, Geography Awareness Week, Geography Bee, newsletters. Contact the Geography Education Program for the name of your state's alliance coordinator.

National Water Information Clearinghouse, U.S. Geological Survey, 423 National Center, Reston, VA 22092-0002. Phone: 800-426-9000.

National Wildlife Federation, 1400 16th Street, NW, Washington, DC 20036-2266. Phone: 202-797-6800.

Natural Resources Defense Council, Public Information, 40 West 20th Street, New York, NY 10011. Phone: 212-727-2700.

Nature Conservancy, The. 1815 North Lynn Street, Arlington, VA 22209. Phone: 703-841-5300.

Sierra Club, Information Center, 730 Polk Street, San Francisco, CA 94109. Phone: 415-776-2211. See *Green Guide* in list of print resources.

U.S. Army Corps of Engineers, Regulatory Branch, CECW-OR, 20 Massachusetts Avenue NW, Washington, DC 20314-1000.

U.S. Environmental Protection Agency, 401 M Street SW, Washington, DC 20460.

U.S. Fish and Wildlife Service, Department of the Interior, Washington, DC 20240. Information on wetlands.

U.S. Geological Survey. National Water Quality Assessment Program: Deputy Assistant Chief Hydrologist NAWQA Program, U.S. Geological Survey, National Center, 12201 Sunrise Valley Drive, MS 413, Reston, VA 22092.

Public Inquiries Office, 503 National Center, Room 1-C-402, 12201 Sunrise Valley Drive, Reston, VA 22092. Phone 703-648-6892; 800-USA-MAPS.

USGS Map Sales, Federal Center, Box 25286, Denver, CO 80225. Phone: 303-236-7477. Map-ordering information.

Water Environment Federation, 601 Wythe Street, Alexandria, VA 22314-1994. Materials on water-quality issues.

Wilderness Society, The, 1900 17th Street, Washington, DC 20006. Phone: 202-833-2300.

Books and Classroom Kits

American Automobile Association, "How to Read a Map" Program kit, Heathrow, FL: AAA Publishing.

Benhart, John E. and Alex R. Margin, Jr. *Wetlands: Science, Politics, and Geographical Relationships.* Indiana, PA: National Council for Geographic Education, 1994.

Costner, Pat and Joe Thornton. *We All Live Downstream: The Mississippi River and the National Toxics Crisis.* Washington, DC: Greenpeace, 1989.

Crews, Kimberly A. and Patricia Cancellier. *Connections: Linking Population With the Environment.* Washington: The Population Reference Bureau, Inc., 1991. Teaching kit: Teacher's Guide, Student Resource Book.

Izaak Walton League. *Save Our Streams.* Arlington, VA: Izaak Walton League of America.

Mitchell, Mark K. and William B. Stapp. *Field Manual for Water Quality Monitoring,* ninth ed. Dexter, MI: Thomson-Shore, 1995. Order from: William B. Stapp, 2050 Delaware Avenue, Ann Arbor, MI 48103.

Posey-Pacak, Melissa L. *Earth at Risk: Instructional Materials on the Sustainable Development and Management of the Environment.* Indiana, PA: National Council for Geographic Education. Annotated resource guide.

Reighton, James F. *Public Involvement Manual: Involving the Public in Water and Power Resources Decisions.* U.S. Government Printing Office. Washington, DC: United States Department of the Interior, 1980.

Robinson, Ann and Robbin Marks. *Restoring the Big River: A Clean Water Act Blueprint for the Mississippi.* Izaak Walton League of America and Natural Resources Defense Council, February 1994. Contact Izaak Walton League of America, 5701 Normandale Road, Suite 5701, Minneapolis, MN 55424, (Phone: 612-922-1608) or National Office, Natural Resources Defense Council.

Sierra Club. *Green Guide.* San Francisco: Sierra Club. Education guide to free and inexpensive environmental materials.

Social Studies Resources Series, Inc. Reprinted periodical articles. The following volumes relate to the River Curriculum Geography Unit: *Energy, Habitat, Pollution, Population, Technology, Third World, Transportation, Earth Science, Life Science,* and *Physical Science.*

Spaulding, Nancy E. *Earth Science Laboratory Investigations: Teacher's Annotated Edition.* Lexington, MA: D.C. Heath & Co., 1989, pp. T4–T5.

Terrell, Charles R. and Patricia Bytnar Perfetti. *Water Quality Indicators Guide: Surface Waters.* U.S. Department of Agriculture Soil Conservation Service, September 1989.

U.S. Environmental Protection Agency. *America's Wetlands: Our Vital Link Between Land and Water.* OPA-87-016.

———. *National Directory of Citizen Volunteer Environmental Monitoring Programs.* EPA503/9-90-004.

———. *The Watershed Protection Approach: An Overview.* EPA/503/9-92/002.

U.S. Geological Survey. *Popular Publications of the U.S. Geological Survey.* Lists the leaflets *What Is Water?* and *The Hydrologic Cycle* as well as other publications. Write for catalog of additional titles in the series from Books and Open-file Reports Section, U.S. Geological Survey, Federal Center, Box 25425, Denver, CO 80225.

Van der Leeden, Frits, Fred Troise, and David K. Todd. *The Water Encyclopedia.* Chelsea, MI: Lewis Publishers, 1991.

World Resources Institute. *Information Please Environmental Almanac.* Boston: Houghton Mifflin Company.

Periodicals

EPA Journal. Superintendent of Documents, Government Printing Office, Washington, DC 20402.

National Geographic. National Geographic Society, 1145 17th Street NW, Washington, DC 20036.

Science. American Association for the Advancement of Science, 1333 H Street, NW, Washington, DC 20005.

Scientific American. 415 Madison Avenue, New York, NY 10017.

Media

National Geographic Society, Educational Services, P.O. Box 98019, Washington, DC 20090-8019. Phone: 800-368-2728. Maps, films, filmstrips, telecommunications, videodisks.

accuracy closeness to the truth.

acid a substance that produces hydronium ions (H_3O^+) in water.

acid rain liquid precipitation containing pollutants that lower its pH.

acid wash to rinse glassware or other scientific equipment with a dilute solution of hydrochloric acid.

aerobic microorganism (er OH bik mi kroh OR guh niz uhm) a microscopic organism that requires oxygen gas in order to live.

algae (AL jee) a general name for numerous unicellular or multicellular chlorophyll-containing plants that occur in fresh or salt water, in the soil, or on rocks and trees.

alkaline (AL kuh luhn) relating to or having the properties of a base.

anaerobic microorganism (an er OH bik mi kroh OR guh niz uhm) a microscopic organism that does not require oxygen gas in order to live.

atmosphere a unit of air pressure.

base a substance that produces hydroxide ions (OH^-) in water.

bioassay an indirect measure of the presence of microorganisms in a given sample of water obtained by measuring their effect.

biochemical oxygen demand (BOD) the requirement for oxygen that matter, organic and chemical, places on water.

buffer a solution used to calibrate a pH meter; a solution capable of maintaining a constant pH even when small amounts of acid or base are added.

Celsius thermometer an instrument that measures temperature on a scale where water freezes at 0 degrees and boils at 100 degrees.

colony a group of microorganisms that propagate from a single organism.

cultural eutrophication the acceleration of eutrophication due to human influences, resulting in overgrowth of aquatic vegetation followed by death and decay, oxygen depletion, and an imbalance of plants and animals in the water.

culture the propagation of microorganisms in a specially prepared environment that enhances growth.

deviation the difference between each measured value and the mean value.

dilution (di LOO shuhn) the process of reducing the concentration of matter per unit volume.

dissolved oxygen oxygen gas dissolved in water.

dissolved solid a solid that dissolves in water and is no longer visible even with the aid of a microscope.

distill wash to rinse glassware or other scientific equipment with distilled water.

erosion (ih ROH zhuhn) the tearing down and transporting of material by wind, water, or ice.

eutrophication (yoo troh fuh KAY shuhn) the overgrowth of aquatic vegetation followed by death, decay, oxygen depletion, and an imbalance of plants and animals in the water.

fecal coliforms (FEE kuhl KOH luh forms) rod-shaped bacteria that propagate in the digestive tracts of humans and other warm-blooded vertebrates.

floc (flahk) a gelatinous or fluffy precipitate that traps solid particles as it forms and settles.

flocculation (FLAHK yuh lay shuhn) a water-purification procedure in which chemicals are added to the water to form a precipitate that entraps suspended solids.

flow volume of a river or stream; the amount of water passing a point on the bank in a measure amount of time, such as cubic meters per second (cms).

flow rate a measure of the speed or current of a waterway expressed in meters per second (m/s).

hard water water that contains large quantities of calcium, magnesium, or iron ions.

hydronium (hi droh NEE uhm) **ion** a charged particle that consists of a hydrogen ion associated with a water molecule (H_3O^+) and gives acids their characteristic chemical properties.

indicator a substance that can determine the presence or absence of a particular chemical. For example, an acid-base indicator changes color as the pH of a solution it is in changes.

infant methemoglobinemia (meht HEE muh gloh bih nee mee uh) a medical condition in infants where oxygen does not properly bind to hemoglobin, the oxygen-carrying molecule in the blood.

Jackson Turbidity (ter BIHD ih tee) **Unit** (**JTU**) a unit of measure for turbidity, which is based on the Jackson Candle Turbidimeter and is numerically interchangeable with Nephelometric Turbidity Units (NTUs).

material safety data sheet (MSDS) printed material that describes the proper safety precautions to observe when using a specific chemical.

medium the environment in which microorganisms live.

© SIU, published by Addison Wesley Longman, Inc.

nephelometer (nehf uh LAHM ih ter) a device for measuring the amount of suspended solids in a liquid by measuring the intensity of scattered light.

Nephelometric (NEHF uh luh meh trik) **Turbidity Unit (NTU)** a unit of measure for turbidity, based on the nephelometer, standardized so that a reading in NTUs is the same as in Jackson Turbidity Units.

neutral a solution with a pH of 7.

neutralization (noo truh luh ZAY shuhn) the chemical reaction of an acid and a base to produce water and a salt.

nitrate (NI trayt) an ion made of one nitrogen atom surrounded by three oxygen atoms: NO_3^-.

nitrogen-fixing plant a plant that can convert nitrogen in the air into nitrogen in the soil.

organic matter anything that is or was alive; a substance containing carbon and other elements chemically combined; such compounds derive from either plants or animals.

overall Water-Quality Index total value of water quality, obtained by adding the weighted percentage scores for all nine water-quality tests.

pathogenic bacteria (path uh JEHN ihk bak TIHR ee uh) bacteria that are capable of causing human disease.

percent error a method for determining data accuracy when the true value is known.

percent saturation the percent of milligrams of oxygen gas dissolved in one liter of water at a given temperature compared with the maximum milligrams of oxygen gas that can dissolve in one liter of water at the same temperature.

pH a number that is used to determine if a solution is acidic, basic, or neutral.

phosphate (FAHS fayt) a compound containing the phosphate ion (PO_4^{3-}); or a salt of phosphoric acid (H_3PO_4).

precipitate (pri SIP uh tayt) an insoluble solid formed in a solution.

precision closeness of readings to one another.

pressure the force exerted over a unit area.

Q-value percent common unit used for comparing the results of different kinds of water-quality tests.

quotient test a statistical test for determining whether data should be retained or rejected.

reported value mean of a series of values, together with the standard deviation.

salt a general term for one product of the reaction of different acids and bases. For example: Acid + Base → Salt + Water.

saturated solution a solution that has dissolved a maximum amount of solute.

scale deposits of metal ions left by hard water in water pipes, water heaters, steam irons, and other appliances.

Secchi (SEHK ee) **disk** a device for measuring the turbidity of a body of water by measuring the depth at which a black-and-white disk is no longer visible.

sedimentation (sehd uh muhn TAY shuhn) the process in which solids settle to the bottom of a liquid.

soft water water that contains little or no calcium, magnesium, or iron ions.

solubility (sahl yuh BIL uht ee) the maximum amount of solute that dissolves in a given amount of solvent; the property of being capable of forming a solution.

solute (SAHL yoot) a substance that dissolves in a solvent.

solution the result of dissolving a solute in a solvent.

solvent (SAHL vuhnt) a substance that dissolves a solute.

standard deviation (d_s) a measure of the variation in a set of numbers.

standard solution a solution of known concentration or pH that provides a true value for testing the accuracy of equipment or procedures.

standard wash to rinse glassware or other scientific equipment with a solution of known concentration.

statistics a branch of mathematics that deals with the collection, analysis, interpretation, and presentation of data.

sterile free from microorganisms.

sterilization (stehr uh luh ZAY shuhn) a process of creating an environment free of unwanted microorganisms.

supersaturated solution a solution that has more dissolved solute than a saturated solution.

suspension (suh SPEHN chuhn) a condition in which solid materials in a liquid do not settle to the bottom on standing.

temperature a measure of how hot or cold an object or substance is.

thermal water pollution the deliberate dumping of waste thermal energy or heat into rivers, lakes, and oceans.

total solids solid matter that is either suspended or dissolved in water.

turbidimeter (ter bih DIHM ih ter) a device for measuring the turbidity of a liquid.

turbidity (ter BIHD ih tee) the degree of lack of clarity in a liquid or gas.

unsaturated solution a solution in which more solute would dissolve if it were added.

weighting factor the percentage value of how much a single test counts in the computation of the overall value of a series of tests.

© SIU, published by Addison Wesley Longman, Inc.